Anna M. (Anna Morris) Holstein

Swedish Holsteins in America

from 1644 to 1892

Anna M. (Anna Morris) Holstein

Swedish Holsteins in America
from 1644 to 1892

ISBN/EAN: 9783743324015

Manufactured in Europe, USA, Canada, Australia, Japa

Cover: Foto ©ninafisch / pixelio.de

Manufactured and distributed by brebook publishing software (www.brebook.com)

Anna M. (Anna Morris) Holstein

Swedish Holsteins in America

Swedish Holsteins

IN AMERICA

From 1644 to 1892.

COMPRISING MANY LETTERS AND BIOGRAPHICAL MATTER
RELATING TO JOHN HUGHES, THE "STAMP
OFFICER," AND FRIEND OF FRANKLIN.

WITH PAPERS NOT BEFORE PUBLISHED
RELATING TO HIS BROTHER OF REVOLUTIONARY FAME
COLONEL HUGH HUGHES OF NEW YORK.

THE FAMILIES OF
DeHAVEN, RITTENHOUSE, CLAY, POTTS,
BLACKISTON, ATLEE, COATES,

AND

OTHER DESCENDANTS OF MATTHIAS HOLSTEIN OF WICACO
PHILADELPHIA, ARE INCLUDED.

THIRTY-FIVE FAMILY PICTURES AND FAC-SIMILE OF LETTERS
OF BENJAMIN FRANKLIN AND REV. NICHOLAS COLLIN, D.D.
ARE GIVEN.

BY

MRS. ANNA M. HOLSTEIN,
UPPER MERION, MONTGOMERY COUNTY, PENNSYLVANIA.

INTRODUCTION.

A FEW of the older members of the family will recall the fact that this Family History was commenced some years ago, and when nearly ready for the press was put aside, thinking it would never be published. But at the solicitation of some of the descendants it was again taken in hand, when the whole labor had to be repeated. How slow and tedious such matter is only those who have been engaged in similar work can judge.

Such as it is, with all its imperfections, I commend it to the kindly favor of the descendants of the worthies whose memory I have tried to preserve. In some few families it was impossible to obtain correct information of ancestors or children. These branches must therefore be imperfect.

This may be but the beginning of what some one of the race may in later time continue, and still gather up and blend together the scattered threads of Family History, making of it a full, harmonious record.

To those who have loaned me valuable papers, and copied or prepared sketches of their respective families, I am under

especially to Mr. Frederick D. Stone, for use of libraries and other important aid; to the American Philosophical Society and the Historical Society of Pennsylvania; also, to Mr. Dixon G. Hughes, of New York; the family and executors of the late Benjamin B. Hughes; Hon. F. P. Dewees, of Washington, D. C.; the family of Hon. Francis W. Hughes, of Pottsville, Pennsylvania; Mrs. James Pollock, wife of ex-Governor Pollock, both now deceased; Miss Emily Clay Pollock, Mr. William John Potts, of Camden, New Jersey; Dr. George W. Holstein, Mr. John Hughes, of Newbern, North Carolina, now deceased; Mr. W. H. Dewees, Mr. Jones Detwiler, of Montgomery county, and others.

Among those to whom I am indebted for personal reminiscences of Family History is Miss Rachel Roberts, of Bridgeport, now deceased, who gave me incidents relating to the family long before I had thought of preserving them in book form. Her niece, Miss Rebecca R. Lane, has continued the same subject, which has been still further enlarged by Miss Hannah Elizabeth Potts, of Philadelphia, whose memory of past events connected with her ancestors was at that time remarkably clear and full.

A late eminent author has said, " Every family should have a record of its own. Each has its peculiar spirit running through the whole line and in more or less development perceptible in every generation.

"We should love our kindred for their glory or their genius, but for those domestic affections and private virtues that unobserved by the world expand in confidence towards ourselves, and flourish with independent vigor in the heart to which a kind Providence has guided them. Why should we not derive benefit from studying the virtues of our forefathers?

An affectionate regard for their memory is natural to the heart.

"They are denied, it is true, to our personal acquaintance, but the light they shed during their lives survives within their tombs, and will reward our search if we explore them."

HOLSTEIN FAMILY HISTORY.

FIRST GENERATION

HOLSTEIN FAMILY HISTORY.

FIRST GENERATION.

I have considered the days of old, the years of ancient times.—Psalm 77: 5.

Matts Hollsten, as the name was written in the earliest Swedish records, the ancestor of this long line of descendants, was born in Philadelphia, Pennsylvania, in 1644, two years after the second emigration of Swedes to America. Who his parents were we have now no means of knowing, but it has been a long established family tradition that they came from Sweden with Governor Peter Minuit in the good ship "Key of Calmar." The date is probably correct.

The name Holstein is at this date widely scattered over Sweden, Germany and the United States, but it is only with those of Swedish descent we are interested. The German name, though largely represented in our country, seems not to belong to this family.

In 1693 Matts Hollsten was one of the Swedish congregation of Wicaco, which is an Indian name, meaning pleasant place. In the list of heads of families sent in that year by Charles Springer to Postmaster Thelin, at the request of the king, Charles XI, of Sweden, is found his name with the seven comprising his household. This corresponds with the record given by Rev. Dr. Nicholas Collin to Colonel George W. Holstein, of Upper Merion, Montgomery county, Pennsylvania, in which the seven names are written in full, with date of birth.

There is a family legend that the name Holstein descended through a noble line. It may be so, though the only evidence I have found to support this claim is in the ancestry of Magdalena Hulings, wife of the third Matthias, which is given in the third generation.

Matts Hollsten died 9th of April, 1708, and was interred in the cemetery at Wicaco, meaning, no doubt, the old cemetery, which was sold in June, 1873, for building purposes, the bodies having previously been removed.

Miss Christiana Holstein, of Philadelphia, who died December 5, 1877, aged 78, stated to the writer some years previous that she remembered having seen in her youthful days, in the burial ground at Wicaco, grave stones brought from Sweden having on them the name of Holstein. None are to be found there at this time. They may have been placed beneath the church, or covered with earth in the cemetery.

The Swedes of that primitive time were a thrifty, industrious people, inclined to farming pursuits more than to trade. Wm. Penn, in a letter to the "Society of Free Traders," written 16th of August, 1683, says: "Philadelphia is at last laid out to the great content of those concerned in this Province. It has advanced within less than a year to about forescore houses and cottages, such as they are, where merchants and handicrafts are following their vocations as fast as they can, while the countrymen are close at their farms."

These few lines give an idea of what this now great city was in the sixteenth century, when the American ancestors of this ancient family were living in cabins upon the banks of the Delaware, or dwelling peacefully upon their farms that are at this present writing in the centre of Philadelphia.

Mathias Holstein, resided in the district of Moyamensing, or Passyunk, according to the list of the Congregation in 1698.
He was buried in the Cemetery of Wicacoa Church, the 7 of April 1708, being 64 years old.

His Children with the first wife, were: — Laurence, born 15 Septemb 1677 — Andrew, b. 19 Jan 1679 — Mathias, b. 1 July 1681 — Fredric, b. 13 Jan. 1684.

He was married to a second wife in the year 1688.
With her he had — Peter, b. 16 Jan. 1691 — Henry, b. 29 March 1694. — Cathrine 10 Jan. 1697.

Peter was buried in Wicacoa Cemetery 1 Nov. 1706.

Fredric Holstein was buried in Wicacoa Cemetery 11 Apr. 1708.

Mathias Holstein was married to Britta Rambo, in Wicacoa Church, 10 Octob. 1705.
Their Children :— Fredric, b. 1 Jan. 1709 Britta, baptized 14 Jan 1712 (time of birth not mentioned)   Debora, b. 5 Sept. 1714 — Andrew, bapt. 15 Apr. 1716 — Mathias, b. 2 Dec 1717 — Maria, b. 23 Apr. 1720 — John, born 26 March 1724. — Fredric, b. 11 Feb. 1726

Britta was buried 31 Nov. 1713, ag. 2 yrs.

personal property, to be equally divided between his wife, Elizabeth, and son Lawrence. He mentions the other children by name, but cuts them off from any portion of his estate.

The dates and names in this will make it almost a certainty that it belonged to the Lawrence, or Lorenz, whose career is lost to us. In Rev. Dr. Clay's "Annals" his name appears as taking part in a meeting of the congregation at Wicaco 17th of May, 1698, which was called for the purpose of locating the site of the new church. Again, in appendix to Acrelius, in a list of members of Piles Grove church, in 1747, near Salem, N. J., Lawrence Holstein, Sr., and Lawrence, Jr., are found. It is probably the Lawrence whose will was written in that year, and Lawrence, Jr., is the son to whom he left his estate.

In Acrelius, under the head of "Baptisms by Rev. Abraham Reincke," is given:

"Mary, infant daughter of Lorenz and Molly Holstein; born in Piles Grove, N. J., 11th of November, 1748. The act of baptism was performed in Yerred Van Emmen's house.

"N. B.—Her mother deceased on the 19th of November, eight days after the birth of the child, and was buried near the new church, on Oldman's creek. Hers was the first interment there after the erection of the new church."

The name of Andrew Holstein appears in the same record in New Jersey in 1747, but beyond the mere date of birth nothing authentic is known of his later history.

Matthias Holstein, 2d, the third son of Matts, moved to Amasland, now Upper Merion, with his wife, Brita Rambo, soon after their marriage, and purchased one thousand acres of land, beginning at the Schuylkill river, comprising what is now the borough of Bridgeport, and extending one and a half miles west to the top of Red Hill. The oldest deed in the possession of the family for this tract is dated 1708.

Matthias Holstein, 2d, resided for a time at Swedesford, and in 1714 built a stone house upon his farm, one and a half miles from the river, on Spring creek. The Swedish settlers of that day invariably chose the site for their dwellings near springs and streams of water. In that dwelling, as it descended from father to son, four generations were born, children, grandchildren, great-grandchildren, and great-great-grandchildren. The house still stands in good condition, though it has been added to and enlarged many times. The large stone barn which Matthias built at the same time was considered a remarkable one, people coming from long distances to examine it.

Prior to and during the building of Christ Swedes Church service was regularly held in it, as the large threshing floors would accommodate all the community.

During the last few years this old barn was torn down to make room for a still larger one. This property is now in the possession of William P. David, of Bridgeport, Penna.

Frederick Holstein, fourth son of Matts, died two days after the decease of his father, aged 24 years, unmarried, and was buried in the cemetery of Wicaco 11th of April, 1708.

Henry Holstein, second son of the second wife, Katharine. There is no further mention made of him, but in 1743 his name appears as residing in Providence township, this county. No descendants of the name are to be found in that locality, or other record of him.

Catharine Holstein, youngest child of the second wife. The date of her birth is all that appears concerning her. If married it cannot be traced.

THIRD GENERATION

THIRD GENERATION.

CHILDREN OF LAWRENCE AND ELIZABETH HOLSTEIN.

Lawrence Holstein.
Matthias Holstein.
Andrew Holstein.
Mary Holstein.
Sarah Holstein.
Susanna Holstein

CHILDREN OF MATTHIAS HOLSTEIN, 2D, AND BRITA RAMBO.

Frederick Holstein, born 1st of January, 1704. Died in infancy.

Brita Holstein, born 1710. Baptized 14th of January, 1712; died aged 2 years.

Debora Holstein, born September 5, 1714. Died at Swedesford.

Andrew, born 15th of April, 1716. Married Mary Jones, of Lower Merion. Died January 3, 1762, aged 46 years. Is buried near the walk, west side of Christ Swedes Church, Upper Merion. Upon his monument, which is remarkably well preserved, is seen this quaint inscription :

> "I pray you, mortals, cast an eye,
> From hence you all must go;
> Beneath this tomb my body is laid—
> For die you must also."

Matthias Holstein, 4th, born December 2, 1717.

Mary Holstein, born 23d of April, 1720. No further record of her.

John Holstein, born 26th of March, 1724. Married Elizabeth ———

Frederick Holstein, 2d, born 11th of February, 1728. Married Magdalena Jones 23d of January, 1753, by Rev. Slof Parkin, by license.

Catharine Holstein.
Elizabeth Holstein.
Brichard Holstein.

Matthias Holstein, 4th, born December 2, 1717. Married Magdalena, daughter of Marcus and Margaret Hulings, of Morlattan (now Douglassville), Berks county, Pennsylvania, about 1744. "The wedding party came to Christ Church (Swedes), Upper Merion, all in their canoes."

Marcus Hulings, the father of Magdalena, seems to have been a prominent man in the community both in church and secular affairs. Day's Historical Collections of Pennsylvania says of the grandfather of Magdalena that Marcus Hulings settled possibly as early as 1735 on Duncan's island, in the Juniata, and established a ferry there. A fight occurred on the island between the whites and Indians about 1766. On one occasion news came to Mr. Hulings that the Indians were coming down the river to attack the settlements. He packed up his valuables in great haste, and putting his wife and child upon a large black horse fled to the foot of the island, ready to cross over at the first alarm. Thinking that the Indians might not have arrived he ventured back alone to the house to try to save more of his effects. After carefully reconnoitering he entered and found an Indian upstairs cooly picking his flint. Stopping some time to parley with the Indian, so that he might retreat without being shot at, his wife became alarmed at his long delay, and fearing he had been murdered by the Indians she mounted the black charger and swam the Susquehanna. This was in the spring when the river was high. Our modern matrons would scarcely perform such an achievement. Her husband soon arrived and in his turn became alarmed at her absence, but she made a signal to him from the opposite side and relieved his anxiety.

Family history states that Magdalena Hulings was betrothed to Frederick Holstein, who invited his elder brother,

Matthias, to accompany him to Morlattan that he might have the pleasure of seeing his intended sister-in-law. When they met Matthias was so charmed with the beauty and loveliness of the fair Magdalena that he continued his visits, and eventually supplanted Frederick in her affections and married her.

Matthias Holstein, the 3d, died 12th of December, 1768, aged 51 years. His grave is covered with a flat monument on which is inscribed:

> "The' pomp nor grandeur
> Swelled his humble name,
> The honest man
> Will reap immortal fame."

His wife, Magdalena, survived him thirty-one years, and died 4th of December, 1799, in her 82d year. Her grave is marked with a head and foot stone. They are both buried at the south end of the old Swedes (Christ) Church, Upper Merion.

In January, 1753, Marcus and Margaret Hulings were sponsors at the baptism of an infant daughter of Matthias and Magdalena Holstein, nee Hulings.

On an old tombstone in the Swedes' churchyard of Morlattan (now Douglassville), is inscribed: "In memory of Marcus Hulings, who departed this life April 2d, 1757, aged 70 years." His wife's grave is not marked. Near that of Marcus is one upon which is recorded: "Here lies the body of Peter Hulings, son of Marcus and Margaret Hulings, who died the 17th of August, 1739, aged 18 years."

Dr. W. H. Egle, State Librarian of Pennsylvania, in an article in the "Harrisburg Daily Telegraph," of February 11, 1882, gives this history of the Hulings family, and states that Ferris, in his "History of the original settlements on the Delaware," gives a list of the Swedish families residing in New Sweden in 1693, &c., in which is given the name of Lars Halling, which later was transformed into Hewling and finally Huling.

Lars Halling is as unquestionably a Swedish name as Olle Derrickson, Nils Mattson, Lasse Cock, or Sven Svenson,

Most of the early Hulings belonged to the Swedish Lutheran Church, as will be learned by examining the early records of Gloria Dei Church, Philadelphia.

The following biographical sketch Dr. Egle found in an old book in Wilkesbarre, Pennsylvania:

"Thomas Paul Frederick Marquis de Hulingues, a distinguished Bearnese nobleman, who followed the fortunes of his prince and kinsman, Henry of Navarre, was one of those heroic men who defended La Rochelle, and finally, in April, 1572, accompanied Henry to Paris to be present at the nuptials of that prince with Marguerite de Valois, daughter of the cruel Catharine de Medicis, on August 18th, and on the 24th of August he witnessed the horrible massacre of St. Bartholomew. He was one of the young noblemen who waited in the ante-chamber of the prince and his bride on that fatal eve.

"He alone of all their personal attendants escaped from the Louvre, as by a miracle, through the gratitude of one of the Catholic soldiers. After various perils he succeeded in reaching Dieppe. Here he was soon joined by his betrothed wife, Isabella de Portal, who, although a protege and maid of honor of Queen Catharine, was a member of one of those rare old French families of Languedoc, descended from the Albigois, whose war cry and armorial device '*Armet nos ultis regum,*' was renowned through Southern France, whose name is inscribed in the 'Book of Capitouls,' which, like the 'Golden Book' of Venice, contained the names of all the patrician families of the ancient nobility.

"She was a native of Toulouse, and was rescued by a caprice of Catharine's from the fate of her once powerful but now persecuted family, and though carefully educated in the Catholic tenets, was secretly faithful to the religion of her family.

"The Marquis and the Lady Isabella de Portal were privately married at Dieppe and sailed for England, but fearful of pursuit and the weather proving stormy they were landed on the Danish coast, whence they afterward proceeded to Gothenberg, Sweden, where they lived but a few years, and left an only son, whose descendants emigrated to America about the year 1700."

Lars Hulings, of 1693 (which is Lawrence Anglicised), had in 1657 a wife Catharine and son Lawrence, and lived in Cinnamensing township.

FOURTH GENERATION

FOURTH GENERATION.

CHILDREN OF ANDREW HOLSTEIN AND MARY JONES.

Martha Holstein.

Peter Holstein, born 1744. Married his cousin, Abigail Jones*, a Welsh girl. He died September 10, 1785, aged 41 years, is buried in the cemetery of Christ (Swedes') Church, Upper Merion. This inscription is found upon his monument:

> "Dear friends, for me pray do not weep;
> I am not dead, but here do sleep,
> Reposited within this clay,
> Until the resurrection day ;
> And here, indeed, I must remain
> Until Christ shall raise me up again ;
> And then with him I shall ascend
> Where boundless joy shall have no end."

Amy Holstein, born 3d of July, 1750; baptized 2d of December, 1750, at Mathzong; godfathers, Abraham and Nicolas Jonson; godmothers, Mrs. Jonson and Mrs. Justice, and the parents, Andrew and Mary Holstein.

Acrelius says the Ford is called by early Swedish writers Matzong, probably a corruption of Matt sons (Matt's son).

Magdalena Holstein, born 30th of November, 1753, at Mathzong; baptized 17th of December, 1753; godfathers, Mons. Rambo, Matthias Holstem ; godmothers, Magdalena Jonse and Lady Rambo, and her father Andrew Holstein.

Stephanus Holstein, born 16th of January, 1755; baptized 9th of April, 1755 ; godfathers and mothers, Ezekiel and Peter Rambo, Mary Rambo and Sarah Priest.

Martha, Amy and Magdalena survived their brother Peter, as reference to his will proves. Magdalena married

---
*In 1766, by Dr. Von Wrangel.

John Black (by license) March 13, 1775, and here the history of these three sisters ends. Their individuality seems to have been lost from that period.

Stephanus probably died in infancy, as his name does not occur in his father's will.

CHILDREN OF MATTHIAS AND MAGDALENA HOLSTEIN, NEE HULINGS.

Samuel Holstein, born 11th of January, 1745. Married Rachel, daughter of Charles and Elizabeth Moore, of Marple, Delaware county, Pennsylvania, November 12, 1771. The Moore family were of English origin. Their daughter Rachel was born August 4, 1746.

Samuel Holstein, the only son of Matthias and Magdalena (Hulings) Holstein, died at the age of 57, on 22d of December, 1802. The following epitaph, written by Rev. Dr. Collin for that purpose, is inscribed upon his tomb in Swedes' (Christ) Church cemetery, Upper Merion, near the east front of the Church.

"He was a dutiful son, an affectionate husband, a kind father, a good neighbor, an upright and benevolent man in all his dealings, an industrious improver of his landed patrimony, a principal promoter of this church in its erection, attendance on divine worship therein, and wardenship of it for thirty-three years. May this candid record be a public benefit is the wish of the framer, Nicholas Collin."

Rev. Nicholas Collin, of Upsala, was sent as Minister Extraordinary from Sweden to this country, where he arrived 12th of May, 1770.

His first charge was rector of the congregations at Racoon and Penn's Neck, and for seven years Provost of the Mission. In 1786 he entered upon his duties as rector of the united Swedish churches of Wicaco, Kingsessing and Upper Merion, and so continued until his death in 1831.

Dr. Collin was held in great esteem by all who claimed a Swedish ancestry. The old people loved and honored him as a nearer tie to their Fatherland, while those of a later time have handed down the name of Collin among their descendants as a memento of their Swedish origin, and in loving remembrance of one of the best men of his day and generation. He was a learned, gifted man, yet of great simplicity of manner. There are still living, 1892, persons who recall with much pleasure his ministrations in this parish. Upon first assuming the charge his visits were monthly, later once in three months, and as age crept on and the strong man became feeble six months or a year would intervene between his services at Swedes' (Christ) Church, Upper Merion, yet he never lost his interest in these distant members of his flock, and thought it not beneath the dignity of his office to have a watchful oversight of the fruit which ripened so temptingly in his garden at Wicaco. It is said that at one time he left his pulpit to drive away the boys from his cherry trees, remarking as he did so, "There was a time for all things."

The good doctor consumed the greater part of a day in his journeys upon horseback from Philadelphia to Upper Merion, always permitting his faithful horse "Tidy" to travel as he liked, resting when so minded, or cropping grass by the roadside. Once when fording the Schuylkill, and again in crossing a smaller stream near Mr. Holstein's, "Tidy" laid down in the water, giving his master an unexpected bath, and soaking the contents of his saddle bags.

Among the children of the parish Dr. Collin was ever a welcome guest. They enjoyed to the full the sugar plums which they knew he always carried in his pockets, and scattered with a liberal hand among them, anticipating his visits with possibly a keener relish than most others in the community.

The last days of his horse "Tidy" were spent upon the farm of Col. George W. Holstein, where he was left by his master, who entrusted him to the kind care of his friend. "Tidy" died at the age of forty-four years.

Hannah Holstein, born 15th December, 1748. Married Isaac Hughes, son of John and Sarah Hughes, of Upper Merion.

The following is a copy of original marriage certificate:

"These are to certifie to whom it may Concern that Isaac Hughes and Hannah Holsten were lawfully married according to the Canons and Constitutions of the Church of England, on the fifth Day of October, 1769.

"p WILL^M CURRIE."

Isaac Hughes served in the various positions of captain, major and lieutenant colonel of the Pennsylvania militia. He was appointed lieutenant colonel of the Flying Camp 15th of July, 1776, and is said to have been twice wounded; was one of the assessors of Philadelphia September 18, 1776, "who or a majority of them shall be a Board of Commissioners for the County of Philadelphia." He was a "member of the Committee of Correspondence," and was twice a member of the Assembly of Pennsylvania.

Tradition says the wedding ceremony of Hannah Holstein and Isaac Hughes was in the parlor of the old homestead of her ancestors, on Spring creek.

In her youthful days Hannah Holstein was noted for her beauty, which can readily be believed judging from the lovely portrait of her as Mrs. Clay, taken in old age, which is in the possession of Miss H. Elizabeth Potts, of Philadelphia. The wedding dress of Hannah Holstein Hughes was preserved until a few years since. It was white satin, the over-dress faintly tinted with rose, and made according to the style of the period, with a court train resembling those that we now see of Mrs. Washington in her early life. The tiny white satin slippers worn with this handsome dress have buckles and high heels. They are still carefully treasured, and retain their beauty to the present time, though showing in color the creamy tint of age.

Her descendants have in their possession some valuable pieces of old china, which are highly prized as belonging to and used by her in housekeeping more than a century ago.

A short time before his health failed Lieutenant Colonel Isaac Hughes built a new home for himself and family about half a mile from "Walnut Grove," on a hill overlooking Gulf creek. Part of that house is still standing and in good condition at the present time. The place has since been known in the neighborhood as the Nugent Farm. They had occupied it but a brief season when in the prime of life the summons came to "rest from his labors," and he entered upon "life eternal." He is buried in Christ Swedes' Church yard, south of the church. Upon his monument is inscribed:

IN MEMORY OF ISAAC HUGHES,
Who Departed this Life April 29th, 1782,
Aged 34 Years and 4 Months.

As a member of society he was called to serve his country in a civil and military capacity. In these he was an advocate for liberty, and the promotion of every design which had for its object the general welfare. In domestic life he was a kind, tender and affectionate husband, an indulgent parent, a humane master.

Free from covetousness, he was a stranger to envy. In his death the poor and distressed have lost a friend. To the merit of others he was ever disposed to do justice, and his kindness and benevolence were great and extensive.

GO AND DO LIKEWISE

ALSO,
TO THE MEMORY OF HANNAH CLAY,
Relict of Isaac Hughes and the Rev. Slator Clay.
Born Dec. 15th, A. D. 1748,
Died June 15th, A. D. 1832.

Rachel Holstein, born 29th of January, 1753; baptized at Matzong 13th of May, 1753; godfathers, the parents and Marcus and Andrew Hulings; godmothers, Margaret and Catharine Hulings. Married Lindsay Coates, of Philadelphia, his second wife, February 6, 1777, by Rev. Andrew Goeransson.

Mr. Coates died November 23, 1798, in Montgomery county, Pennsylvania, aged 55 years.

Mrs. Coates died April, 1829, in the 77th year of her age.

Lindsay Coates was a prominent man in the eventful times in which he lived. Educated as a lawyer, he never practiced at the bar, but made a frequent beneficent use of his knowledge of it by gratuitous counsels through an extensive vicinity. As senator and in other public offices of trust he enjoyed the confidence of the community. His descendants preserve and value his diploma, received May 1, 1760, from the Academy of Pennsylvania, now known as the University of Pennsylvania. His signature appears on some of the Continental money of that date.

Rebecca Holstein, born 19th of October, 1750; baptized at Matzong 16th of December, 1750; godfather, John Garret; godmother, Susanna Rambo. Married Jesse Roberts, son of Joseph and Sarah (Eastburn) Roberts, of Upper Merion, 1st of March, 1781.

Mrs. Rebecca Roberts died 29th of August, 1823, in her 78th year.

Throughout a life lengthened beyond the Psalmist's limit she was remarkable for devoted love of her church. In her latter days, when mind and body were failing together, her prayer-book seemed suited to her daily needs. Wherever she moved about, in doors or out, a large prayer-book was constantly under her arm, and frequently carried with her to bed. When quietly sitting in an easy chair she would bend over the open book as it rested upon her knee, and with her finger follow line for line the precious words it contained. When she "entered into rest," Dr. Collin was sent for to attend her funeral. His friend, Hugh DeHaven, was to accompany him from Philadelphia. Becoming absorbed in conversation they missed the road and traveled in an entirely different direction, not discovering the error in time to reach Norristown for the services, which were delayed until a late hour in the afternoon, when the doctor and his friend retraced their steps to the city. The following Sunday was Dr. Collin's stated time for holding service at Christ (Swedes') Church, Upper Merion, when he explained to the family how the mistake occurred, and suggested that they should then accompany him to the churchyard, where they would have the burial service over her grave, which was done, greatly to the comfort of the survivors.

Jesse Roberts, the husband of Rebecca Holstein, was a soldier of the Revolutionary war, and was with the army during the encampment at Valley Forge. Upon one occasion, having a short furlough, which was spent among friends in the valley, he called at Samuel Holstein's, and taking his son Matthias, who was but a little child, carried him upon his shoulder through the woods. As they passed along a shower came up, when the young soldier stopped and turned his coat wrong side outward, for the purpose of preserving it bright and untarnished. Doing so exposed a red lining. The color attracted the notice of a Federal picket, who would have shot him for a British soldier had it not been for the little boy he was carrying.

Jesse and Rebecca Roberts ever entertained a feeling of great interest for the lad, who in later life was widely known in this community as Major Matthias Holstein, of Norristown.

Sarah Holstein, born 31st of July, 1755; baptized 9th of November, 1755; sureties, Michael Hulings, Magdalena Holstein and the parents. Married Hugh DeHaven, son of Peter and Sarah Hughes DeHaven, of Philadelphia, 27th of April, 1775.

The father of Hugh DeHaven was prominently known in the troublous days of the Revolution. In Colonial Records and Pennsylvania Archives, second series, is found a history of his transactions with the government in the manufacture of powder and superintendence of the gun-lock factory before and after its removal to French creek, Chester county, Pennsylvania. At this place were stored arms that were forwarded by order of "Council of Safety," as the wants of the army required.

Hugh DeHaven was appointed assistant to his father while arms and stores were at French creek, by order of the "Board of War."

From 16th of November, 1776, to 20th of January, 1778, the accounts of Peter DeHaven show that he received from the government $60,000 during that period. It is not stated for what purpose this sum was applied, though it is probable a portion of it was for the expenses of the powder manufactory.

The following is the early history of the DeHaven family as I have been able to obtain it:

In 1698 Evert Inden Hoff, with his wife, Elizabeth Schiphower, and their three sons, Gerhard, Herman and Peter, came from Holland and settled in Whitpain township, Montgomery county, Pennsylvania. In 1706 Evert Inden Hoff took up 200 acres of land in Whitpain township, this county. In 1708 Evert Inden Hoff and his three sons took the oath of allegiance in this country.

Evert is an abbreviation of the German name Eberhard. In one of the church records of the Reformed Church the name is written Evert Ten Heuven. They all seem to have been members of the Reformed Church, and Evert a " Ruling Elder," his sons holding the same position in the church after him. Evert was buried at the Skippack Church. This place has long since gone to decay, and no trace is now to be found of his grave.

In 1713 the sons of Evert signed a petition for a road in Skippack township, this county, and wrote it In Hoven. The son Gerhard was at that date a " Ruling Elder" in the Skippack Church, where his father had held the same position before him.

About 1730 Evert sold a tract of land to his son Peter. In the deed for this land he signs his name Evert Inden Hoff. From the year 1708 until the year 1763 the name was variously written.

The first attempt with the Holland name was In Hoff, next Ten Heuven, then Inde Hoffen, and finally, as they became familiar with the English language, we find it in the assessment list of the township written by five families as DeHaven. From that date there has been no variation, except that of one branch, who for convenience, they say, use but one capital. Of this number is John Dehaven, a lineal descendant of the emigrant Evert, who still owns a portion of the original tract, and resides in Philadelphia.

Not one of the name now lives in Whitpain township, where in 1698 Evert settled. This family of Hollanders, and

VON (DE) HAVEN.

those who came with them, were of the farming class, though not known as the peasantry. They brought some money with them, because they all eagerly sought land. The cities had no attractions for them. They soon took the oath of allegiance that they might become land holders.

Peter DeHaven, the son of the first emigrant, died May 23, 1768, aged 82 years, and is buried in Boehm's Church yard, Whitpain township, this county. That would make him a lad of 12 years when his father Evert and his three sons came to America. He was therefore born in 1686, and was 22 years old when he took the oath of allegiance.

The early members of Boehm's Church came chiefly from the Palatinate during the great emigration between the years 1734 and 1738.

From the earliest writing of the name in authentic records it has always been with two capitals, from the first attempt In Hoff, Ten Heuven, Inde Hoffen, DeHaven. The trouble was to angleize the Holland name.

In Pennsylvania Archives, vol. 7, page 114, Peter DeHaven and Elizabeth Knight were married January 18, 1763. If this Peter was the father of Hugh, who married Sarah Holstein April 22, 1775, it was a second marriage.

Mary Holstein, born 11th of July, 1758. Married Septimus Coates, son of John and —— Coates, of Montgomery county, Pennsylvania.

CHILDREN OF JOHN HOLSTEIN AND ELIZABETH.

Surname and date of marriage not known.

Jeremiah Holstein, born 29th of January, 1751, at Ammasland; baptized 20th of March, 1751; godfather, Jonas Marten, godmothers, Catharine Curlin and Mary Fleck, with the parents.

Matthias Holstein, born 16th of January, 1754, at Ammasland; baptized 27th of January, 1754; godfather, Andrew Curlin; godmother, Rebecca Bonde, with the parents. He married Mary Jones about 1783, and died September 5, 1814

The name Jeremiah is not now known in the family. It is presumed he died in infancy.

The date of Matthias' birth is preserved with the comment that he was the only child of John Holstein, who died when Matthias was an infant. The widow of John Holstein married again.

CHILDREN OF FREDERICK HOLSTEIN AND MAGDALENA JONSE.

Matthias Holstein, born November ye 24th, 1755, at 4 o'clock in the afternoon. Married Jane Johnston, of Irish parentage. Resided near Gray's Ferry, and owned land in what is now West Philadelphia. Hamilton Terrace, West Philadelphia, was part of his farm.

About 1803 he moved, with his wife and family of little children, to Westmoreland county, Pennsylvania, spending a winter in Carlisle, Cumberland county, while on his way westward. The remainder of his life was passed in Westmoreland county on the farm upon which they then located. He died there January 8, 1822, aged 66 years; was buried at New Alexandria. His wife died November 18, 1834, aged 70 years.

After the death of Matthias this property came into the possession of his son, Abraham Holstein, who sold it to Robert and Sarah Love, the latter his niece.

Isaac Holstein, born November ye 20th, 1757; died in infancy.

Peter Jonse Holstein, born at Swede's Ford May 25, 1759; baptized November 14, 1759, by Rev. C. M. Wrangle; godfathers, Peter Jonson Morfradren, Henrik Priest; godmothers, Sarah Rambo and Maria Priest. Married Catharine Blake, of Jacobstown, New Jersey, September 25, 1783.

Copy of Marriage certificate, Philadelphia, October 20, 1783.

"These are to certify, That on the Twenty-fifth day of September, in the year of our Lord one Thousand seven hundred and eighty-three, Peter Holstein and Catharine Blake are joined together in holy matrimony.

"As witnesseth my hand.

"HENRY HELMUTH,
"Protestant Minister."

There are three commissions preserved by the descendants of Peter Holstein, the first issued by "The Supreme Executive Council appoints Peter Holstein, Gentleman, Ensign in a company of foot, in the Fifth Battalion of Militia, in the City of Philadelphia, May 1, 1785."

The second appoints him lieutenant in the Third Battalion of militia, May 1, 1789. The third commission of captain is from Thomas McKean, Governor of the Commonwealth of Pennsylvania, August 2, 1800.

Christiana Holstein, born 30th of June, 1761; died aged 20 years.

Elizabeth Holstein, born 9th of August, 1766; baptized 24th of December, 1770; sureties, Andrew Geeranson, Anne Jones, and Peter Jones and wife. She died unmarried, aged about 40. A portion of her hair, light-colored, bright and glossy, is in the possession of and highly prized by her great-nieces.

FIFTH GENERATION

FIFTH GENERATION.

CHILDREN OF PETER HOLSTEIN AND ABIGAIL JONES.

Mary Holstein, married Levi Bartleson in 1785. She was familiarly known among her relatives and friends as "Polly"; was admired for her many pleasing qualities, and considered a young lady of some note in the circle in which she moved. As an only child her every wish had been gratified, and when among her admirers came one whose persistent attentions were agreeable to her, though disapproved by her father and family on account of his intemperate habits—no other objection—the wilful maiden still determined she knew best, and asserted that in time her father surely would yield his judgment to hers. While this was in abeyance her father died. Having every confidence in his daughter his large estate was left to her without any restrictions.

As soon as Peter Holstein died the suitor called at the house, and entering the room where the body lay, remained a few moments, and when he came out remarked in a cheerful, well-satisfied manner "that they would now be married, for he had asked her father, and as silence gives consent there could be no further objection." Soon after, to the surprise of all her friends, they were married, when Levi rapidly squandered in drink the fine estate left Polly by her father.

In 1786, the year following the death of Peter Holstein, the Swedes Ford Inn was kept by Levi Bartleson. In 1791 Jesse Roberts was living there. In 1793 Mr. Roberts was at the Rising Sun Hotel in Norristown, and in 1795 moved back again to the Swedes Ford farm and purchased the property, where he resided until 1800, when he sold it to Major Matthias Holstein, of Norristown, so that Polly Holstein and her hus-

but I could not have retained her father's valuable property over five years, an incredibly short period in which to lose a farm that had been the pride and delight of her father and grandfather.

This, with all the rest of the estate left her by her father, disappeared in the same manner, and they were left entirely destitute, when she who had been esteemed an heiress thankfully accepted the home offered by her cousins, Rebecca and Jesse Roberts, at the Swedes Ford farm, formerly her own inheritance. She remained there receiving pay for her services.

Levi Bartleson occasionally visited his wife at Jesse Roberts.' During these interviews she never failed to reproach him for bringing her and their children to want, and sacrificing her comfortable home to his passion for drink. Their four little children were cared for by her relatives.

Levi at length died and General DuPortale (whose farm joined that of the Swedes Ford, and included what is now, in 1892, known as the borough of Bridgeport, his farm house located where the Evans House, DeKalb street, is now standing) offered Mrs. Bartleson a more lucrative position as his housekeeper, which she accepted with the approval of her cousins.

While there she became interested in the General's farmer, a clever young Irishman named Blaney, and in course of time married him.

During these years of privation and hardship they had both accumulated some money, and taking it as a beginning went to make for themselves a new home in what was then the far west, Ohio or Indiana. Some years later, when Jesse Roberts was again living in Norristown, a man and woman, riding handsome horses, and leading a fine one, were remarked as they passed through the town for their quaint attire and valuable horses they rode. Their destination was the " Rising Sun," and here they were soon recognized as Polly Blaney and her husband, who had returned from their home in the West for her children.

MAJOR MATTHIAS HOLSTEIN.

It is not known whether the children accompanied them when they left the neighborhood, or when and where Polly died. All trace of her family is lost except a little grave directly below the monument of her grandfather, Andrew Holstein. On the headstone of this is carved, "Hilary Bartleson, died September 2, 1706, aged one year." This is without doubt one of Polly Holstein Bartleson's children.

CHILDREN OF SAMUEL HOLSTEIN AND RACHEL MOORE.

Matthias Holstein (the fifth of the name in direct descent), born 12th of October, 1772. Married Elizabeth Branton, daughter of Samuel and Elizabeth Branton, of North Carolina, October 15, 1795, by Rev. Slator Clay, at the residence of Judge Jones, Lower Merion, Montgomery county, Pennsylvania. Mrs. Elizabeth Holstein died February 22, 1815.

Major Holstein married the second time—Sarah Eastburn, of Norristown. He died August 10, 1850, in his 77th year, and is interred near the southeast corner of Swedes' (Christ) Church, Upper Merion.

In early life he started as a merchant at Darby, Pennsylvania; afterwards he was engaged in the milling business in Norristown. His recollection of local events was remarkably accurate. He was the accredited authority in the county for every incident of note that had transpired since his boyhood. Though but a little child at the time Washington and his army, on their march to Valley Forge, crossed the Schuylkill at Swedes Ford on December 15, 1777, yet the bridge of wagons upon which they safely passed the river was often described by him, and also the appearance of the trees upon the bank. The scene made such an impression it was never forgotten.

In his reminiscences of family history he has stated that on the 4th of July, 1778, he walked in the grand procession in Philadelphia with two other kinsmen of the same name, Matthias, the son of Frederick; Matthias, the son of John, and he, Matthias, the son of Samuel, making the third. "This great procession in Philadelphia was for the double purpose of celebrating the adoption of the Constitution, and commemorating the Declaration of Independence of the 4th of July, 1776. It was computed that 5000 persons walked in line, which was one mile and a half in length."

There are now in the rooms of the Historical Society of Pennsylvania two flags which were carried upon that occasion. On a blue ground are thirteen silver stars. Three of them are only outlined, unilluminated, to show that these three states had not at that time adopted the Constitution.

At that day the common mode of travel for both men and women was on horseback. His earliest remembrance of Swedes' (Christ) Church, Upper Merion, was associated with seeing persons arriving there, the women taking off their "safe-guard petticoats" before entering the church and hanging them along the fence.

He frequently pointed out the stump of a black-oak tree upon the farm of Wm. H. Holstein, near the corner of his land upon the turnpike, where, about 1790, he shot the last bear seen in the county. The tree stood upon the edge of a limestone sink, where tradition says cannon balls were secreted during the Revolution. Some years ago numbers of balls were found in the vicinity.

Major Matthias Holstein gave this statement to his nephew, Wm. H. Holstein, of the large landed estate which came by inheritance to his grandfather. He divided it equally among his three sons. To Matthias, the homestead upon the creek, and farm containing something over four hundred acres. To Andrew, the Swedes Ford farm, which was over three hundred acres. Frederick had the balance of the above thousand-acre tract, making his farm three hundred acres, which he afterwards sold to his brother Andrew, and Andrew again sold to their brother Matthias. He, by his will, devised it to his three eldest daughters, Hannah Hughes and Clay, Rebecca Roberts and Rachel Coates. The deed for this property is dated March 1, 1774. The portion left to John was in or near Philadelphia.

The three daughters of Matthias Holstein sold this farm to Andrew Shainline for £170, when Continental money was at its greatest depreciation. Rebecca purchased with her portion of this estate a silver cream pitcher, six tablespoons, six teaspoons, one soup ladle, sugar tongs, and a calamanco petticoat. This material was a heavy woollen stuff, sometimes mixed with silk or goats' hair, and was much used for riding skirts.

It was always understood that the three sisters purchased the same articles with the proceeds of the farm sale. The silver which belonged to Rebecca Holstein is still in the possession of her descendants, Miss Rebecca R. Lane, of Bridgeport, Pennsylvania.

ARTICLES OF AGREEMENT, Indented and made between Samuel Holstein and Isaac Hughes, both of the Township of Upper Merion, in the County of Philadelphia, of the one part, and Andrew Shainline, of said township and county, of the other part. Whereas, Matthias Holstein, by his last will, devised a certain plantation, containing about one hundred and twenty-six acres, now in the occupation of Martin Waters, to his three daughters, Hannah, Rebecca and Rachel, and their heirs and assigns forever, to be equally divided between them share and share alike; and whereas, the said Rebecca Holstein, one of the said daughters, is desirous of selling her undivided third part of the said plantation; now it is hereby covenanted and agreed upon by and between the said parties by these presents, that for and in consideration of the sum of one hundred and sixty-eight pounds, to be paid by the said Andrew Shainline in such manner as is hereafter expressed and appointed, they, the said Samuel Holstein and Isaac Hughes, for themselves, their heirs, executors and administrators, doth covenant and agree with the said Andrew Shainline, his heirs, executors and administrators, that if the said Rebecca Holstein attains the age of twenty-one years, that she will well and truly convey and assure, or cause to be conveyed and assured, to the said Andrew Shainline and his heirs forever, all her right, title, interest and claim whatsoever which the said Rebecca Holstein hath to one undivided third part of afore described plantation, in consideration of which said agreement to be well and truly done. He, the said Andrew Shainline, for himself, his heirs, executors and administrators, doth covenant, promise and grant to and with the said Samuel Holstein and Isaac Hughes, and their heirs, by these presents, that he, the said Andrew Shainline, shall and will well and truly pay unto the said Rebecca Holstein, her heirs, executors or administrators, the sum of fifty-six pounds, on the first day of April now next ensuing, and will moreover then give his bond or obligation for the further sum of fifty-six pounds to be paid by the said Andrew

Shantline, his heirs, executors or administrators, on the first day of April which will be in the year one thousand seven hundred and seventy-two; and also one other obligation for the remaining sum of fifty-six pounds to be paid by the said Andrew Shantline, his heirs, executors or administrators, on the first day of April which will be in the year one thousand seven hundred and seventy-three; said bonds nevertheless to bear no interest till the above times of payment herein specified. It is agreed that if the said Rebecca Holstein should not attain the age of twenty-one years then this obligation to be void, and the said Shantline is to have his money returned to him. In witness whereof we have hereunto put our hand and seals this twenty-seventh day of December, one thousand seven hundred and seventy.

Witnesses present:
  Michell Shenlein.
  Bernhard Shenlein.

SAMUEL HOLSTEIN.
ISAAC HUGHES.
ANDREAS SHENLEIN.

Charles Holstein, born 25th of December, 1774; unmarried; died May 3, 1794, aged 20 years.

He studied law in Norristown with Hon. Seth Chapman, and passed a successful examination. When just previous to being admitted to the bar in Norristown his health failed, finally terminating in consumption. It was of that form which ever deludes its victims to the close. Continuing his rides to the last day of his life, he came into the house after having been over the farm, remarking that he was tired, sat down to rest, and in a few moments was gone beyond the reach of pain and weariness.

George Washington Holstein, born 10th of April, 1778; baptized January 15, 1779.

His parents evidenced a spirit of pure patriotism and bravery in naming the boy without delay in honor of the great general who was at that very time encamped with his soldiers six miles distant upon the hills of Valley Forge.

Miss Christiana Holstein, of Philadelphia, speaking of this fact, remarked to the writer that her mother, with some young friends, had been sent at this time from Philadelphia, because of its occupation by the British, to the safer country home of their relative, Samuel Holstein. The first morning after their arrival his greeting was, "Girls, George Washington arrived last night." Of course there were great demonstrations of joy, but not knowing whether it was in Philadelphia or at the

farm house, their delight was none the less in either case, as they imagined that wherever *he* was there was safety and protection, but the advent thus noted was George Washington Holstein. When but a youth, in his 18th year, he responded to General Washington's call for 15,000 men to suppress the "Whiskey Insurrection," and was among the number who proffered their services, and with his companions was sent to the seat of war; but before the advance party reached the scene of disturbance the insurgents had laid down their arms, and the volunteers returned to their homes.

At the earnest solicitation of his father, George W. Holstein became a tiller of the soil, following the occupation of his father, and assisting him at the homestead farm. On the 5th of November, 1801, he was married to Elizabeth Wayne Hayman, daughter of Captain William and Ann Hayman, of Chester county. Captain Hayman was born in the city of Exeter, England, was captain of a merchant vessel, and for many years followed a sea-faring life.

The marriage ceremony was performed by Rev. Slator Clay, at Waynesboro, the residence of the bride's uncle, Major General Anthony Wayne, in the presence of a large and brilliant assemblage. Both were quite young, the groom being a little over 23, the bride two years younger. The residence which he built at the time of their marriage was but a few hundred yards from his father's, and is now owned by the family of his youngest son, Isaac Wayne Holstein.

Colonel George W. Holstein was a prominent man in the community in which he resided, giving much attention to whatever was for the public good. He was greatly interested in the cause of education, was one of the pioneers in opening up the Schuylkill navigation, and a director in the company for many years; was one of the party who passed up in the first boat at the opening exercises; was active in the erection of the Schuylkill river bridge at Norristown, and an influential director of the company from its organization to the close of his life.

He was a leading member of the Board of Directors of the old Bank of Montgomery, and in this capacity was exceedingly popular as a friend of the industrious laborer. His doctrine was that banking institutions were not intended simply for the benefit of the wealthy business man whose securities were undoubted, but also for the industrious mechanic and artisan whose efforts for success in life were equally deserving of aid.

He was a reliable counsellor and advisor among his neighbors, and by his judicious advice many troubles were settled and kept out of court. He continued as vestryman and warden of the old Swedes' (Christ) Church, Upper Merion, for a period of nearly forty years. Of manly, attractive bearing, and cheerful, genial manners, he was always a cherished guest among his friends and neighbors. His life was passed upon the farm on which he was born.

He died March 10, 1841, aged 62 years and 11 months, and is buried with his kindred in the cemetery of Christ (Swedes') Church.

William Holstein, born 29th of October, 1782; died unmarried, July 1, 1847, in the 65th year of his age.

With his death the old homestead passed out of the name and ownership of the Holstein family into the hands of strangers, on the 4th of November, 1847. It had then been in the family one hundred and forty-two years. There then remained of the thousand-acre tract in their name and possession three hundred and eighty acres.

A daughter of Samuel and Rachel Holstein died in infancy.

CHILDREN OF HANNAH HOLSTEIN AND ISAAC HUGHES.

Sarah Hughes, born 29th of July, 1770; baptized August 26th by Rev. Andrew Goeranson; died in infancy.

John Hughes, born 28th of March, 1772; baptized May 31, 1772, by Rev. John Wickrell. Married Hannah, daughter of Captain Benjamin and Hannah Bartholomew, of Chester county, Pennsylvania.

THE NEW YORK
PUBLIC LIBRARY.

ASTOR, LENOX AND
TILDEN FOUNDATIONS.

WILLIAM LUKENS POTTS.

Benjamin Bartholomew was first lieutenant in General Wayne's Battalion of the Line; commissioned captain October 2, 1776, 5th Pennsylvania Line, and continued as captain of a company of cavalry throughout the Revolutionary war; retired January 1, 1783; died March 31, 1812; buried in Tredyffrin Baptist Church yard, Chester county.

Rachel Hughes, born 18th of April, 1774; baptized October 30, 1774, by Rev. Charles John Sweet, assistant minister of the Swedish congregation. Married March 31, 1801, by Rev. Dr. Abercrombie, of Philadelphia, William Lukens Potts, son of Thomas and Elizabeth Potts, residing in or near Whitemarsh, Montgomery county, Pennsylvania.

The Potts family came originally from North Wales. David Potts, a substantial farmer, a Quaker, appears to have been here as early as 1696, probaby ten years earlier. Of his ten children, John Potts, of Upper Dublin, Quaker, had two sons. The second, Thomas, owned Chelsea Forge, was the high sheriff of Sussex county, New Jersey, in 1772, and member of the Provincial Assembly of 1775 and 1776, and died July 20, 1777. One of his sons, William Lukens Potts, iron merchant, removed to Philadelphia in 1817, and died in 1854.

Ruth Hughes, born 23d of April, 1776; baptized 30th of June, 1776, by Rev. Andrew Goranson. Married David Jones. She died March 2, 1817, aged 40 years and 10 months. Buried in Christ (Swedes') Church cemetery, Upper Merion, at the east or river side of the church.

Sarah Hughes, the second, born 22d of February, 1778; baptized by Rev. Wm. Currie. Married David Rittenhouse, son of Benjamin Rittenhouse and Elizabeth Bull, who was the daughter of General John Bull, of the Revolutionary army, on April 8, 1801, by Rev. Slator Clay. This David Rittenhouse was a nephew of David Rittenhouse, the great astronomer.

Hannah Hughes, born 28th of November, 1780; baptized 20th of April, 1781, by Rev. W. Hultgren. Married Francis Wade, son of Colonel Francis Wade, of the Revolution, and Sarah Nelson Wade. Marriage ceremony performed by Rev. George Sloan, of Frenchtown, N. J.

Isaac Hughes died April 26, 1782, aged 34 years and 4 months.

The Hughes name being closely allied to the Holstein, DeHaven and Clay families, their ancestry and history is given from the earliest dates known in America, and enlarged by reminiscences of some of the older relatives, with the addition of papers relating to John Hughes, the "stamp officer," and his brother, Colonel Hugh Hughes. Many of these have never before been published.

John Hughes and his wife, Jane Evans, resided in Merionethshire, Wales. In this place, in the year 1671, a son, Hugh, was born to them, who was their only child. In 1680, when a lad of but 9 years of age, Hugh Hughes left his parents and home and came to this country. They supposing that he had gone to America, followed him to Pennsylvania, where they found him, to their great joy. John Hughes and his wife, preferring the country as a home, purchased a tract of land in Upper Merion township, then Philadelphia county, now Montgomery. This farm has been known from that date to the present time as "Walnut Grove." Here they resided until their death.

This place is so often mentioned and associated with the history of John Hughes, the "stamp officer," that a short sketch of it may not be out of place. The date of the marriage of John Hughes and his wife, Sarah Jones, is not known, but in 1743 they were living there.

At the time he received his commission as "stamp officer" for the Province of Pennsylvania, in October, 1765, they were living in Philadelphia. In 1770 his son Isaac was at Walnut Grove, and upon that farm the greater part of his short married life was spent. It is said by family tradition, whose authenticity has never been questioned, that General Washington was a frequent visitor to the Hughes mansion while encamped upon the hills of Valley Forge during the winter of 1777-78. A number of his letters are dated "Gulf Mills." They were probably written at "Walnut Grove," and dated from this then well-known land mark. After the close of the war Washington visited his friend, Isaac Hughes, at this place, where he remained over night, and did so at various times.

Persons now living who remember that house recall it as a long, rambling kind of stone building two stories high, having seemingly been added to at various times, as the needs of the family occupying it required.

In 1885, Mr. Benjamin B. Hughes, considering the old house unsafe, begun the work of tearing it down, but the walls were stronger and better than any one supposed, and might well have stood for another century, part of it having to be removed by blasting, as in solid rock. The inside timbers and roof were really all that were unsound. It was always a source of regret to Mr. B. B. Hughes that finding them so durable he had not stopped the work of destruction and renewed the heavy timbers and roof. The new house was then built near it, but not on the same foundation.

In May, 1884, fire destroyed the barn, though the walls were not injured, and on them a new roof was placed the same year, so that of the original buildings at "Walnut Grove" the spring-house is the only one unchanged.

Hugh, their only child, settled in Philadelphia, his residence being on Third street. He married Martha, only child of Hugh and Martha Jones, of Lower Merion. Her parents came from Pembrokeshire, Wales, to Lower Merion. Hugh Hughes carried on in Philadelphia the business of a tanner until the failing health of his parents obliged him to move with his family to their country home, Walnut Grove farm. Soon after this change his parents both died, and, it is said, were buried in the cemetery of St. David's Episcopal Church, Radnor, Delaware county, but no marked graves of the family are now to be found there.

The name Radnor was no doubt given by the early Welsh settlers in that vicinity in loving remembrance of the county of that name in Wales, and the title of their little church among the hills, St. David's, perpetuated the name of a bishopric in their native land.

The Rev. Israel Acrelius, in his History of New Sweden, states that the corner stone of St. David's, Radnor, was laid May 9, A. D. 1715. The Swedish pastor, Sandel, of Gloria Dei, was invited, a service was held, and a sermon preached in a private house.

In 1736 Rev. John Hughes was missionary at Radnor. In his report he states that he visited many Welsh and English gentlemen who " lived far back in the woods." In 1734 Mr. Hughes was the only person officiating in Welsh. At that date there were thousands of Welsh people in Pennsylvania. Mr. Hughes may have belonged to the family of that name in Wales, and possibly a relative of Hugh Hughes, who came to America in 1680, though there is no record to confirm this theory, nothing beyond the fact that they were a clannish people, and where one ventured to establish a home in the new world his kindred would probably follow. Wm. Penn, in early colonial days, said of the race, Welshmen were " mightily akin."

At the time of the marriage of John Hughes to Sarah Jones he resided at Walnut Grove farm. He was a man of remarkably pleasing address and deportment, affable and genial. While yet a young man he seems to have been prominent in his own neighborhood as well as among the noted political and distinguished men of Pennsylvania, where his presence and counsel were eagerly sought.

Hon. Jonathan Roberts, of Upper Merion, in a memoir written over fifty years ago for his immediate family, says of him : " In 1743 John Hughes, of Philadelphia, was then living on his own farm,' Walnut Grove,' about three miles from the residence of my father. He was a man of distinction and cultivation, with the tone of fashionable manners. He was also a man of leisure and social habits, and looked around for intercourse, and in the search called on my father. Their interview was long, perhaps interesting to both. His friendship was no doubt useful to my father. Inclined to a pulmonary affection, Mr. Hughes sought the benefit of a southern climate, and went to Charles Town, South Carolina, in some public capacity, and soon after died there."

Mr. Hughes had probably resided in Philadelphia previous to his marriage. It may have been at that time that the friendship with Benjamin Franklin was formed, which continued through his life. It was through his influence that he was appointed stamp officer for the Province of Pennsylvania. Dr. Franklin wrote to him in May, 1765, that he had recommended him for the position. His commission was received in October of that year.

The Stamp Act was passed in the English Parliament March 22, 1765. It directed that every document used in trade, to be valid, must have a stamp affixed to it, the lowest of these in value costing one shilling, and thence increasing indefinitely in proportion to the value of the writing. This created great excitement in America, and everywhere the people determined not to use the stamps. Associations calling themselves "Sons of Liberty" were organized in opposition to the act, and for the general defence of the rights of the colonies. So powerful were these combinations, and so intense the popular indignation, that when the 1st of November came, the day on which the obnoxious law was to go into effect, it was found that all the stamp distributors had resigned their office. The bells throughout the country were tolled, and the flags lowered to half-mast, to indicate "the funeral of Liberty."

These demonstrations led Parliament to consider the repeal of the act. Among other witnesses, they called Benjamin Franklin, who stated that these acts of Parliament were lessening the affections of the colonies, and unless repealed all commerce between them and the mother country would be broken up, etc. The colonies had also warm friends in Parliament, who advocated their cause, the result of which was that on March 18, 1766, the Stamp Act was repealed.

It must be remembered that at this date the colonies were presumed to be loyal to the English government. This was ten years before the Revolutionary war. Mr. Hughes, as a good and true citizen, desired to support and enforce the law, but prior to the final disposition of the act there had been great excitement in Philadelphia. Mr. Hughes' life and position then were unenviable. Several times a mob collected about his house, threatening his life and property if he did not resign his office. His commission had not then been received, and his answer was he "could not resign what he had not."

During the month of September, 1765, he was critically ill for twenty-five days, and his life was despaired of. While in this condition a deputation from the mob waited on him with muffled drums and muffled church bells ringing. The son of Chief Justice Allen was the leader, accompanied by James Tilghman, Robert Morris, Charles Thomson, Archibald McCall, John Cox, Wm. Richards and Wm. Bradford. They insisted upon seeing him, low as he was, and obtained his written promise not to attempt to perform the duties of the office until his Majesty's further pleasure was known.

In Hazard's Register of Pennsylvania, vol. 2, are a number of very interesting letters from Mr. Hughes upon this subject. These, including those of the Stamp Commissioners in England, also those of Benjamin Franklin and Mr. Galloway, were republished in Bradford's Pennsylvania Journal, and with the comments they called forth were the means of defeating Mr. Hughes for the assembly.

There can be no question of John Hughes' loyalty to the United States. His letters to his valued friend and neighbor, Jonathan Roberts, which follow, show conclusively that he changed his views after the Stamp Act was abolished. From these letters it is learned where and how he was received in Portsmouth, New Hampshire, when he held the position of "Collector of Customs" there in 1769. He was the honored guest of men in high social and political standing. He was appointed "Collector of Customs" for Charleston, South Carolina, in 1771, and died there February, 1772.

These notices of the death of Mr. and Mrs. Hughes were written by his son-in-law, Lindsay Coates, on the leaf of an old Bible:

"John Hughes, my wife's father, departed this life in Charles Town, South Carolina, far from his children and native country, Pennsylvania, the 1st day of February, 1772, aged 60 years. In the various stations of a public and active life He conducted Himself with Stability and Integrity, and displayed a Strength of mind never to be acquired by Education, but which is always the Gift of Heaven. His private character was truly amiable and exemplary in every Relation.

> "Such were thy virtues! With distinguish'd Light
> They shone till shaded by one gloomy night.
> Indulgent Father! O had we been near
> The last sad Rites to pay, and grateful Tear!
> Yet still, tho' on a distant Shore inurn'd,
> Thou wert by Strangers honour'd and by Strangers mourn'd.'

"Sarah Hughes, my wife's mother, left this mortal State the -- day of October, 1774, aged 55 years. Her Temper was mild, averse to affectation and shew. Her attention was confined to its proper sphere, Domestic Life. She was eminent as an affectionate wife, a tender mother, a kind mistress, and benevolent neighbor. Throughout this tedious and painful Illness she was all Gentleness and Patience, cheerfully expecting the welcome summons, being assured that—

> "The Day of Death is not a fatal Day.
> No! 'tis our great Pay Day; 'tis our Harvest,
> Rich and ripe. What tho' the Sickle, sometimes keen,
> Just scars us as we reap the golden grain,
> More than thy Balm, O Gilead, heals the wound.'"

Mr. William John Potts, in a recent letter commenting upon those addressed to Mr. Jonathan Roberts, says: "John Hughes would not have received introduction to Boston patriots from the hand of Franklin, a public act, committing his Patron to the course of the one introduced, and making him responsible for his views, if he was not then, several years after the Stamp Act, in unison with his party."

James Otis and his father, whose flaming patriotism is mentioned at that very time when John Hughes went to Boston, would not have received him so warmly, and handed him about among that most patriotic American society, "The Sons of Liberty," if his views had not been in accordance with theirs. Mr. Otis and son were both active in public life. Mr. Hughes' letters show that his intercourse then with Franklin was a cordial one.

Governor Wentworth, of Portsmouth, New Hampshire, was afterwards a noted Tory. During the time John Hughes was Collector of Customs for the Province of New Hampshire he met the Governor frequently in Portsmouth, where he lived in great state. The representatives of the family who still reside there endeavor to keep this grand old mansion in the exact condition it was a century ago, the same paper, furniture, portraits, etc., which must have been in the house when John Hughes visited it.

The house now known as the Pemhollow House was then called the "Sherburne House." It is highly probable that Collector Hughes was wined and dined there. Broad halls, full-length portraits, rich silver, and stately furniture, are the characteristics of these famous mansions. The state in which the wealthy citizens lived was not excelled by any northern town.

While Collector, John Hughes resided in two American towns which are unsurpassed for their splendid style of living, which more nearly resembles stately English homes. Mr. Potts visited Drayton Hall, ten miles from Charleston, South Carolina, in 1874, and has seen nothing to compare with this great house in any part of the country except Portsmouth. It was built in the decade of 1670, and as the Draytons and their kinsmen, the Middletons, were among the most prominent of the South Carolina families of that day, John Hughes must have been a visitor to this beautiful place.

LONDON, Aug. 9, 1765.

Dear Friend:

Since my last I have received your Fav'r of June 20. The Account you give me of the Indiscretion of some People with you concerning the Government here I do not wonder at. 'Tis of a Piece with the rest of their Conduct. But the Rashness of the Assembly in Virginia is amazing.

I hope, however, that ours will keep within the Bounds of Prudence and moderation, for that is the only way to lighten or get clear of our Burthens. As to the Stamp Act, tho' we purpose doing our Endeavor to get it repeal'd, in which I am sure you would concur with us, yet the Success is uncertain. If it continues, your undertaking to execute it may make you unpopular for a Time, but your Acting with Coolness and Steadiness, and with every Circumstance in your Power of Favour to the People, will by degrees reconcile them. In the meantime a firm Loyalty to the Crown and faithful Adherence to the Government of this Nation, which it is the Safety as well as the Honour of the Colonies to be connected with, will always be the wisest course for you and I to take, whatever may be the Madness of the Populace or their blind Leaders, who can only bring themselves and Country into Trouble, and draw on greater Burthens by Acts of rebellious Tendency.

In mine of June 20, I sent you the Bill of Fees I had paid, amounting to £5. 10. 0. Since which I have paid another Demand of £2. 4. 6. Treasury Fees for a Second Warrant, &c., the first not having included the Lower Counties. I now send with this your Commission, with a letter from the Secretary of the Stamp Office, with whom you are to correspond.

As to our Petition, the new Secretary of State, General Conway, has appointed next Wednesday to give us an Audience upon it, when I suppose it will be presented. And I have very little doubt of a favorable Progress and advantageous Issue.

I am my dear Friend,

Yours Affectionately,

B. FRANKLIN.

To JOHN HUGHES, Esq.

STAMP OFFICE, LINCOLN'S INN, LONDON,
13TH SEP., 1765.

Sir:

There was sent you on Board the Ship Philadelphia Packet, Richard Budden, Commander, a parcel of stamped parchment and paper, directed to you, No. 2, which you are to take care of as soon as the ship arrives, and by the first opportunity acknowledge the receipt thereof by letter directed to the Board, and if you find the stamps to agree with the consignment sent with them, you are to sign and return the said consignment. You are desired immediately to forward the parcel directed to Mr. William Coxe, Distributor for New Jersey.

I am your humble servant,

JOHN BRETTELLEY, Sec'y.

P. S.—Herewith your instructions are sent, which you are punctually to observe.

JOHN HUGHES, Esq.

STAMP OFFICE, LONDON, 10TH MAY, 1766.

Sir:

    I am ordered by the Commissioners to acquaint you, it is the direction of the Lords Commissioners of His Majesty's Treasury, to have all the stamped parchment and paper consigned to you sent back to this office, and the Commiss'rs will endeavor to get directions from the Admiralty for the ships of war returning to England to bring all the stamps home.

    Therefore, if you have any stamps in your custody or power you will please to apply to the Commanders of such ships to take the stamps on board, in order that they may be brought to England by them.

                  I am
                          Your humble serv't,
                                        JOHN BRETTELEY.

JOHN HUGHES, ESQ.

PISCATAQUA, SEPTEMBER 5TH, 1769.

My Dear Son:

    I arrived here after a pleasant journey of 15 days, and have met with the most kind as well as Genteel Treatment in every place I past through, and particularly in the Town of Boston, where not only Doctor Franklin's friends and Relations Treated me with Respect, But the Sons of Liberty shew'd me high marks of Respect also, and I was with the approbation of the Great Mr. Otis Invited to Liberty Club, where I spent an Evening in the most agreeable manner.

    And upon my arrival here, I was Received in the most obliging manner by all Ranks of People, and particularly so by his Excellency, the Governor, who is of the first family in this place, who by their wealth, marriages and Great Offices, are Strictly connected with most of the best families in the province—and are not only a gay and Genteel, But a polite and Hospitable people.

    I am not yet Got into Lodgings, for the Comptrouler has Got me to his house, and will not suffer me as yet Even to mention Lodgings, for some Time, as he says. This Gentleman is young Mr. Traill's father, and is Excessively kind and obliging, and I should be glad if you and your brother John would Treat his son kindly at each of your houses, in acknowledgement of the kind Treatment I receive from his father and mother. And I do assure you, that the story you have heard of the young man, is Groundless as to an old woman, but it seems that woman has a Daughter, that has conceived a passion for the young fellow, who has not the same for her by any means.

    And I now learn that the father had proposed some man as a Husband for his Daughter—and she frankly told him that young Mr. Traill was the man of her choice.

    And this so nettled the father that he Deliver'd the young man his Indentures, and turned him away. I also understand, that some overtures have been made to the young man by her friends since he has been away, and that with the approbation of the father. But the young Gentleman has not been wounded with Cupid's arrow as yet, it seems.

Let me now Recommend attention to your Business, and an amicable agreement amongst yourselves. But above all be obedient to your mother, and strive to make her Situation as agreeable to her as possible. And Rest assured that altho' I have left you in my place or Sted, yet you must always consider your mother as sole and absolute mistress of my fortune in my absence, and all her Commands must by you be Cheerfully Comply'd with at all Times.

From what you Inform'd me before I left home, I suppose I shall upon my Return find you a married man, and you may then Expect to Receive a Deed for Wickerline's place. I shall also give you part of the stock, but your mother will Remain mistress of the old place and every thing that is not given to you or your Sister.

And altho' I have no Intention to prevent your having the use of the old place, nor do I believe your mother has, unless your future behaviour should Render such a step necessary, and if it shou'd, She must and shall During her life be absolute mistress there.

So that it is Greatly your Interest to make her life Easy in all Respects—for when your Sister is Settled, I suppose your mother will be mostly with her Daughter, for some time at least. But if that shou'd be the case, you are not to Expect less than that your mother will have the Command, and it is very fit she shou'd. And if it shall so happen, that your wife should so Choose to live by her self, and not with her mother in law, a house shall be built for yourselves, on your own Land. But as your mother is not hard to please, I expect you will live Lovingly together, and I am sure it is both your Interests so to Do. Yet nevertheless your wife shall always be her own mistress, while she is our Daughter-in-law.

Let Jacob Supplee and his wife know that their son is in good health, and has not yet, I believe, once wish'd himself at home. Give my Respects to Peter Matson and wife, and let me hear how well you succeed in the farming Business, and be particular in Everything, whether you succeed or not succeed. Give my Respects to Miss Hannah, and tell her I shall take a particular pleasure in Receiving a line from her when she condescends to become my Daughter in law. Give my Respects also to the family, and to all my Good neighbors and friends, Especially Mr. Roberts, and Mr. Anderson, and Magdalena Morgan and family, and—

        I am, my Dear Son, your father,

               JO'N HUGHES.

To ISAAC HUGHES.

         PISCATAQUA, SEPTEMBER 7TH, 1769.

De Sir:

In 15 Days from the time I left Philad'a I arrived in this place, and had a very agreeable Journey, both by Land and Water, as the stage served, viz. from Philad'a to New York, a stage wagon from New York to Rhode Island, to Boston in a stage coach and four, and from Boston to Piscataqua in a stage coach and four; which travels better than 40 miles a Day, with Great Ease, the

Roads being mostly very good, but the lands not very Good near the Road in many places for miles together.

In going this long Journey, I often thought of Ovid's Metamorphosis, and cou'd hardly forbear Laughing when I recollected the old Grayheaded fellow, who used to be trotting up and Down a meadow at Walnut Grove, with the Resemblance of Grubbing hoe on his shoulder, and his feet wet and Dirty, and often times his Legs also, but now—Riding in Great state, in a coach and four, prink'd off like a Bean, and treated as a person of consequence, with—your most Humble Servant Mr. Collector. You are heartily welcome to our Town, &c., &c.

Then comes a card with the — compliments of the Collector, &c., to Request the favor of his Dining or supping with him, as the time admitted—And to see the old fellow sent to his lodgings in a Chariot, with a Postillion behind, and sometimes a servant into the bargain. I say, when I considered these things seriously, I cou'd not help reflecting upon the folly and vanity of those persons, who upon such a change (which is but Temporary) forget not only their former acquaintance, but themselves also, and thereby render themselves Ridiculous and Contemptible.

The Province I am in is by no means a wheat country, there being little or none raised in it latterly, Indian corn, Rye, Oates, and Barley, being the Grain Raised here.

These people from Rhode Island Eastward, work oxen chiefly, and it is Rare to meet a Team with a horse in it. And I am told, that many of these ox teams, come 80 and 100 miles to Boston market, and it is much the same here.

To do Justice to the people in this part of the world, it must be allow'd, that notwithstanding the common people have some oddities in their behaviour and speech, yet the better sort are a Polite, Genteel, Hospitable people. And with Respect to myself, must say, that I never met with better usage in my life; than I have met with in this Journey, in every place I passed through, particularly Boston, where not only my own friends, and Doctor Franklin's friends, treated me with Great Civility, but I was by the Sons of Liberty Introduced to Liberty Club, and that with the approbation of Mr. Otis—and the evening was spent very agreeably. And I was next Day accompanied by several Sons of Liberty, and shew'd their manufactory, where upwards of 300 Little Girls, from 6 to 10 years of age, are kept spinning with the Little wheel, Either Flax, cotton, or Lamb's wool; and when these Girls are perfect in their business, they leave the manufactory, and spin for it at their several homes. And they told me that numbers that had left it, now Earned near 3£ Sterling pr week. And so they make those little Girls useful to the Community, and useful to themselves also.

Pray present my best Respects to Mrs. Roberts. Let little Polly know that I expect she has been to see my Wife before this time, or Else I shall complain of her as a bad neighbor. My Compliments to your brother David and Wife, and all friends that enquire for the old Welshman—who is D'r Sir, your Real fr'd,

J'N HUGHES.

TO MR. JONATHAN ROBERTS.

P. S. I am so much hurried between the business of my Office, and the paying and Receiving visits &c. that I have only just had time to write this scrole, and am now call'd upon to Dine with old Coll Atkinson, who is of the upper house, and Chief Justice &c., and as it is now past one o'clock I Inclosed this without ever perusing it, and so you have it from the mint just as it is, without further apology.

John Hughes to Deborah, wife of Benjamin Franklin, from the original in the possession of the American Philosophical Society:

PORTSMOUTH,
SEPTEMBER 8TH 1769.

Dear Madam

After my kind Respects to your Self, and your Daughter, and from the Regard I have for the family, be pleased to make my Compliments to your Son in law, altho' a stranger to me.

Upon my Arrival at Boston I Did my Self the pleasure to wait upon your Sister Meacum. And altho' I am not very forward in Saluting Ladies, Yet it was not in my power to Refrain taking the Sister of my Good friend in my Arms and Saluting her. Perhaps the Good Lady may think that as a Stranger I have been rather Rude, and as I Expect you will have the pleasure of seeing her this fall before I shall, I beg you will Excuse me to the Good Lady if any part of my Conduct has been thought too free, but at the same time I must Confess that it woul'd be Laying a Great Constraint upon my Temper not to Act in the same Manner was I to meet with another Sister of Doc'r Franklin's.

I received on the Account of Doctor Franklin, Great marks of Civility from Mr. Jonathan Williams, and Mr. Hubbard, as well as from Mrs. Meacum, to each of whom I am Under Great obligations for favors Received.

I hope, Dear Madam, your Little Grandson thrives Apace, and that your Daughter is well Recovered from this Little flutter that perhaps may happen a Dozen times yet.

There is nothing strange in this place to Communicate. I shall only say that the Journey was very Agreeable, the people both by the way and kind and hospitable, and I received particular marks of Civility from the Sons of Liberty, and that with the Approbation of Mr. Otis, at Boston.

My Compliments to all Enquiring friends, and believe me, Dear Madam, an Affectionate friend to your family

whilst

JO'N HUGHES [lives.]

CHARLES TOWN, JULY 24TH, 1770.

My Dear Friend:

I take this opportunity to tell you I am yet in the Land of the Living, having arrived safe in this port on the 16th Instant, and have been very kindly Received by the merchants of this place. But must in a great measure, if not altogether, allow, that I stand Indebted for this happiness to the hints very

and Letters sent by me, from my new friends in Boston, Newbury and Portsmouth, many of which have since been shewn me, by the gentlemen here.

The town stands on a Level neck of Land, between the two Rivers, and fronting a large Bay, which lies open to the Sea, save a Bar, at about six miles from the Town, which seems a protection in time of war, much more than any Fortification which they have, in my opinion. Almost all the 1st Settlers were French Refugees, which the persecution of Louis the 14th drove out of France. And the Tempers of the Generality, seem French, to this Day, that is—they are polite, hospitable, and seemingly very friendly, but not overburdened with sincerity. I am told, however, it is much too soon for me to give any opinion of them.

Trade is Dull at this Time, but the Controuler tells me, that my Fees are not less than a Thousand a year sterling, but as yet I do not know how far he is right.

    Believe me to be with Great Regard—
          Your Real Friend
               J'N HUGHES.
To MR. JONATHAN ROBERTS.

         CHARLESTOWN, FEBRUARY 1ST, 1771.
Dear Son:

We arrived in this place in 13 days, but we were but four days from your capes to sight of our port, but then bad weather came on, and we were drove off to sea, and were six days getting to the same place again; however, it was not a bad passage, tho' a long one. Your mother was sea-sick until the last two days, when she grew better—came upon deck, and began to eat. Since we have been here she has been very hearty, until three or four days ago she was a little ailing, but is now getting bravely again.

My cough continues bad, but I have a good appetite, and mend in flesh fast, and I expect shall get into a good state of health before the hot weather comes on. It has rained almost every other day since we have been here.

We long to hear from you all, therefore let no opportunity slip without writing.

I am, with compliments to all enquiring friends, and love to your wife,
         Your Father
To   JO'N HUGHES.
 ISAAC HUGHES.

         CHARLES TOWN, FEBRUARY 1ST, 1771.
My good friend:

It seems almost an age since I had the pleasure of your company, and therefore now sit Down to tell you that we arrived in this place safe after a passage of 13 Days, and what was most Disagreeable we went in four Days from your Capes within 30 miles of Charles Town Bar, and expected to be in port in 6 or 8 hours, but bad weather came on, and we were glad to fly to sea for safety, and it took us six Days to get to the same place again; however, it was not a bad passage tho' long.

My wife was sea-sick most of the time, but since we have been here she has been very hearty Except a Day or two, but is now well again and Eats hearty and looks well, and for aught I see may get fat in this country, as her longing for her children is now moderated, and new Acquaintance Daily coming in.

It rains in this country almost without intermission, and there is a kind of raw moist Cold in the air that is very Disagreeable, but they brag much of their spring months; how it may be then I know not.

Pray let me hear from you by Every Opportunity. My Respects to your good wife and all Enquiring friends, and believe me to be your Real friend,

JOHN HUGHES.

To JONATHAN ROBERTS.

CHARLES TOWN, FEBRUARY 14TH, 1771.

D'r Son:

I only write to let you know we are in health, having several other letters since our arrival here, which must come to hand before this.

I hope you take care to keep your farm in Good order, Especially the meadows, Because it is not only your own loss, but will give me pain if I either hear, or should see the contrary.

I hope Hannah and the child is well, as your mother and I are at present, (my Cough Excepted.)

Let Mr. Roberts know I shall write to him, as soon as I have seen a little of y'e Country, and have something to Communicate worth his perusal.

Be sure to write by Every Opportunity, and as you are in the Country, Mr. Marigeault will forward your letters if left with him.

My Compliments to all Enquiring friends, and my love to Hannah.

I am your father,

JOHN HUGHES.

To ISAAC HUGHES.

CHARLES TOWN, MARCH 20TH, 1771.

My dear Children:

I have sent to the care of your brother John, 7 ounces of silk worm eggs, to be divided as directed in his letter.

Not less than two ounces will fall to your share, and if properly tended will, in six weeks, spin near 140 lbs of silk, which, if properly reeled, will be worth near 140 Pounds Sterling, besides a bounty of 25 £ Sterling, on every £100 value at market. You have mulberry leaves plenty, and may if you properly improve this scheme, make it worth a considerable sum Sterling pr Annum.

There is a young woman on 3rd Street, above Chamber's shop, a carpenter's daughter, who as her father told me is very expert at reeling the balls, and she will instruct you in any thing you may want to know. It will give me great pleasure to hear of your proficiency in this matter, as well as in all other things. The eggs must be kept in a cool part of the house, where no sun comes, nor no fire, and where no mice can get at them. I have put them in flour as you will see; and if they are kept cool, they will not hatch before the leaves come out, but if the sun or fire heats them, they will hatch, and then must perish; no leaves can be got to support them. There has been two vessels from Philadelphia, and no letter from any of you. It will give me great pleasure on my return, to find your plantation in good order, that is—the fences in good repair, and the meadows well watered, and dunged; and I desire you may attend to it.

I am your Father
JO'N HUGHES.

N. B. The best way to keep the eggs, is to hang them up, as I have sent them, in a cold room, where the sun does not come, and where no mice can get at them, because the mice are very fond of them. The worms must be tended night and day, when they are in the eating strain; practice and observation will direct you what to do.

For
ISAAC HUGHES,
at
Walnut Grove.

Pr favor
of Captain Hull.

CHARLES TOWN, S. C.,
APRIL 13TH, 1771.

Dr Sir:

"Give me leave, my Dear Friend, to commend my Son and Daughter Coates to your kind friendship, and assistance, as they are both strangers to the way of life they are now in, and will frequently want both Mrs. Roberts' and your Direction, in almost everything, for some time at least."

"My situation in this Province is Rendered Daily more agreeable by the Respect shewn me by all Ranks of people, from the Governor Down to the Planter, and I have been particularly fortunate in obtaining the friendship of an old Gentleman of a most amiable character, and one of the first fortunes in this very affluent Province. His Son is Speaker of Assembly, and exceedingly popular, and the Father may truly be call'd the mentor of Carolina, being not only wise and judicious but humane and Charitable, in every sense of the word, and is allow'd on all hands, to be the most sincere friend, when he makes but moderate professions of it. Such is the Gentleman's Interest and Influence in this Province, that he is Esteem'd and caress'd, by all Ranks, and all Professions, and I look upon it as a peculiar happiness to me, to have been Recommended to him in so warm a manner, by my much Honor'd friend, Governor Wentworth of New Hampshire."

J'N HUGHES.
April 13th, 1771.

To JONATHAN ROBERTS.

CHARLES TOWN, MAY 24TH, 1771.

My Dear Son:

I write only a short Billet, to be shew'd to your Brother and Sisters Coates and Pratter, to let you all know we are in moderate health. We have vessels often from Philadelphia, and not a scrape of a pen from any of you. Your mother is by no means pleased with your conduct, nor am I, as a letter might be lodged in Marignault's hands, who must know of every vessel that comes here from thence, and I am persuaded w'd Readily Do you that Service.

I long to hear from you all, and so does your mother. I expect Coates' account of his farming, and how they like the Country. I hope Potner and Cary go on Cordially. Give my Respects to Mr. Jonathan Roberts and his wife, and let him know I expect to hear from him by Every Convenient opportunity. My Respects to your mother in law and her family, and to all my old neighbors.

Be particular in giving an account of the Silkworms, and how you go on with farming, and let me advise you all that if you Desire to be Easy, and out of Danger, keep out of Debt, whatever you Do. My love to Hannah.

I am your father,
JOHN HUGHES.

To Isaac Hughes.

CHARLES TOWN, JULY 25TH, 1774.

My Dear Child:

I wrote you by Cap't'n Blewer, to the care of Peter Hughes, which I hope got safe to hand. In it I gave Liberty for you to sell Julius, and buy a boy of 15 or 16, and keep the Remainder of his price for your Brother John.

But I think it is better to Divide the money Equally between you, and I will make up what Each is obliged to advance in his purchase, and that will be more Just to John, who has had but one negro Girl from me.

There is a Gentleman Going to Philadelphia for his health. His name is John Sealy. He is a man of figure and fortune in this country. He is a Justice of the peace, and a Captain of the militia, and as I am kindly Treated by all ranks of people in this place, I w'd wish you on the Rec't of this to wait upon him, and let him know you are my Son, and invite him up to your house, and send your carriage for him if necessary, and Endeavor to make that part of the Country agreeable to him, but Do not permit him to be at any Expense at your house.

My health has been but very Indifferent for three or four weeks past, and if you knew the Difficulty I have to prevent the people from almost Carrying me on their Backs to such a place on the Sea shore, as each thinks will contribute to my health, you will not begrudge some small pains to oblige a single Individual Recommended to your care by me.

Your mother has been poorly for three or four Days past, but I hope will soon Recover.

Whatever may be the Sentiments of Pennsylvania Relative to me, I have now the pleasure to say that in the Greatest of my Popular Credit in that province I was not by any means as happy as I am now. It is true whilst I sacrificed my time, and Consequently my fortune, to support a party, I was a Clever fellow. But when it became me to Discharge my Duty to my Sovereign, I was then with both parties a very bad man. Here I have the pleasure to know that from the

Governor to the meanest merchant I am highly Esteemed. Nor is there a single man in the Province but heartily wishes me to remain amongst them.

My love to Hannah.

I am your father,

JOHN HUGHES.

To ISAAC HUGHES.

CHARLES TOWN,
JULY 25TH, 1771.

My Good Friend:

I do not enjoy my health well in this country, nor my wife either, for some Days past, but both hope for better Times.

I shall send some seed Rice to Isaac to Divide among his Brothers and you. I am of opinion that any Rich up Land will bear it very well, if Drill'd in and the ground kept clean, and often stir'd with the plow. But in this country Rice is confined to Swamps, and what may properly be call'd Drowned Land for a great part of the year, which is the Reason that most Planters suffer more or less every year by Rains overflowing their Rice fields before the Rice is strong enough to live in the water, which it will do very well when it is near a foot high. The Rich upland is Imploy'd in Raising Indigo, as also the highest parts of the Swamps, where common Freshets do not Reach. But they very often suffer in this article also by floods and Inundations, and it has been fatal this year to great numbers of Planters in several parts of the country. I know some Planters that have been obliged to plant 3 or 4 times over in the same ground, and have not 100 acres of Rice standing, altho' near 400 was planted several times over, three Quarters being Destroy'd by the heavy Rains in May and June. If the Season admits their planting in April they have two crops, for after it is Reaped, which is done while the straw is green, it will sprout again and bear another crop. Therefore, I shall send seed, and Expect that amongst you it will have a fair chance.

I shall send some Indigo Seed, and the best account I can get of the manner of making it.

You give us great pleasure in the account you give us of our children. I hope their conduct towards you will be thankful and obliging. Coates has in the amplest manner acknowledged both your and Mrs. Roberts Father and Motherly kindness to them, for which you have our most grateful thanks.

Your account of Isaac is not Disagreeable. I have allowed him to sell Julius, and advised his buying a lad of 15 or 16 years age. I have no Doubt of the New Husbandry, and am pleased to hear of your success. Isaac tells me his Drill'd wheat looks well, and should have been glad to have heard how Sam'l Holstein's turns out. I do not learn by your letter that you have paid my son John a visit, and given him the necessary directions, he being but a young Farmer.

Believe me to be with Real Regard,

Your Sincere Friend,

J'N HUGHES.

To MR. JONATHAN ROBERTS.

CHARLES TOWN, SEP. 25TH, 1771.

My Good Friend:
Your kind favor of the 1st Inst. came to hand by Cap't Wright, and I do myself the pleasure of answering it by him.

I hope Mrs. Roberts is in good health, and able to give my Daughter Ruth some useful Directions as a country wife. As to my son Coates, it seems by your account he never has been in his Right Element until he commenced Farmer, and if he continues to make proficiency in the farming way he will, I dare say, give his Father Coates great pleasure as well as myself. I thank you for the agreeable account you gave of my Son and Daughter Pratter. Perhaps the method I have taken with him may answer as well as if some wiser head had had the management. I sent Caty two, and her mother one half Joe, by Capten Moor, who arrived before Cap't Wright sail'd.

Let Mr. Coates know that I wrote to my Son Hugh, but it is Time must Discover its Effects.

As to my health, it is but very indifferent, being reduced to a skeleton; but hope to recruit when the weather becomes moderate, but if I should not it is not very material. My children are all settled for themselves, and I have seen and known as much of this world as can give a rational being any pleasure, and when that is the case what matter how soon we proceed to survey the boundless universe, and with wonder and amazement admire the Great Creator's works, not only in this but in numberless other worlds, and gain, perhaps, an acquaintance with Innumerable other beings of much Superior knowledge, abilities and Sincerity.

My wife (excepting some few days) has had her health moderately well, and looks as well, or better, than she did when she left Pennsylvania. I shall be glad to hear from you as often as you have opportunity, and if Peter Hughes in Phil'a was spoke to by Coates, and the letter sent to him, he would readily undertake to put them on board from time to time as vessels sail'd for this place.

Yours affectionately,
JO'N HUGHES.

To Mr. JONATHAN ROBERTS.

These two letters and Articles of Agreement from John Hughes, the Stamp Officer, were received from Mr. E. P. Dewees, of Washington, D. C., who has the originals in his possession:

PHILAD'A, MARCH 23D, 1765.

Reverend Doctor:
It is with the greatest deference that we beg leave through your influence and assistance, to inform the Honorable Society that for many years past we have with no small uneasiness of mind observed how much the several missions in Pennsylvania and the Western Division of New Jersey (or at least many of them) are pinched for want of a competent revenue or support for the several clergymen that fill them. It is expected that a clergyman of the Church

of England, and his family, should make a decent, reputable appearance. Not withstanding the diligence and good economy of many of these missionaries, yet such is the narrowness of their present income that they are but barely able to support their families. If death chance to take away the husbands the poor widows and helpless orphans are left destitute of the common necessaries of life.

Moved with the consideration of such distressing circumstances, and extremely sensible at the same time of the extensively pious and charitable design of the Honorable Society for propagating the Gospel, and being desirous to throw in our mite to the aid and assistance of so useful an institution, beg leave to inform the Society that we have with pleasure conceived that the following information, if properly pursued, may in a few years add to the Society's annual income a very considerable sum, which May be rendered perpetual, and we think the best method that can be pursued in such case.

Give us leave to say that upon considering that the Province of Pennsylvania is bounded to the Eastward by the river Delaware, and that New Jersey is bounded to the Southward by the Ocean, and to the Westward by the Delaware aforesaid, whereby there remain yet undisposed of by the Crown several islands along the seashore, and many others within the river Delaware as far as that river is the boundary of the two provinces, which we conceive to be not much short of 300 miles, and as the boundaries of the two provinces are as aforesaid, these islands are not the property, nor yet subject to the law of either Province, but in many cases are the asylum of dishonest men to screen themselves from paying their just debts.

It is also true that several of them are settled by people of both provinces under different pretences of claims, but it is as true that most of them have no legal right by any means, but at the same time there are some few, for which there is the late Duke of York's patents. This we conceive to be at best an equitable title.

We would further beg leave to observe that there is in one of the three lower counties or territories of Pennsylvania several manors or tracts of said property located for the Duke of York, the property which we conceive to be at this time vested in his majesty, and we also believe that some other tracts of land are located in Pennsylvania and elsewhere for the use of the Duke of York, which must also at this time be vested in the crown.

We therefore beg leave to say that we are honestly of the opinion that if so august and respectable a body as the Honorable Society were to apply to his majesty for the Donation or Grant of these Islands as aforesaid, and also all such manors or tracts of land as have been heretofore located by actual survey in any part of North America for the use of the late Duke of York, we cannot in the least doubt but what his most gracious Majesty would, for the pious intent of propagating the gospel, be graciously pleased to make such a grant, and at the same time render these Islands subject to the laws and the government of New Jersey.

It is with grateful pleasure that we embrace this opportunity to inform the Honorable Society that the Assembly of Pennsylvania have, on the application of the Warden and vestry of the united churches of Christ and St. Peter's, &c., passed an Act for raising, by way of Lottery, £3000 for building and repairing churches in different parts of the province where wanted. And it is with no small concern that we behold the thinness of churches in this part of the world, for in so great an extent of country from Burlington to the Cape, which is 150 miles, there is no mission, and from the Cape to Rev. Mr. Cook's mission is near the same distance, and not one mission in all that extent of country. Under these circumstances great advantages are given to dissenting preachers and Romish priests to seduce the people and add to their own numbers, already too great.

Wherefore, to remedy these growing evils as far as in us lies, we have taken the freedom to trouble you with these lines, and do assure the Honorable Society that we have reason to believe that there are some persons at this time taking measures for obtaining a grant of those Islands for their private use, so that it may not be amiss to be early in the application.

If we may be so far indulged, we w'd further observe that it gives us great concern to see some restless, ambitious spirits dabbling in politicks and religion at the same time, and thereby endeavoring to cover under the last the low duty, party views of the first, to the very great scandal, but we forbear this most disagreeable theme.

And most humbly beg leave to add that if these grants can be obtained we offer our best and most vigilant aid and assistance in getting possession of those islands, and shall freely take every measure in our power to get them surveyed, settled and improved, so as to produce an annual income that will be of great use to the churches here, and at the same time we offer our services in discovering the several tracts of land surveyed and returned for the late Duke of York, most of which are at this time entirely waste. And we have not the least doubt but we can manage these matters so as to net the Honorable Society a very handsome income in after years, if they succeed in obtaining the Grant.

The motives that have induced us so far to trouble you and the Honorable Society we hope will plead our excuse, and therefore we very sincerely wish the grant may be obtained, and do most earnestly pray for the propagation of the Gospel in this part of the world.

We are, reverend doctor, with great esteem,

Your most obedient humble servants,

W. S.

L. H.

P. S.— If these hints shou'd meet with the approbation of the Honorable Society, we have some other proposition to make, from which we expect considerable advantage to the Society's pious undertakings, for as we are Americans it may not perhaps be immodest to presume that we are better acquainted with some advantages that may be had in this great, new world than gentlemen in Great Britain with ten times our abilities, who are altogether unacquainted with every part of the country, and the particular modes of settlement, and the advantages that can be made of small grants of land, &c. If we are fortunate enough to be the instruments of increasing the Church of England in North America, happy, indeed, shall we think ourselves. Yet we must confess that it gives us great concern to see in many parts of these two flourishing provinces at least five presbyterian meeting houses to one church, and from the ambitious and restless disposition of that society in this province no pleasing prospect appears, and especially from late riots and extraordinary proceedings of that sect much is to be feared.

N. B. We would further beg leave to say that it is his majesty's real interest to make the grants aforesaid, for by that means not only the islands but those tracts of land that are now wasted would be settled and improved, his subjects increased and wealth added to his provinces.

Sent by way of New York by young Mr. Bard, to go by Franklin's ship.

PHILAD'A, FEBRUARY Y^E 24TH, 1766.

May it please your Grace:

Having lately perused a pamphlet which your grace wrote in answer to Doctor Mayhew I was very much pleased, and upon considering the great strides that the presbyterians in America are now making in order to throw off their dependence on Brittain, and consequently the forming of a republican government of their own, and being Lords and masters themselves, I am induced once more to address your Grace in behalf of the Church of England. I do most sincerely beg your Grace to turn your eyes to America, and receive information from those that have no interest to deceive you, nor can possibly have any motive in view but the support of the church.

I did myself the pleasure some time ago to give your Grace some honest information of the state of things here, and I have from other hands been informed that the letter came to hand, but whether my state or address was disobliging, or whether your Grace imagined that I was some restless, weak mortal that apprehended danger when there were no ground for it, or perhaps your Grace may have apply'd to some of our clergymen here, and from them received different accounts of the state of things. If any or all should have happened, I cannot but say your Grace is excusable. But be the cause what it may, I must declare to your Grace that it is with astonishment that to this day I behold presbyterian teachers and presbyterian influence govern the College in this province, and mould the minds of the youth who will compose the next generation.

It is true also that Mr. Smith, who passes under the Denomination of a Church of England Clergyman, is at the head of this seminary, but may it please your Grace that gentleman's conduct is too well known to all his majesty's loyal subjects here to require any comment of mine, nor w'd your Grace stand in need of much information if you knew the pains and pleasure that gentleman takes to inform the people that his majesty and council have rejected petitions for a change of the Government proprietary to Royal. Can your Grace believe that man a friend to the church who w'd chuse to throw off the sovereignty of Britain. If your Grace can believe it I must confess your faith is great, but for my part I have no such faith, and make no doubt if his majesty and ministers do not support the power of the crown in America, and resume the powers of Government in this province and elsewhere, but what the time will soon come when the presbyterians in America will say (Thank God) we have no King and no Bishop.

Give me leave to inform your Grace for the last time that every Society of Christians on the Continent begins now to be apprehensive of the growing power of the presbyterians in America. Should his majesty or his ministers neglect or refuse at this time to resume the Government in this province and elsewhere, and at the same time not exert the powers of the crown and support the sovereignty of Great Brittain in America, and increase Churches and the Church of England principles on the Continent, I may venture to predict that Brittain's sovereignty and the Church of England will be no more in America in a few years.

I perceive that your Grace is well apprized of presbyterian violence and want of charity, and I trust in God that not only your Grace but my Lord of London and every Bishop in England will exert yourselves on this most alarming ———— ———— and whatever may be the accounts given his Lordship and you by the clergy in America, depend upon it that the downfall of the church is intended by the presbyterians in America, who are avowedly at the head of these riots and opposition to the power of parliament.

If your Grace has any doubt of the truth of what I write I must refer you to their Lordships of the Treasury, who are possessed not only of my letters and account of things but the letters and information of all my brother officers on the Continent, and it appears that not one of them had interest enough in his colony to hold his office and stand his ground but myself, notwithstanding most of them were men of great interest and reputation in their respective colonies, but whether all or any of them have distinguished the presbyterian from other societies in their letters I know not, but as many of them are of that society I presume they have not. Yet it is considered that the colonies particularly inhabited by presbyterians, viz.: Boston, New Hampshire, Connecticut, Road Island, New York, &c., have been the most violent. All that I have alledged is demonstrated, and I must add to this that the presbyterians are active in colonies where they are not yet in a majority. But unless the state of the church is attended to they will soon be in a majority in every colony on the Continent, for they spare no pains in promoting their principles. I will give your Grace an instance in my own family. When my eldest son, who served his time to the law, entered into matrimony, he chose to decline the law and settle upon an estate I had in the Jerseys with £1000 works upon it. As there was no church he went to the presbyterian [several words illegible] and the clergy from all quarters appeared very fond of him, call'd at his house, let him know they would use their interest for his being a Justice of the Peace, &c., and if he happened to stay one Sunday from meeting great inquiry was made for him, and the minister call'd at his house and let him know that it gave the congregation great uneasiness at his being absent, &c. This continued a year or better, and by that time they thought they had him, and ventured to acquaint him that it was expected he w'd make himself master of the lesser catechism, and appear at meeting and make his responses. But this was coming too close upon a Welshman, and a lawyer too. He immediately resented it and declared himself a Church of England man. They soothed him and said he w'd not rise in the world if he behav'd refractory, for their interest would be powerful for him. He gave them for answer that he had an independent fortune and wanted no office, but if he did he would not all his religion to purchase the best office in the government, for as God had given him understanding and his parents had given him good education and a good estate, he was determined not to be duped by them, nor should he treat them with common civility if they ventured to give him any further trouble on that score.

I have only mentioned this as one instance to show your Grace what measures these incendiaries pursue, and the necessity there is to counteract them and promote the Church of England doctrine. I should imagine that if application was made to his majesty for two or three hundred thousand acres of land in each colony, free of quit rent for 15 or 20 years, to be ——— the support of the church forever; if proper persons were employed to get ——— to settle it on low terms, I am persuaded that in ——— than twenty years ——— be brought to produce a very considerable sum annually, and in time come to be such an income as wd enable the society for propagating the Gospel to build churches and fix missions in such parts as are destitute and unable without such aid ever to have any. And I must further premise that unless some good discreet person be made a Bishop and enabled to reside constantly in North America, the church will not flourish, for it is very expensive for common men to send their sons to England for ordination, and rich men in America very seldom make clergymen of their sons. This is one principal reason that the Presbyterians swarm with preachers and fill every new settlement with them, and then they grow up with the settlement and make Presbyterians of all that come amongst them, and by degrees have rich parishes and a handsome salary annually. As the parsons are mostly poor men's sons that are thus settled, ——— think themselves well off if their salary and perquisites at first amount ——— more than hire ——— to labor for them and support the family ——— practice has made ——— church people rank Presbyterians, and will continue to do so if something is not done to prevent it.

The manuscript ends here. Additional might have been added, but if so, it is not in my possession. F. P. D. March 1, 1891.

ARTICLES OF AGREEMENT, made, Indented, Concluded and ——— on this twenty ninth day of March in ——— of our Lord one thousand, hundred and sixty six. Between His ——— William Franklin, Esq., ——— one part; The Honorable Sir William ——— of the second ; G——— Crohan, ——— of the third part; ——— the City of ———, Merchant, of ——— fourth part; Samuel ——— of the said city, ———, of the fifth part; George Morgan, of the ——— merchant, of the ——— part; Joseph Wharton, senior, of the seventh part; ——— Junior, eighth part; John Hughes, Esq, of the ninth part; and Joseph Galloway, ——— of the tenth part.

Whereas it is expected that a Civil Government will be established by his Majesty in the Illinois Country near Fort Chartres, and that a sufficient quantity of land for the settlement of an English Colony there will in a short time be purchased from the nations for that purpose; and whereas the said parties have agreed to apply to the Crown for a grant of *Twelve hundred thousand Acres* or more thereof, if to be procured under such terms and conditions as shall be obtained for the settlement thereof.

Now this Indenture Witnesseth, that the said parties respectively have covenanted, granted and agreed to and with each other in manner and form following: that is to say, that they and each and every of them shall and will from and immediately after the date of these presents enter into and become a joint company and partnership, and do hereby agree to make application to His Majesty, the King of Great Britain, for a Grant or Grants of the said Twelve hundred thousand acres of land to be located in the said Colony, or more if it be procured, and that each and every of them shall immediately after the execution of the said grant or grants so to be procured stand and be seized of the same and the lands thereby granted in manner and form following: that is to say, that each and every of them shall stand and be seized from and immediately after the time aforesaid, of one undivided equal tenth part thereof, the whole into ten equal parts to be divided to hold the same to the said parties respectively, their respective Heirs and assigns forever, provided always nevertheless, that in case it should be thought convenient or necessary in order to obtain the said grant, that any two other gentlemen should be taken into said partnership by the said Company, or by the person or persons who shall be appointed to apply for and procure the said grant, that then and in such case the said lands shall be equally divided between the said parties and such two other persons, and that they and the parties aforesaid and each of them shall stand and be seized of the said lands in manner and form following: that is to say, that each and every of them shall stand and be seized of an equal undivided twelfth part thereof, the whole into twelve equal parts to be divided, to hold to them respectively and their respective Heirs forever. And the said parties do hereby further covenant, grant and agree to and with each other that they and each and every of them shall and will pay his and their reasonable and just part and share of the costs and charges which shall arise, accrue and happen in making the application aforesaid, and in obtaining the said grant in a rateable proportion according to their said respective shares and purparts. In Witness Whereof the said parties have hereunto interchangeably set their hands and seals the day and year above written.

Sealed and delivered in }
the presence of us. }

John Hughes, Junr.
Thos. Hood,
Isaac Hughes.

(Sig.) WM. FRANKLIN. [Seal.]
(Sig.) GEO ROGHEN for
    SIR WILLIAM JOHNSON. [Seal.]
(Sig.) GEO. ——— [Seal.]
(Sig.) JOHN ——— [Seal.]
(Sig.) SAML. WHARTON. [Seal.]
(Sig.) GEO. MORGAN. [Seal.]
(Sig.) JOSEPH WHARTON. [Seal.]
(Sig.) JOS. WHARTON, junr. [Seal.]
(Sig.) JON. HUGHES. [Seal.]
(Sig.) JOS. GALLOWAY. [Seal.]

Mr. William John Potts, speaking of these two letters from John Hughes, the Stamp Officer, says:

"From the time and initials given, one was a joint letter with the Rev. Wm. Smith, Provost of the University of Pennsylvania, whom, as Mr. Hughes shows in his single letter, he does not like; who was the enemy of Franklin, notwithstanding he pronounced the eulogy upon him before the American Philosophical Society. They were always opposed to each other in his life time."

Thomas Seeker was the Archbishop of Canterbury to whom John Hughes wrote, who took a great interest in the Church in the Colonies.

Hugh Hughes was the youngest son of Hugh Hughes, of Wales, and his wife Martha Jones, of Montgomery county, Pennsylvania, and youngest brother of John, the "stamp officer." He was a man greatly esteemed in the community where he was known; trusted, respected and beloved through all the troublous times of the Revolution.

He continued his father's business in New York, on Ferry street near Cliff; was a member and Corresponding Secretary of the "Sons of Liberty" for several years, many of the posters and inciting notices emanating from him. He was Deputy Quartermaster General of the Continental army and Quartermaster General of the State of New York during the Revolutionary war.

Appendix A, "Life and Times of General John Lamb," has this memoir of him:

"Of the many officers of the Revolution who served in the armies of America, and by their fidelity and zeal contributed to the successful issue of the war, few were more distinguished for promptitude and efficiency and very few have had so little justice done to their merits as Col. Hugh Hughes."

In 1765 he warmly opposed the acts of the British Ministry; and although his brother was appointed Stamp Distributor for Pennsylvania, he used every effort to put down the Stamp act.

At the time of these transactions he was residing in New Jersey, but soon afterwards removed to New York. In 1766 he taught a select grammar school in the consistory room of the French church in Nassau street, New York.

He was an energetic writer, and although not a member of the Committee of Vigilance of 1765, he used his exertions and employed his pen in this patriotic work.

On the 16th of February, 1776, he was appointed Commissary of Military Stores for New York by the Provincial Convention, and shortly afterwards was made Deputy Quartermaster General of the forces under the head of that department, Colonel Mifflin.

When Colonel Moylan, the senior deputy, acted as aid to the Commander-in-chief, the management of the department then entirely devolved upon Colonel Hughes, who was indefatigable in performing the onerous and responsible duties required of him.

At the battle of Long Island under his direction the troops were passed over to the Island as the exigencies of the day required, the signals for the dispatch of each detachment being a flag raised on the top of the house at headquarters; and after the retreat was determined on Colonel Hughes received by Joseph Trumbull, the Commissary General, a verbal order from General Washington to impress every kind of water craft from Hell Gate on the Sound to Speyghten Duyvil creek that could be kept afloat, and that had either sails or oars, and have them all in the east harbor of the city by dark. Secrecy was enjoined, as well as dispatch; and although the rendezvous was fifteen miles distant from the anchorage of some of the vessels, they were ready for service at the appointed time. The order was delivered at noon, and at eight o'clock in the evening, such was the celerity of the movements of those employed, that everything important to the occasion was in readiness to be placed in the most favorable situations to secure the retreat; so judiciously were the vessels posted that no delay or confusion occurred, and all material of the army that could possibly be secured was brought off.

At this alarming crisis, when the fate of the campaign and probably the success of the Revolution depended upon the Quartermaster, Colonel Hughes never dismounted from his horse until ten o'clock the day after the order was given, having kept the saddle unremittingly employed for twenty-two hours. Had not the duties of the Quartermaster's department been well performed on that day, the army might have been lost or its artillery and stores captured, and Washington could not have been able to make head against the superior force which menaced the city.

The opinion of the Commander-in-chief in relation to that service was expressed in general orders, and in after times was reiterated in a letter written to Colonel Hughes from Mount Vernon, which is given in Colonel Hughes' memorial to Congress.

He retained the position of Deputy Quartermaster General as long as Colonel Mifflin continued in office. And when General Greene assumed command of the department, he was desirous to secure the services of Colonel Hughes as assistant; but owing to some disgust relative to rank Colonel Hughes declined the appointment, but continued to perform all the services required of him by General Greene until his successor could assume his duties.

When the obstinate contest of Compo Hill, Connecticut, was raging, he sought out General Arnold in the thickest of the fight, and offered his services as aid, which were gladly accepted; and continued throughout the day bearing orders to different parts of the field, and escaping unharmed the severe fire of the enemy.

Throughout the campaign of 1777 he was indefatigable in the discharge of his arduous duties, obeying exactions from every quarter. The army, under Lord Sterling in the South and that of Schuyler in the North, were both indebted to his exertions.

On a certain occasion, the date of which is not now recollected, a British vessel loaded with entrenching tools and other munitions was taken by an American privateer, and her lading ordered to be sold. Colonel Hughes applied to the head of the department for orders to purchase a large portion of the cargo and for funds to enable him to do so, but received for answer that there were no funds disposable for that object.

So confident was Colonel Hughes that these articles would soon be found indispensable that he raised funds by means of loans of his friends, among whom was Governor Clinton, and purchased as many of the implements as he was able. It was not long until they were needed, and few being in the market they were supplied by Colonel Hughes without any advance in the cost, although the market price had risen fifty per cent. after his purchases. His friends thought him over liberal to the Government in not claiming from it the full value of his supplies; but he disclaimed all idea of speculating upon the necessities of the army. In after times he was made to feel that the public generosity was not commensurate with his own, and that even its justice might be fruitlessly invoked.

When Colonel Pickering was made Quartermaster General in 1780, he urged Colonel Hughes to resume the command he had relinquished in 1778, which he did, and continued to serve in a double capacity until the close of 1781, when he relinquished the first in order to devote himself more closely to the duties of the second appointment. The following is an extract of the general orders issued by the Commander-in-chief:

HEADQUARTERS, HIGHLANDS,
December 6, 1781.

Colonel Hugh Hughes having resigned his appointment of Deputy Quartermaster to the army, the General returns him his hearty thanks for his attention to and discharge of the several duties of his office while in service, under innumerable embarrassments. Colonel Hughes still retains his office of Deputy Quartermaster for the State of New York. H. STEWART, *Aid de Camp*.

While acting in this capacity he went from Peekskill to Albany with funds of the department to provide boards for quarters for the army at and near West Point. Arriving at the ferry after the boats had been withdrawn for the night, he fastened his horse and went in search of means of conveyance across the river. During his absence his saddle-bags were rifled and the money, nearly fifteen hundred dollars, stolen, a loss which afterwards occasioned him much inconvenience.

Colonel Hughes continued to perform the functions of his office throughout the war until it was abolished in 1783. In January, 1784, he was elected to the Assembly from the city of New York, with many others of his old associates of the war. The infirmities produced by the severe duties of his department induced him to retire from the city, and he rented a farm at Yonkers, the property of his friend, Col. Lamb; and there, in order to gratify attachments formed in early life, he undertook the charge of the younger children of his friend.

Gen. Anthony Lamb, of New York, was for many years an inmate of his family; and at a later period the children of Major Charles Tillinghast, his deceased assistant in the Quartermaster's department throughout the war, enjoyed the same advantages.

Colonel Hughes had made several attempts to settle his accounts with the War department, but such was said to be the pressure of business upon those employed there that he was unable to effect it. On the 22d of January, 1789, when he was absent from home, a fire broke out in the house he occupied, which, being remote from inhabitants, obtained such ascendancy before help could arrive that it baffled the exertions of the members of his household to arrest its progress, and all the important papers of Colonel Hughes, together with his accounts and vouchers, were consumed, depriving him of the means of proving the indebtedness of the government for his services and expenses, which amounted to nearly nine thousand dollars. Colonel Hughes afterwards made several efforts to procure from the officers of the government the just settlement of his accounts, the loss of the vouchers of which had been owing to former delays on their part, and offered to

GENERAL JAMES MILES HUGHES.

supply the evidence necessary to establish his claims as well as circumstances would admit. But the too rigid construction of the laws by the government officials shut out the equity of his demands, and threw him upon the action of Congress for redress.

But every effort to obtain justice from Congress was unavailing; and three days after his return from his last fruitless journey to Washington, disappointment and its concomitants hastened the ravages of a disease contracted in the public service, and he died at Tappan, March 15, 1802, in the 75th year of his age.

Colonel Hughes was a man of spotless integrity and unsullied honor, sagacious to discern right, and inflexible in his determination to pursue it. His fortitude in the most trying times was never shaken, and in physical and moral courage he was exceeded by none. His attachments were imperishable, and no change of circumstances or mutabilities of fortune could weaken his friendships so long as their objects were deserving. He survived most of his early coadjutors, and in the close of his life was made to realize the ingratitude of the government which, at the hazard of that life and the sacrifice of his fortune, he had assisted to establish.

Two sons of Colonel Hughes were in the army of the Revolution, and both served on the staff of Major Generals in the memorable campaign of 1777.

The elder, Major Peter Hughes, was aid to Gen. Arnold, and bore his orders to various parts of the field in the battles of the 19th of September and the 7th of October. He was for many years clerk of the county of Cayuga. His descendants reside in New York and New Jersey.

General James Miles Hughes, the younger son, served as aid to General Gates so long as his own service with the army continued. Before the termination of hostilities he commenced the study of the law, and was for many years a practitioner in the city of New York, his office being on Wall street, where he was extensively known as one of the public notaries of the

State. His children are now all deceased. He was a member of the New York State Society of the Cincinnati.

Mr. William John Potts, who is greatly interested in the history of Colonel Hugh Hughes, has found some interesting details concerning his early patriotism under difficulties in 1765. A letter-book lately offered for sale by Bangs & Co., Broadway, New York, in a catalogue entitled "Autographs: American, Foreign, Dramatic," etc.; letter-book containing official copies of numerous letters during 1780, 1781 and 1782, to and from Col. Hugh Hughes, Deputy Quartermaster for the State of New York, stationed at Fishkill. Folio unbound.

This correspondence, covering two hundred and thirteen folio pages, presents many items of historical interest, and illustrates the difficulties under which, at that period, the Quartermaster's department labored.

In "The Evelyns in America," compiled from family papers and other sources, 1608–1805, edited and annotated by G. D. Scull. * * * Printed for private circulation by Parker & Co., Oxford, 1881. Pages 286, 287 and 288.

From Francis Bernard, Governor of Massachusetts, to Sir Henry Moore, Bart., Governor of New York:

BOSTON, Feb. 23, 1766.

SIR:—I am favoured with yours of the 17th inst. and would not miss the return of the post to answer it, as far as I can in so short a time.

The account of the affair at New London I had from the mouth of a gentleman of undoubted credit, who dined at a Tavern in New London on the first of January, the day after the meeting with the New York messengers. In the company was one of the Persons who had been at the Meeting the Evening before; and he, in open company, gave the account of what passed at the Meeting, in manner as I have informed you. I don't think myself at liberty to mention the name of the Gentleman who informed me, nor the name of the person who gave the account to him, without their leave; nor do I think this a proper time to make an inquiry into a business of this kind. But if Mr. Sayers is very zealous of his character so as to admit of no delay, he may easily procure Evidence of these Declarations at New London, for, as I am assured, it is known to every one in Town; and as there were seven persons, at least, in company with Mott and Hughes upon this occasion, *Sons* *Sons*, of *New York*, it is hard if he can't prevail upon one of them to testify the declarations concerning him.

When I see the gentleman who informed me, I will acquaint him with this, and if he gives me leave, will inform you of the name of the person who informed him; but it is so little a secret at New London, that information cannot be wanted from hence. I received your packet from Lord Colville, and delivered it to Captain Bishop of the "Fortune," who put it on board the Halifax packet the same day.

I am with great respect, sir,

Your most obedient, humble servant,

FRA. BERNARD.

Sir Henry Moore, Bart.

"DECLARATION.

"On the 31st of December, 1765, two persons came to New London and went to a Tavern there. They said they came from New York. One of them called himself Hughes, and said he was brother to Mr. Hughes, of Philadelphia, appointed distributor of Stamps there.* The other called himself Mott. They sent for six or seven Inhabitants of New London, who were known to be most violent against the Stamp Act, and produced to them a Letter from one Sears, of New York, a noted Captain of the Mob there, recommending them and their Business to the people of Connecticut; that it was expected that Troops would be sent from England to enforce their submission to the Stamp Act; that it was also necessary for them to unite in opposition to the English Forces upon this occasion; that most probably New York would be attacked, and Connecticut ought to march in defence of New York; that they were therefore to learn what number of men from Connecticut might be depended upon to assist the people of New York to support themselves against the English forces. They added that they were to go from thence to Norwich, and from thence to Windham, at both of which places they were to make the same enquiry, and they said that two other persons were gone to Boston on the same business. This Company spent the Evening at the Tavern, and some Resolutions were framed and reduced to writing, but the substance of these has not as yet been discovered.

"These two persons set out the next day in very bad weather to Norwich, from whence they returned to New London the third day, without going to Windham."

Copy of Memorial and Documents in the case of Colonel Hugh Hughes, Deputy Quartermaster General during the war for American Independence, respectfully submitted to Congress by the Memorialists, Washington City, January, 1802.

The claim in this case was laid before the period prescribed by the act of limitation, and was taken up by Congress in February, 1793, and ordered by that honorable body to the Executive for report, but neglected by the proper officer.

The original MSS. of the above-mentioned documents are in the hands of the Clerk of the House.

---

*Appointed through Dr. Franklin's influence.

To the Senate and House of Representatives in Congress Assembled:

The Memorial of Hugh Hughes, of the State of New York, Respectfully Sheweth: That your Memorialist served as a Commissary of military Stores, and as an Assistant and Deputy in the Department of Quarter Master General in the American Army, during the whole period of the Revolutionary war, in the course whereof he rendered many and essential services to the United States, and thereby greatly impaired his health and circumstances.

That anxious to settle his accounts, he did, several years ago, apply repeatedly for means to enable him to accomplish that object, but which he could not obtain. That a considerable balance was and still remains due from the United States to your Memorialist, for which he put in his claim before the Limitation act expired, but after waiting on expences a considerable time he could not obtain the desired settlement, owing to a press of business of superior importance, which the gentlemen then of the treasury alleged precluded their attention to that of your Memorialist. That thus discouraged by expensive attendance, your Memorialist then returned home, when on the night of the 22nd of January, 1789, his house took fire, and his papers, with most of his private property to a considerable amount, were almost entirely consumed. Notwithstanding this unfortunate event, your Memorialist prepared another statement of his claim in the best manner he could, with a conscientious regard to justice, and again applied for a settlement of his accounts, upon which he was told that he must apply to Congress to authorize a special settlement of his claims and demands.

That on the 22nd of February, 1793, your Memorialist did apply by a respectful Memorial to Congress, praying a liquidation and settlement of his accounts and claims, which Memorial was, by the honorable the house of Representatives referred to the then Secretary of the Treasury, " To examine the same, and report his opinion thereon." That the Secretary stated that he was so much occupied by other concerns that he could not attend to your Memorialist, and in fact never did attend to the business of your Memorialist, though called on and pressed so to do. That a copy of that Memorial is hereunto annexed, to which your Memorialist prays the attention of Congress.

That having faithfully served the United States through the whole course of a perilous war, and encountered many hardships and dangers in the promotion of the cause of American freedom, having impaired his health and circumstances by an incessant application of his time and strength, and private resources, to the advancement of the Public Good of the United States, your Memorialist humbly conceives that under the difficult circumstances of his situation, he is entitled to a settlement of his claims, and a full payment of the balance justly due to him.

He therefore, still confiding in the justice and wisdom of Congress, and in the essential services he has rendered the United States, Respectfully prays Congress to provide that relief for him which the necessity of his case, the merits of his services, and the justice of his claims demand.

HUGH HUGHES.

Washington, Dec. 31st, 1801.

PHILADELPHIA, JULY 31ST, 1784.

No

In obedience to your Excellency's verbal order, which was delivered to me by Colonel Joseph Trumbull, on the 27th of August, 1776, the Quarter Master General acting on that day as one of your Excellency's Aids, I impressed, with the assistance which General Spencer was directed to furnish, all the Sloops, boats and water craft from Spyghten Duyvel, on the Hudson, to Hellgate, on the Sound. By which means many of them fell into the hands of the enemy, some of which have since been paid for, but others have not.

As I never expected to be prosecuted for executing your Excellency's orders, that were evidently and eventually the preservation of the army, I never applied for a written order, which is now demanded, and in case of non-compliance prosecutions are directed to be immediately commenced against me.

In justification of my conduct, as above stated, I am compelled to solicit your Excellency to favor me with a written order for that particular service, or a certificate of the verbal one, if more agreeable.

Should my other services, whilst honored with your Excellency's commands, have generally met with your approbation, I will thank your Excellency for such sentiments concerning them as your candour may think that they merit.

This I always intended to ask at the end of my service, but was prevented making the application by a tedious indisposition. Colonel Pickering, having very politely offered to frank this to your Excellency, it will be an additional mark of your favor if you will be pleased to order whatever may be intended for me, to be put under cover to the Colonel, who has engaged to forward it to my Son in New York, as I have not yet returned from Connecticut.

Your Excellency will be pleased to permit me by this opportunity to offer my best wishes for the happiness of your lady and yourself.

With the purest respect and esteem,

I have the honor to be, Sir, Your Excellency's

Most Obedient and Humble Servant,

HUGH HUGHES.

His Excellency, GENERAL WASHINGTON.

MOUNT VERNON, AUGUST 22ND, 1784.

No

I have received your letter of the 31st ult., from Philadelphia. My memory is not charged with the particulars of the verbal orders which you say was delivered to you, through Colonel Joseph Trumbull, on the 27th of August, 1776, "for impressing all the Sloops, boats and water craft from Spyghten Duyvel, on the Hudson, to Hellgate, in the Sound." I recollect very well that it was a day which required the greatest exertion, particularly in the Quarter Master's Department, to accomplish the retreat which was intended under cover of the succeeding night, and that no delay or ceremony could be admitted in the execution of the plan. I have no doubt, therefore, of your having received orders to the effect and extent you have mentioned, and you are at liberty to adduce this letter in testimony thereof.

It will, I presume, supply the place of a more formal certificate, and is more consonant with my recollection of the transactions of that day.

It is with pleasure I add that your conduct in the Quarter Master's line, so far as it has come under my view, or to my knowledge, was marked with zeal, activity and intelligence, and met my approbation accordingly. With grateful thanks for your good wishes, I remain, Sir,

Your Most Obedient, Humble Servant,

GEO. WASHINGTON.

COL. HUGH HUGHES.

In this Memorial are letters from Major General Horatio Gates, Thomas Mifflin, Colonel Stephen Moylan, Brigadier General Samuel H. Parsons, Brigadier General James Clinton, Geo. Clinton, seven from Colonel Timothy Pickering, all speaking in the highest terms of Colonel Hugh Hughes' "honor and fidelity, assiduity and zeal in the public service."

Another dated "Camp Valley Forge," 31st of March, 1778, from Quartermaster General Nath'l Green, begging Col. Hugh Hughes to "forward the supplies then expected from Boston and Rhode Island, to their Camp without delay. They will be directed to your care." And wishing him to continue in the same position.

Also one from General H. Knox, dated New York, April, 1786, stating the artillery service required incessant demands on the Quartermaster General's Department, which gave him an opportunity of knowing the merits of Mr. Hughes, and that "his integrity was untainted by suspicion."

Col. Timothy Pickering writes from Newburgh, May 22d, 1781, instructing him, as Quartermaster General, to dispose of certain United States property, wagons, &c., the public buildings at Bennington, and also in New York. "The iron in the old boom to be sold. The commanding officer at the Point will, at your request, turn out fatigue men to get it out and secure it," &c.

General Horatio Gates, Albany, December 16, 1777, writes for Col. Hugh Hughes to attend to the lumber for barracks, cannon, &c.

In a letter dated Philadelphia, July 19, 1784, Col. Hugh Hughes says: "For almost two years there was not half a sufficiency of paper to transact the daily business of the army and office on; nay, it was not uncommon to tear up old books, write on the covers of letters, wrapping paper, &c., or borrow a little, now and then, where we had credit." This was to show the utter impossibility of rendering his accounts quarterly, as no paper could be had to do it. To show the large amount of money passing through his hands, this letter is given, dated—

TREASURY OFFICE, YORKTOWN, 5TH MARCH, 1778.

SIR:

In consequence of letters transmitted to Congress from Mr. Hugh Hughes and Mr. Wadsworth, an order has been issued on the Treasury for 150,000 Dollars, to be forthwith transmitted to the first, together with another to the Loan Office of New York for 100,000 more.

And the Board suppose that you have remitted to him part of the 400,000 Dollars which you lately received.

A warrant has also been sent to Mr. Wadsworth, on the Loan Office of Connecticut, for 75,000 Dollars, for each of which sums you are to be accountable.

By Order of the Board.

WM. GOVETT, A. Audt. Gen'l.

Mr. Dixon G. Hughes, of New York, has four printed notices of the "Sons of Liberty," one signed H. Hughes, New York, July 16, 1774; another of March 25, 1775. A third one has the signature of Hugh Hughes, and others, calling for "the Citizens to meet at the Liberty Pole, New York, April 28th, 1775." Another to the inhabitants of the city and county of New York, drawn up by Hugh Hughes, dated Thursday night, April 13, 1775.

Mr. Dixon G. Hughes has the Articles of Agreement between Noble Townsend & Co., proprietors of the Sterling Iron Works, in the State of New York, of the one part, and H. Hughes, Quartermaster General to the army of the United States, of the second part, who agreed to make a chain of the following dimensions, at their works, in the space of nine months from the 2d day of February, 1778, provided their teams and artificers were exempted from impress by the Quartermaster General's Department during that time; the chain to be of the following dimensions and quality: In length, five hundred yards, each link about two feet long, to be made of the best sterling iron, two inches and one-quarter square, or as near thereto as possible, with a swivel to every one hundred feet, and a clevis to every thousand weight, in the same manner as those of the former chain.

The said company also engage to have made and ready to be delivered at least twelve tons of anchors of the aforesaid iron, and of such sizes as the said Hugh Hughes, or his successors in office, should direct in writing, as soon as the completion of the chain will permit.

Hugh Hughes, Quartermaster General, on behalf of the United States, engages to pay the said company the sum of four hundred and forty pounds for every ton weight of chain and anchors delivered as before mentioned.

The parties to this agreement subscribed their names to it on the 2d of February, 1778. Signed, Peter Townsend, on behalf of Noble and Townsend. Witness, C. Tillinghast.

Letter from Col. James Miles Hughes to his half-brother, Captain Porter, concerning the death of his father, Colonel Hugh Hughes:

NEW YORK, 1ST OF APRIL, 1802.

My Dear Sir:

It is my misfortune to be under the painful necessity of informing you of the death of my Father, on the 15th of last month, about half after 12 o'clock in the morning. He expired with great serenity, and in the full occupation of his mind. His Death was occasioned by a variety of causes. On or about the first of December last he set out for Washington, in order to make application to Congress for a remuneration for his services as Deputy Quarter Master General in the Revolutionary War, and with pretty warm hopes from the justice of his claims, the merits of his services, and the honorable Documents he could produce, together with a confidence he had in the Justice of the Government, that he would be successful. He continued thereat until about the middle of February, when the Committee of Claims determined on his affairs against him, when he immediately set out for home in a very languishing state. His mind some time before must have anticipated that he would not be successful, which sensibly affected him and bro't on Diabetes, a disorder that fixed itself upon him in his sickness about seven years ago, but not in any violent degree.

These sensations, with the Debility from the disease, produced a total loss of appetite, and for two weeks before he left Washington, he told my Uncle De Haven, at Philadelphia, that he had not eaten one ounce of meat or bread. Thus weakened, he set out, and arrived in Philadelphia, where he stayed about five days. He was attended by physicians, but their art, or any energy of his constitution, could not restore his appetite. He saw his glass was nearly run, and with a wonderful Resolution determined to die in the arms of his family. He therefore set out in a covered carriage, about the 6th of March, from Philadelphia, in company with my Uncle De Haven, an old man of 80 years, who accompanied him as far as Trenton, under the additional hardships of bad roads and cold weather. Here he peremptorily insisted on my Uncle's return, and then journeyed alone, in increasing Distress, for six Days longer, when he arrived at Tappan nearly speechless, and so exhausted with an extreme soreness of flesh, caused by the jarring of the wagon, that it took four Persons an hour to extricate him from the carriage. He continued progressively decaying for about three days, and expired at the Time I have before mentioned, in the 75th year of his age, an honest, neglected, abused Patriot and man, an indefatigable officer, and by the high Testimonials he produced in his Documents presented to Congress, was perhaps an Instrument twice in this war, by his Sole Exertions, of saving his Country. These Documents in Print I shall transmit you by an early opportunity. All the foregoing Facts of my Father's situation on his journey I never knew until he had passed Newark. I immediately set out and arrived about ten hours before he expired. He knew me, asked me indistinctly how I did, and pressed my hand in token of love and Adieu.

Our Mother and Sisters are much depressed for his loss. I attended to his funeral, and interred him in the Tappan Church yard. On his grave I have placed a horizontal Tombstone, with an inscription of his name, Title, age and Time of his Death only. My Mother, Ruthy and Caty, together with Mrs. Gamble's child, I transferred to the Yonkers on this side of the Hudson, in the neighborhood they last lived among. Mrs. Gamble goes with Mrs. Stotesbury and Charry comes to me.

Thus, my Friend, I have given you an account of this unhappy event, and the arrangements made with the family. Our Mother and Sisters desire to be affectionately remembered to you and Mrs. Porter, and to hear from you as early as possible. Remember me, with great Kindness to Mrs. Porter, and believe me,

Your Affectionate Brother,

JAMES M. HUGHES.

CAPT. JOHN PORTER.

Mr. Dixon G. Hughes has in his possession the commission of General James Miles Hughes as First Lieutenant, dated 24th of February, 1776, signed by order of the Congress, John Hancock, President; attest, Chas. Thomson, Secretary. Also, a letter written by General James Miles Hughes to his mother, on the battlefield of Saratoga, and dated, Headquarters, October 15, 1777.

DEATH OF GENERAL JAMES MILES HUGHES.

Our dear Brother, James Miles Hughes, departed this life on the 27th of December, 1802, of an apoplectic fit, in the 46th year of his age. He had had two before. Left his house in expectation of returning in fifteen minutes, was a corpse in less than ten minutes, and brought home dead. He was Aid to General Gates in the Revolutionary war, and was at the Surrender of Burgoyne. At the close of the war he went to the study of the Law, was Master in Chancery, General of the Militia of the City and County of the State of New York; was buried in the New Dutch Church Vault, which was corner of Cedar, Liberty and Nassau Streets, New York.

The Mutual Life Insurance Company's Building now stands on this ground. The body of Colonel James Miles Hughes was removed to Trinity Church yard, New York City.

Hugh Hughes, of Wales, married Martha Jones, of Lower Merion, Montgomery county, Pennsylvania.

SECOND GENERATION.

Children of Hugh Hughes and Martha Jones:

John Hughes (stamp officer) married Sarah Jones in 1738.

William Hughes. His history unknown.

Sarah Hughes married Peter DeHaven, of Philadelphia.

Hugh Hughes, born in Upper Merion 20th of April, 1727, married Charity Smith, nee Porter, in New York, Saturday, July 14th, 1748.

THIRD GENERATION.

Children of John Hughes (stamp officer) and Sarah Jones:

Prudence Hughes, born July 7th, 1740.

Jane Hughes, born June 15th, 1741.

Hugh Hughes, born September 7th, 1742; married very young and settled in New Jersey.

Ruth Hughes, born November 16th, 1743; married Lindsay Coates, May 1st, 1765.

John Hughes, Jr., born December 14th, 1745; married Margaret Paschall, June 11th, 1767.

Isaac Hughes, born December 1st, 1747; married Hannah Holstein, daughter of Matthias Holstein and Magdalena Hulings.

Catharine Hughes, born June 29th, 1750; married Mr. Pritner.

James Hughes, born November 29th, 1752.

Children of Sarah Hughes and Peter DeHaven:

Hugh DeHaven, born 1750; married Sarah Holstein, daughter of Matthias and Magdalena Holstein, April 27th, 1775.

One of the daughters of John Hughes married a Mr. Blankley, of Lower Merion. The name is still found in the vicinity of Philadelphia, and could probably be traced with little trouble, but I have made no attempt to do so. The descendants of his oldest son, Hugh, may possibly be found in New Jersey, where the name is still seen. All that has come to my notice of him is from his father's letter to Benjamin Franklin, dated Philadelphia, September, 1765, where he says: "I shall be exceedingly obliged to you, if consistent with your judgment, to recommend my son, Hugh, for Mr. Cox's successor (as Stamp Distributor). My son is married and settled in New Jersey, has a good estate, both real and personal, and can give any security that may be required. My Son, I hope, will be the better for the office in that Province, which may be some compensation for what property may be lost out of the family."

FOURTH GENERATION.

Children of Ruth Hughes and Lindsay Coates:

Ruth Coates married William Elliott.
Sarah Coates married Charles Moore, of Ohio.
Mary Coates died unmarried, in Ohio, in advanced life.
Lindsay Coates, Jr., died unmarried.

He chose the law for a profession, but his retiring, reticent nature unfitted him for its practice, and he found enjoyment and pleasure in the quiet of a country home, where his life was spent. His greatest delight was in exploring the lonely, unfrequented forests of the vicinity. In one of these rambles it was supposed he had lain down to rest among the rocks, and there death came to him. Though his family, friends and neighbors searched in every direction, no trace of him was found until long after the death of his parents, when his fate had been forgotten except by the oldest residents. In making the Philadelphia and Reading railroad, and cutting through a rocky embankment not far from his home, the laborers discovered the perfect skeleton of a man lying in a depression of the rocks. The size and peculiar formation of the teeth identified it as Lindsay Coates.

Children of Isaac Hughes and Hannah Holstein are six:

Sarah Hughes, born 29th of July, 1770; died in infancy.

John Hughes, born 28th of March, 1772; married Hannah, daughter of Capt. Benjamin and Hannah Bartholomew, of Chester county, Pennsylvania.

Rachel Hughes, born 18th of April, 1774; married March 31st, 1801, William Lukens Potts, of Philadelphia, by Rev. Dr. Abercrombie.

Ruth Hughes, born 23d of April, 1776; married David Jones.

Sarah Hughes, the second, born 22d of February, 1778; married David Rittenhouse, April 8th, 1801, by Rev. Slator Clay.

Hannah Hughes, born November 28th, 1780; married Francis Wade, by Rev. George Sloan, of Frenchtown, N. J.

Children of Catharine Hughes and Mr. Pritner:

Hughes Pritner, died.

Elizabeth Pritner, married Benjamin Bartholomew, youngest son of Capt. Benjamin Bartholomew, of Revolutionary fame, and brother of Benjamin B. Hughes' mother.

Lindsay Coates Pritner.

John Thomas Pritner, was a doctor.

CONSTANCE PRITNER HOLSTEIN.

Caroline Pritner, married Dr. John T. Huddleson.

Catharine Pritner, unmarried.

Isaac Hughes Pritner, the second, married Rebecca Conard, whose family came from Krefelt, near Dusseldorf, on the lower Rhine, Germany, in 1683. At that date they spelled their name Kunders. They settled in Germantown, near Philadelphia, Pennsylvania.

William Pritner.

Constance Pritner, married Branton Holstein, of Mercer county, Pennsylvania, March 15th, 1836. She died August 4th, 1889, aged 73 years.

Martha Pritner, unmarried.

Henry Pritner, died.

Rebecca Pritner, married John A. Colwell.

Henry Pritner, the second.

The descendants of Sarah Hughes and Peter DeHaven, of Isaac Hughes and Hannah Holstein, of Catharine Hughes and Mr. Pritner, will be found further on among Holstein names, carried down to the present time. When the family record of Colonel Hugh Hughes was received the other branches were completed, which will account for the irregular manner in which this is arranged.

DESCENDANTS OF COLONEL HUGH HUGHES, OF NEW YORK.

FIRST GENERATION.

Children of Colonel Hugh Hughes, of New York, and Charity Smith, née Porter:

Sarah Hughes, born 1749; married Captain John Stotesbury.

Peter Hughes, born 1751; married Sarah Ann Ward, January 8th, 1783, and second wife, Naomi Gould.

Susannah Hughes, born 1753; died.

James Miles Hughes, born 1756; married Maria Bailey.

Charity Hughes, born 1758.

Susan Hughes, born 1759; married William Gamble.

Ruth Hughes, born 1762.

A. W. Sidney Hughes, born 1768; died aged 10 years.

SECOND GENERATION.

Children of Sarah Hughes and Captain John Stotesbury:

Susan Stotesbury.

Sydney Maria Stotesbury, married Philemon Dickerson

Mr. Dickerson was in Congress in 1833-5, and in 1835-7 resigned; was Governor of New Jersey, 1836-7; again in Congress, 1839-41; U. S. Judge, 1841-62.

Children of Peter Hughes and Sarah Ann Ward:

Charles Hughes, married Ann Dixon.

Hugh Hughes, married Laura Bostwick.

Stephen Ward Hughes, unmarried; died.

John Lamb Hughes, unmarried; died.

Sarah Ann Hughes, married Dr. Nathan Farnsworth.

Child of Peter Hughes and second wife, Naomi Gould:
Peter Gould Hughes.

Child of Susan Hughes and William Gamble:
Ruth Hughes Gamble, died unmarried, April, 1891, aged 97 years.

Children of Sydney Maria Stotesbury and Judge Philemon Dickerson:
John Henry Dickerson, married Maria Kirby.
Theodore Dickerson.
Mary Dickerson, married John M. Gould.
Edward Nicoll Dickerson, married Mary C. Nystrom.
Philemon Dickerson.

Children of Charles Hughes and Ann Dixon:
Stephen Decatur Hughes.
Jasper Ward Hughes, married Catharine Conely.
Harriet M. Hughes, died unmarried, aged 72 years.
Charles Hugh Hughes, married Ann Lauton.

Children of Sarah Ann Hughes and Dr. Farnsworth:
Monroe Farnsworth, died.
Nathan Hughes Farnsworth; residence unknown since 1860.

THIRD GENERATION.

Children of John Henry Dickerson and Maria Kirby:
Maria E. Dickerson, married Nathaniel Coles.
Susan S. Dickerson.
Philemon Dickerson.

Children of Mary Dickerson and John M. Gould:
Sydney Maria Gould.
Catharine Holsman Gould.
Ann Eliza Gould.

DIXON G. HUGHES.

Children of Edward Nicoll Dickerson and Mary C. Nystrom:
Mary Caroline Dickerson.
Edward N. Dickerson.
Louise Adele Dickerson, married Charles W. Gould.

Children of Jasper Ward Hughes and Catharine Condy:
Harriet M. Hughes, died.
Dixon G. Hughes, married Mary L. Storer.
Stephen D. Hughes, died.
Emma Augusta Hughes, unmarried.
Jasper W. Hughes, unmarried.
Henry Warden Hughes, died.
Catharine Louise Hughes, unmarried.

Child of Charles Hugh Hughes and Ann Lauton:
William M. Hughes, married Annie Gould.

FOURTH GENERATION

Children of Dixon G. Hughes and Mary L. Storer:
Catharine L. Hughes, died.
Mary Ada Hughes.
Emma Augusta Hughes.
Charles Wood Hughes.

Children of William M. Hughes and Annie Gould:
Charles M. Hughes.
Harriet M. Hughes.

Edward Nicoll Dickerson, third son of Sydney Maria Stotesbury and Philemon Dickerson, and great-grandson of Colonel Hugh Hughes, of Revolutionary fame, was born February 11, 1824, and died December 12, 1889.

Extracts from "Memorial Addresses" before the Bar of the city of New York, December 16, 1889, in the U. S. Circuit Court. Mr. Samuel A. Duncan presented the following resolutions:

The Bar of New York have learned with profound sorrow of the death of Edward N. Dickerson, one of the most eminent and useful members of the profession, whose career of more than forty years has adorned and added the lustre of genius to the profession of the Lawyer and Advocate. Assembled in accordance with the time honored custom, in the temple of justice where he was so often seen and was so conspicuous a figure, it is incumbent on us, his associates, to recount his merits, and pay an appropriate tribute to his memory.

Be it therefore Resolved, That in the highest and best sense our departed brother deserves commemoration as a man of lofty character, of irreproachable life, and of qualities that won and held the esteem of friends and the confidence of the public. As a citizen he was patriotic, courageous in the expression of his convictions on all political questions, and ever guided by a strong attachment to the union of the states.

As a member of the legal profession Mr. Dickerson was eminently fitted by nature and training to be serviceable to his fellow-men. Earnest in his convictions, with a great faculty for lucid statement, and persuasive of speech, he enforced his views with an eloquence and a power that won him many noted victories. Concerned in many of the most important patent litigations of his day, Mr. Dickerson has left his mark upon that branch of our jurisprudence.

He has left it also upon the mechanic arts, in some of which he made highly useful inventions of his own. He has left it too upon many of the sciences which are concerned with the material progress of the age. His proficiency in scientific knowledge made him always a welcome guest among its special professors.

By his many brilliant qualities and his largeness of heart Mr. Dickerson gained a host of friends both among the members of the bar and in other walks of life.

Mr. Grosvenor P. Lowrey said of him:

"He was lawyer, inventor, explorer, builder, engineer, philosopher, and, above all, friend. How many among us here have felt the warmth of that friendship? I cherish it as among the best of my possessions that at different times I have been permitted to deal, open heart to open heart, with Edward N. Dickerson, not because there ever arose between us any particular occasion for great trust, but because it was natural to him to be open, and I thank heaven it was possible for me to reciprocate. He was in all respects a stalwart and a great man. Nothing was small about him. His physical stature was like his moral and his spiritual stature.

"We have seen this rare man pass before us in life's procession. Some who are here now have been witnesses to the whole of an unique career. It was the figure of a visigoth that strode across the stage of our professional and social life and disappeared. The heroic limbs were clad in modern habiliments, it is true, and the features, derived from some far-off ancestor of an heroic epoch, were illuminated with high thinking on every subject which engages the attention of our more civilized times. Still it was the figure of an ancient warrior and champion. And now it is a memory and a shade. For me, I prefer to retain the idea of a man who exists, and forever will exist, as we have known him here. We have witnessed his entrance and his exit, and without in any way abandoning the expectation of seeing again that stalwart figure and high bearing, and that illuminated face, we may pronounce the salutation, Hail and Farewell! His like will not, I am sure, be seen again among the Bar of this generation."

Mr. Charles C. Beaman, his law partner, says:

"Gentlemen, you will agree with me that Mr. Dickerson was a great man. No man that I have ever seen enjoyed more the conflict of a law suit than he, and no man that I have ever met was in a conflict more impressed with the absolute justice of his own side, not only in its justice morally, but in its justice intellectually. Therefore he struck with strength and without fear. There was nothing small about Mr. Dickerson. Was he ever small to a court? Didn't he always stand straight up and set out all there was in the case? Did he not generally base his arguments not upon the testimony of his own witnesses but upon his cross-examination of the witnesses of the other side? Has he not as a strong man and as a just man battled and reasoned for his clients through this court and through every court?

"I only utter the tribute of you all in saying that when you met Mr. Dickerson you met a man that you were glad to meet, proud to defeat, and when defeated by him felt that he had fairly whipped you. The recollection of that great-limbed, great-minded, great-hearted man will be to us all a joy forever."

Judge Wallace said:

"His great ability and his very exceptional accomplishments as a lawyer in that specialty to which he devoted his professional life are known to all of us. Among the leaders of the patent Bar he stood pre-eminent. His towering stature typified with but little exaggeration his intellectual supremacy. He threw his whole heart and judgment into the cause of his client. When he was on the right side he was irresistible. Usually his diction and delivery were simple and even homely, rising at times to heights of rugged eloquence, but on occasions when the subject was worthy of the best forensic oratory he soared in the azure beyond. He was one of the most generous, loyal and magnanimous of men, and his thousand unremembered acts of kindness and of charity were so intermingled with his daily life that they were its woof and warp, and invested it as with a garment of which they were the fabric. He sleeps well after life's fitful fever, and the flowers of a fragrant memory will blossom upon his resting place."

At the time of the marriage of Mrs. Hannah Holstein Hughes and Rev. Slator Clay she resided on the farm known as "Poplar Lane," but a short distance from "The Gulf," and about half a mile from her former home at Walnut Grove. The location of the house at Poplar Lane was upon a hill near Balligomingo creek. That house still stands, many additions and improvements having been made to it, so that it is now an attractive country house. In the settlement of the estate of John Hughes, Poplar Lane was sold, and Walnut Grove came by inheritance to the children of Isaac and Hannah Holstein Hughes, whose descendants retain it in the name at the present time.

The slaves, Jack and Dinah, his wife, who were given to Isaac Hughes by his father in 1770, were bitterly opposed to their mistress marrying again, and behaved so badly when Rev. Mr. Clay was at the house that their dislike to him could not be concealed. Soon after their marriage, while at breakfast with his wife and children, Mr. Clay was the first one to taste the coffee. Finding something very peculiar and unpleasant about it, he desired that none of the family should touch it until he returned. Upon going into the kitchen he found the coffee pot filled with poke root, which Dinah had put in hoping it might sicken him and end his life. When charged with the crime she did not deny the accusation, not seeming to have realized until that moment that there might have been a fatal termination, but simply anxious that Mr. Clay should not be in the same house with her mistress. When told that she could not be trusted and would have to be sold she entreated them most pitifully that they would pardon her, exclaiming that she would never do a wicked act again. They did forgive her, and ever after she continued to be a faithful, trusty servant.

As the descendants of Rev. Slator Clay and Hannah Holstein Hughes comprise many important families, the history of the Clay ancestry is given as it was received from his granddaughter, Mrs. Emily Clay Pollock.

The first ancestor of the Clay family of whom an authentic record is given is Robert Clay, of Chesterfield, England (date of birth not given).

He married Hannah Slator, of Chesterfield, England, January 15, 1687; he died July, 1737, is buried in the east end of the Parish church, Sheffield, England.

The children of Robert and Hannah Slator Clay are Slator and Thomas. The latter emigrated to North Carolina, and died there about the year 1744. Slator, the eldest, married his first cousin, Ann Curtis. She was the daughter of Jehu Curtis, Speaker of the Delaware Assembly, Judge of the Supreme Court and Treasurer of the Loan Office, upon whose tombstone, near the porch of Immanuel Church, at New Castle, Delaware, is the following epitaph, written by Benjamin Franklin:

IN MEMORY OF
JEHU CURTIS, ESQ.,
LATE SPEAKER OF THE ASSEMBLY,
A JUDGE OF THE SUPREME COURT,
TREASURER AND TRUSTEE OF THE LOAN OFFICE,
WHO DEPARTED THIS LIFE, NOV. 18TH, 1753.
AGED 64 YEARS.
If to be prudent in Council,
Upright in Judgment,
Faithful in Trust,
Give value to the Public Man;
If to be sincere in friendship,
Affectionate to relations,
And kind to all around him,
Make the private man amiable,
Thy death, O Curtis,
As a general loss,
Long shall be lamented.

The children of Slator and Ann Curtis Clay were thirteen in number, nine boys and four girls. Slator, the second, being their fifth son. He was born in New Castle, Delaware, October 1, 1754.

Slator Clay, the second, studied law and was admitted to the Bar in 1779 or 1780. He went to the West Indies with a friend who was a sea captain. This was during the Revolutionary war. A British privateer captured the vessel, and Mr. Clay was put ashore on the island of Antigua with only one piece of money in his possession. He took passage in a vessel bound for New York, which was then held by the British. A mutiny occurred among the sailors, and they were afterwards wrecked on Bermuda Rocks. At Bermuda he taught school for six years, and returned to Philadelphia in 1786, and on the 31st of December in that year he was married to Mrs. Hannah Holstein Hughes, widow of Isaac Hughes, of Upper Merion, Montgomery county, Pennsylvania, by Rev. Dr. N. Collin. She was the daughter of deceased Matthias Holstein, and his relict, Magdalena, in Upper Merion.

He was ordained deacon in Christ Church, Philadelphia, by Bishop White, December 23, 1787, and on the 17th of

February, 1788, he was ordained priest in St. Peter's Church, Philadelphia. He became rector of St. Peter's, Great Valley, Chester county, of St. James', Perkiomen, and St. David's, Radnor; was also assistant minister of Christ (Swedes') Church, Upper Merion, under Rev. Dr. N. Collin's rectorship. At that date Episcopal clergy were scarce, and their fields wide.

In 1790 Mr. Clay removed to Perkiomen, where a parsonage had been erected, with a glebe of thirty acres. He also gave a part of his time to St. Thomas', Whitemarsh. He was highly honored for his sincere piety, which shone in his life; he was a natural and earnest speaker, and his voice was agreeable. Where he began his ministerial work he ended it, and died at Perkiomen September 25, 1821, aged 67 years, closing a life of faith on earth, in a sure hope of entering on a life of glory in eternity. Upon his tombstone in the churchyard at St. James', Perkiomen, is inscribed:

"Sacred to the memory of the Rev. Slator Clay, who for nearly 33 years was rector of St. James', Perkiomen; St. Peter's, Great Valley; and Swedes' Church, Upper Merion. Who departed this life Sept. 25th, 1821, aged 67 years." (Two Scripture quotations are here omitted.)

Robert Clay, Slator Clay's elder brother, was also a church clergyman. He was born October 18, 1749, was ordained by Bishop White in 1787; was for thirty-six years rector of the church at New Castle, and died there in December, 1831. He was unmarried.

FIFTH GENERATION.

Children of Mrs. Hannah Hughes and Rev. Slator Clay are four:

Ann Clay, born at "Walnut Grove," Upper Merion, Montgomery county, Pennsylvania, March 16, 1788; married Samuel Hepburn, son of James and Mary Hopewell Hepburn, of Northumberland county, Pennsylvania, December 21, 1811, by Rev. Slator Clay, in Montgomery county, Pennsylvania. Samuel Hepburn was a prominent lawyer of Milton, Pennsylvania. He died October 16, 1865. His wife, Ann Clay Hepburn, died December 5, 1865.

George Clay, married his cousin, Emma, daughter of Hugh DeHaven and Sarah Holstein, December 5, 1822; no children; both deceased.

FIFTH GENERATION.

Children of Mrs. Hannah Hughes and Rev. Slator Clay are four:

Ann Clay, born at "Walnut Grove," Upper Merion, Montgomery county, Pennsylvania, March 16, 1788; married Samuel Hepburn, son of James and Mary Hopewell Hepburn, of Northumberland, Pennsylvania, December 21, 1811, by Rev. Slator Clay, in Montgomery county, Pennsylvania. Samuel Hepburn was a prominent lawyer of Milton, Pennsylvania; he died October 16, 1865; his wife, Ann Clay Hepburn, died December 5, 1865.

George Clay, married his cousin Emma, daughter of Hugh DeHaven and Sarah Holstein, December 5, 1822; no children; both deceased.

Jehu Curtis Clay, born February 3, 1792. He was ordained by Bishop White in St. Paul's church, Philadelphia, in 1813. In 1814, married Margaret Annan, of Philadelphia, by Rev. Dr. Pilmore, in St. Paul's church; Mrs. Margaret Clay died April 16, 1826. At that time Mr. Clay was assistant to Rev. Dr. Collin, of Gloria Dei Church, at Wicacco, but soon after was called to St. John's, Norristown. From there he went to Newbern, North Carolina, but on account of the unhealthy climate removed to Hagerstown, Maryland, where he remained until his father's death; when he succeeded him as pastor of Perkiomen, Norristown, and old Swedes' (Christ) Church, Upper Merion, which charge he retained until the death of Rev. Dr. Collin in 1831, when he was called to the rectorship of Gloria Dei, Philadelphia, where he remained until his death, October 20, 1863. Rev. Jehu C. Clay married the

"Gloria Dei" Old Swedes Church, Philadelphia.

second time, Simmons Edy, daughter of Thomas Atkins Edy and Julian Edy, both of the island of Barbadoes, West Indies, by Bishop H. U. Onderdonk, November, 1828. (The name Simmons was the surname of a gentleman, a friend of Mrs. Clay's father.)

Bishop Potter, in his sermon at the funeral of Dr. Clay, says: "The death of Dr. Clay was no ordinary death. He had gone in and out of this diocese during his long ministry without a reproach. The ministry is a power for weal or woe, his was certainly a ministry for good. The innocence of his life, and the doctrine of his preaching, were all directed to this end. In sunshine and storm he was at his post; no sufferer ever appeared to him in vain. The prominent traits of his ministry might be summed up in punctuality, fidelity, kindness and gentleness. In the exercise of these traits, he had erected a monument that would last for generations." The Bishop closed his sermon by saying that "he had gone to his rest, full of years and honors." Another notice of his death says: "As a pastor he was greatly beloved and esteemed by the people for whose spiritual welfare he had given the largest portion of his life. To the poor he was a warm and steadfast friend, whose loss it will not be easy to replace. Of an affectionate, loving disposition, he was hailed alike by both old and young as a privileged counsellor and adviser."

Charles Holstein Clay, married Maria, daughter of Owen and Ellen Lane Evans, of Evansburg, 22d of March, 1822, by Rev. Slator Clay.

Children of Rachel Holstein and Lindsay Coates, six:

Rebecca Coates, married Nathaniel Henderson, of Upper Merion; no children. Mrs. Rebecca Henderson died April 11, 1843, aged 56 years.

Rachel Coates, married Nathaniel Smith; died December 1, 1853, aged 65 years.

Matthias Coates, married Sophia, daughter of Captain William and Ann Wayne Hayman, of Chester county, Pennsylvania.

Hannah Coates, married John Young; children all died in infancy.

Betsy Coates, died unmarried in early life.

Emma Coates, unmarried; resided in Bridgeport; died July 11, 1882, aged 83 years.

Children of Rebecca Holstein and Jesse Roberts, of Norristown, four:

Rachel Roberts, born 31st of December, 1781; died January 14, 1859, in her 79th year.

Sarah Roberts, born November 5, 1783; died October 25, 1862, in her 79th year.

Hannah Roberts, born December 17, 1786; died August 2, 1854, in her 68th year.

These three sisters all died unmarried. As the eldest of the family, Rachel was the controlling power among them, managing with marked ability the business affairs for all. Her memory is lovingly cherished throughout the parish of "old Swedes'," Upper Merion, where she was known as aunt and cousin by more than half the community. The happy influence of so good a life still lingers among the people by whom she was beloved, revered and respected. When Rachel died Sarah naturally took her position as head of the household, retaining the love and respect she had always commanded. Previous to this time, each of the sisters filled her allotted place in the home circle.

Magdalena Roberts, born February 21, 1789; married Edward, son of Samuel and Phœbe Lane, of Chester county, Pennsylvania. Edward Lane died in Bridgeport, March 10, 1858, in his 70th year. Mrs. Lane died August 13, 1871, in her 83d year. In 1822, the heirs of Jessie Roberts, dec'd, owned all the land on the east side of DeKalb street, Norristown, from the river to Lafayette street, and from DeKalb street to Green. In the Spring of 1826, one portion of it was sold to Major Matthias Holstein, of Norristown, for $2,500. A few years later, the other three shares were sold to Mr.

MISS RACHEL ROBERTS.

Jamison, Benjamin Evans and Jesse Keesy, for $3,600. All of it is now closely built up, and very valuable.

Children of Sarah Holstein and Hugh DeHaven, eleven:

Peter DeHaven, born 21st of January, 1776; baptized by Rev. Jacob Duché; married 25th of January, 1801, to Sarah, daughter of Col. Samuel Atlee.

Sarah DeHaven, born 18th of November, 1777; died July 16, 1778.

Harriet DeHaven, born October 1, 1779; baptized by Bishop White; married Nathaniel Barber, April 20, 1809. Mr. Barber died in Philadelphia about 1840. Mrs. Barber died on the 8th of March, 1857, aged 77 years and 6 months. No children.

Mary DeHaven, born May 30, 1781; died April 18, 1782.

Maria DeHaven, born January 16, 1783; baptized by Bishop White; died same year.

Amelia DeHaven, born January 5, 1785; baptized by Bishop White; married 2d of January, 1809, Joseph Augustus Atlee, who was born near Lancaster, Pennsylvania, March 10, 1781. They settled first in Marksboro township, New Jersey; afterwards resided near Bellefonte, Centre county, Pennsylvania, where Mrs. Atlee died 7th of October, 1854. Mr. Atlee died January 20, 1867. Both are buried at Pine Grove Mills, Pennsylvania.

Holstein DeHaven, born September 9, 1786; baptized by Bishop White; married January 18, 1818, Sophia, daughter of John and Sophia Jolly Elliott, of Philadelphia.

Hugh DeHaven, born June 30, 1788; baptized by Rev. Jos. Clarkson; married Christiana Lyng Bunting, daughter of Charles and Ann Bunting, of Octorara, West Nottingham, England, February 3, 1825. Mrs. DeHaven was born March 28, 1796; died November 30, 1830, aged 34 years and 8 months.

Hugh DeHaven married the second time—Zipporah Dill White, daughter of Samuel and Sarah White, April 11, 1832, by Rev. Jos. Holdrich; she died March 19, 1871. Hugh DeHaven died February 16, 1860.

Juliana DeHaven, born October 18, 1790; baptized by Rev. Jos. Clarkson; died March 3, 1802.

Lindsay Coates DeHaven, born April 20, 1793; baptized by Rev. Nicholas Collin; died November 16, 1839, aged 40 years; is buried at south side of Swedes' (Christ) Church yard, Upper Merion.

Emma M. DeHaven, born February 18, 1795; baptized by Rev. Slator Clay; married George, son of Rev. Slator Clay, December 5, 1822; died 1857; no children.

The name Hugh, which is carried down in many branches of the DeHaven family, is evidently derived from Hugh Hughes, who was born in 1671, and whose daughter, Sarah Hughes, married Peter DeHaven. Their only son was named Hugh, and married Sarah Holstein April 27, 1775.

The names of the sons of Sarah Holstein and Hugh DeHaven are clearly traced to their direct ancestors—Peter, the eldest, having the name of the great grandfather; Holstein, bearing his mother's surname; Hugh, carrying down the line his father's; and Lindsay Coates, that of his father's uncle.

Children of Mary Holstein and Septimus Coates, seven:

Hannah Coates, died aged 14.

Sarah Coates, married Ebenezer Rambo, son of Tobias and Margaret Knox Rambo, of Upper Merion.

Magdalena Coates, died unmarried, June 16, 1868, at the residence of Mrs. Samuel Coates, Norristown, aged 83 years.

John Coates, married Martha, daughter of Henry and Hannah Pugh, of Lower Merion, Montgomery county, Pennsylvania. John Coates died 27th of January, 1857, aged 70 years. Mrs. Coates died January 5, 1881, aged 81 years and 11 months.

Ann Coates, married Wm. Holloway, February 11, 1819. She died October 21, 1822.

Samuel Holstein Coates married Margaret, daughter of John and Mary Owens, of Radnor, Delaware county, Pennsylvania, November 30, 1815, by Rev. Nicholas Collin. Samuel H. Coates died 22d of December 1856. Mrs. Coates died October 21, 1872, aged 78 years.

Slator Clay Coates, died in his 22d year, unmarried.

Children of Matthias Holstein and Mary Jonse, eleven:

Elizabeth Mattson Holstein, June 11, 1784; died June 16, 1811.

John Jonse Holstein, born October 8, 1785; married Elizabeth Williamson about 1811. He died January 21, 1818; Mrs. Holstein died March 12, 1849.

Ann Holstein, born April 11, 1787; died October, 1852; unmarried.

Hannah Holstein, born December 29, 1788; died August, 1845.

Rachel Holstein, born November 8, 1790; died August 15, 1803.

Nicholas Collin Holstein, born July 12, 1792.

Peter Jonse Holstein, born February 23, 1794; died October 18, 1824.

Rebecca Holstein, born May 11, 1796; married Evan Davis; 4 children, all died in infancy. Mrs. Davis died February 15, 1875.

Mary Holstein, born July 1, 1798; died August 5, 1838.

Christiana Holstein, born September 5, 1799; unmarried; died December 3, 1877, aged 78.

Susanna Jonse Holstein, born October 31, 1802; married Charles Vaugn. Died May 8, 1866.

Children of Matthias Holstein and Jane Johnston, seven:

Rebecca Holstein, born in Philadelphia; unmarried; died in Westmoreland county, Pennsylvania.

Samuel Holstein, born in Philadelphia; married Mary, daughter of Samuel and Jane Henderson, of Westmoreland county, Pennsylvania.

Andrew Holstein, born in Philadelphia; married Miss Patterson; one child died in infancy; all deceased.

Elizabeth Holstein, born June, 1798; married Samuel Love 8th of January, 1822, by Rev. Mr. Lee, in Westmoreland county, Pennsylvania. Mrs. Love died 1st of July, 1871. No children.

Abraham Holstein, born in Philadelphia; unmarried; resided in Westmoreland county.

Mary Holstein, born in Philadelphia 1803; died, unmarried, in Westmoreland county, Pennsylvania, on the 23d of December, 1824, aged 21 years.

Sarah Holstein, born 3d of June, 1807, in Westmoreland county, Pennsylvania; married January 15, 1829, to Robert Love (brother of Samuel, who married her sister Elizabeth), by Rev. Mr. Davis. Removed same year to Butler county, Pennsylvania, to a farm.

Children of Peter Jones Holstein and Catharine Blake, twelve:

Frederick Holstein, born July 17, 1784; died 7th of October, same year.

John Holstein, born December 30, 1785; married Jane Parkinson (who was of English descent) September 29, 1808, by Rev. Dr. N. Collin, in Kingsessing township; died March 18, 1821, in the 36th year of his age. Upon his monument is inscribed these lines:

> "Lo! where these silent marbles weep,
> A husband and his children sleep."

Mary Holstein, born February 3, 1788; died 1867, unmarried, aged 80.

Christiana Holstein, born January 31, 1790; married Henry, son of James and Catharine Makemson, of Kingsessing, in 1815.

THE NEW YORK
PUBLIC LIBRARY,

ASTOR, LENOX AND
TILDEN FOUNDATIONS.

SIXTH GENERATION

ELIZA B. HENDERSON.

Sarah Holstein, born March 29, 1792; married George Brandt, son of James and Mary Brandt, of Kingsessing township; died in 1884.

Mary Magdalena Holstein, born October 5, 1794; married Abel Lodge, son of John and Elizabeth Lodge, of Kingsessing township.

Peter Jones Holstein, born May 29, 1797; married Hannah Leech. No children.

Ann Holstein, born August 23, 1799; unmarried; resided at Darby; died 1884.

Nathan B. Holstein, born November, 1801; died in infancy.

James Bartman Holstein, born June 16, 1803; died in infancy.

Eliza Holstein, born April 2, 1804; died, aged 5 years.

Catharine B. Holstein, born April 2, 1807; married John De Hart, son of Abraham and Catharine De Hart, of Kingsessing. Mrs. De Hart died June, 1848.

SIXTH GENERATION.

Child of Mary Holstein and Levi Bartleson:
Hilary Bartleson, died September 2, 1796.

Children of Major Matthias Holstein, of Norristown, and Elizabeth Branton:

Elizabeth Branton Holstein, born October 1, 1798, at the old homestead on Spring creek; married John Henderson, a talented lawyer of Norristown, son of Samuel and Mary Henderson, of Upper Merion, Montgomery county, Pennsylvania, October 21, 1819, the ceremony being performed by Rev. Bird Wilson. Mrs. Henderson removed to Mercer county, Pennsylvania, in 1850, where the remainder of her life was spent. " Entered into rest" December 11, 1871. Interred at Christ (Swedes') Church, Upper Merion.

Rachel Moore Holstein, born November 22, 1800; married Thomas Mayberry Jolly, son of John Adams Jolly and

Rebecca W. Mayberry Jolly, a lawyer of distinction in Norristown. Mrs. Jolly died October 16, 1884, in her 84th year.

Samuel Holstein, born May 30, 1803; married Anna, daughter of Abram and Elizabeth Kintzing Pritchett, of Philadelphia, on April 30, 1840, in the Church of the Epiphany, Philadelphia, by Rev. Stephen H. Tyng. Samuel Holstein settled in Mercer, Mercer county, Pennsylvania, on the 3d of December, 1827, having left Norristown a few months previous with the intention of locating in Detroit, Michigan. He moved from Mercer to Neshannock Falls, Lawrence county, in the spring of 1855, relinquishing the practice of law from that date and finding pleasure and occupation in the oversight of his farm and mills to the close of his life. He died May 29, 1870, aged 66 years.

Charles Holstein, died in infancy.

Matthias Holstein, died in infancy.

Branton Holstein, born March 18, 1808; married Constance, daughter of Isaac Hughes Pritner and Rebecca Pritner, of Kittanning, Armstrong county, Pennsylvania, on March 15, 1836, by Rev. Bryan Bernard Killikelly (Episcopal). Isaac Hughes Pritner was the son of Catharine Hughes and Mr. Pritner, and grandson of John Hughes, the "stamp officer." Branton Holstein moved from Norristown to Mercer in 1834, but finally settled on a farm at Neshanock Falls, Lawrence county, where he remained eighteen years. In 1852 he moved to a farm five miles north of the town of Mercer. Constance, wife of Branton Holstein, died August 4, 1889, aged 73 years. After the death of his wife Mr. Holstein resided with his daughter, Mrs. David M. Hadley, in Sharpsville, Mercer county, Pennsylvania, where he died October 8, 1890, aged 82 years.

Children of Col. George W. and Elizabeth Wayne Hayman:

Ann Sophia Holstein, born August 24, 1802; married Andrew, son of Jacob and Rebecca Shainline, of Upper Merion, Montgomery county, May 17, 1826, by Rev. Slator

Clay. Their home was an adjoining farm, about one-half mile distant, which had been purchased in the year 1774 by Andrew Shainline from the heirs of Matthias Holstein. Here their happy married life was spent, and in the same house, surrounded by all most dear to her, she "fell asleep" on the 9th of April, 1847, in the 45th year of her age, leaving a family of nine children, the youngest an infant three months old. Captain Andrew Shainline married a second wife, Mrs. Mary Naile Sell, and died November 5, 1869, aged 74 years.

Rachel Moore Holstein, born October 6, 1804; baptized by Rev. Slator Clay; married Thomas J., son of James Molony, of Kingsessing, 27th of May, 1830, by Rev. Jehu C. Clay. Mrs. Rachel Molony died Tuesday morning, 29th of March, 1831, aged 26 years and 6 months. Remarkably attractive in person, gifted with a happy, cheerful disposition and refined, winning manners, she gained the love of all who knew her. An infant son a week old survived her; her body was laid to rest beside her kindred, in the cemetery of Old Swedes Church, Upper Merion, March 31, 1831.

Elizabeth Wayne Holstein, born January 4, 1806; baptized by Rev. Slator Clay; married Dr. Joseph Brookfield, of Philadelphia, son of William and Elinor Irvin Brookfield, of Gloucester county, New Jersey, 19th of June, 1849, by Rev. Edwin N. Lightner, at the residence of her sister, Mrs. Mary H. Amies, of Bridgeport, Pennsylvania.

Mrs. Elizabeth W. Brookfield, died in Philadelphia, March 29, 1887, in her 81st year, and was interred in the Friends' Cemetery, Lower Merion township, by the side of her husband, Dr. Joseph Brookfield, who died December 17, 1872, aged 84 years. An extract from an obituary notice of her says: "Hers was a life of love, of duty, of devotion to the happiness of the many who were near and dear to her, and it was fitting that as the evening shades began to gather devoted hearts and willing hands were near to minister to her every want. The loveliness of her Christian spirit added a charm to her fourscore years that endeared her to all around her, and made it a struggle for our selfish hearts to give her up, but the fragrance of her pure life will be ever with us."

Mary Atlee Holstein, born September 15, 1807; baptized by Rev. Nicholas Collin; married William, son of Thomas and Susan Amies, of Philadelphia, April 24, 1828, by Rev. Jehu C. Clay. He was a prominent paper manufacturer at Darby, Delaware county, Pennsylvania. Mrs. Mary H. Amies died in Philadelphia, at the residence of her son-in-law, Abram Walker, July 9, 1888, in the 81st year of her age. There is in the possession of Mrs. Amies' daughters a looking-glass, in fine preservation, which formerly belonged to Magdalena Hulings Holstein; it descended to Mrs. Amies through her uncle, William Holstein, by whom it was highly prized, as having belonged to his grandmother.

Emily Wilson Holstein, born March 18, 1810; baptized by Rev. Nicholas Collin; married William Brooke Thomas, son of Reese and Rebecca Brooke Thomas, of "The Gulf," Montgomery county, Pennsylvania, September 22, 1836, by Rev. Jehu C. Clay. William B. Thomas succeeded his father as proprietor of the "Gulf Mills," and in 1843 removed to Philadelphia, where he began the manufacture of flour, at Thirteenth and Willow streets, and soon after added another mill at Thirteenth and Buttonwood streets. He was one of the founders and first president of the Corn Exchange Association, Philadelphia, now known as the Commercial Exchange, and was a prominent member of the Board of Trade. On the breaking out of the Rebellion he enlisted in the Hon. C. M. Clay's Company, and soon afterwards was appointed to the Collectorship of the Port of Philadelphia. In 1862 he organized two companies, known as the "Revenue Guard," which he armed and equipped at his own expense. He was elected Captain of Company A, and was afterwards promoted to Colonel of the Twentieth Regiment Pennsylvania Volunteers. In 1863 he responded to the call for more troops, and reported at Harrisburg, where the duty of guarding the Northern Central Railroad was assigned him. He was ordered to the command of all the troops in York and vicinity. In 1864,

MARY HOLSTEIN AMIES.

having obtained leave of absence as Collector, he organized the One Hundred and Ninety-second Regiment Pennsylvania Volunteers, which were garrisoned at Fort McHenry. He also served on Lake Erie, on the Ohio River and in West Virginia. After his return to Philadelphia, he was elected Brigadier-General of the Fourth Brigade, First Division of the Pennsylvania State Guard, which position he held until the reorganization of that body. Col. Wm. B. Thomas died on the 12th of December, 1887, in his 77th year.

Gustavus Adolphus Holstein, born June 26, 1812; died August 12, 1813.

Louisa Brooke Holstein, born May 23, 1814; baptized by Rev. Nicholas Collin; married George W. Dewees, son of Waters and Ann Bull Dewees, of the Marsh, Chester county, Pennsylvania, January 8, 1846, by Rev. Edwin N. Lightner. George W. Dewees died March 7, 1859.

William Hayman Holstein, born February 17, 1816; baptized by Rev. Slator Clay; married Anna Morris, daughter of William Cox Ellis and Rebecca Morris Ellis, of Muncy, Lycoming county, Pennsylvania, in St. James Church, Muncy, September 26, 1848, by Rev. Edwin N. Lightner; and settled upon the farm which is part of the thousand acre tract purchased by Matthias Holstein, the second, in 1709; it then extended from the Schuylkill river to Red Hill. Upon this farm they have since resided.

At the time of the battle of Antietam, on the 17th of September, 1862, William H. Holstein enlisted in the Seventeenth Regiment Pennsylvania Militia, in response to the call made by Governor A. G. Curtin. Upon his return he and his wife left their home to engage in the Field Hospitals of the Army of the Potomac; remaining at Antietam caring for the sick and wounded until all were removed to Frederick City, Maryland. The remainder of the winter of 1862 and 1863 was spent in General W. S. Hancock's Second Corps Hospital, near Falmouth, and at Potomac creek; while there living in tents, William H. Holstein making frequent trips to Philadelphia to renew supplies of needful hospital stores, which were abundantly furnished from this and adjacent counties, Mrs. H. continuing as nurse in Second Corps Hospital.

Remained there until the 14th of June, 1863, when orders were given to send all sick and wounded to Washington, D. C., by railway.

They moved with the hospital department of the second corps, traveling in an ambulance from that point to Fairfax Station with them, bringing up the rear of this grand army of the Potomac while on its hurried march to Gettysburg, having a little tent for their use whenever the train halted, a rubber blanket upon the earth their bed, and satchel for pillow. At Union Mills, near Fairfax Station, where the last night of this march was spent, were in sight of rebel camp-fires almost within bugle call of their troops. These contending hosts moved northward, in parallel lines; day by day each could trace very nearly the route of the other by the vast clouds of dust which hung over them. At this point General Hancock advised proceeding by railroad to Alexandria, thence to Washington, and there await results. After a few days of rest in that city, returned home to recuperate, when, on the 2d, 3d and 4th of July, 1863, came news of the great battle of Gettysburg; went from Baltimore in the first train through, seated in box cars upon rough boards; joined the Second Corps Hospital, and resumed the work that had so lately been laid down. They found the wounded lying just where they had been placed when carried from the battle-field; large numbers of both armies kindly cared for by the same surgeons and attendants. On the 17th of August, 1863, the general hospital, known as "Camp Letterman," was organized; here were collected from the various corps and division hospitals three thousand of the worst cases of the wounded of the two great armies. Mrs. Holstein filled the position of matron-in-chief, remaining there until it was broken up in November, when, after a few days' rest and glimpse of home, returned to Gettysburg, to be present at the dedication of the Soldiers' Cemetery, and were so fortunate as to be seated within a few feet of President Lincoln when he delivered his ever memora-

WILLIAM H. HOLSTEIN.

ble address. Part of the winter of 1863 and 1864 was devoted to work for hospitals, in visiting various parts of Pennsylvania, to make known to those who were working for the sick and wounded their wants, as had been learned while resident among them.

May, 1864. Again in Virginia, Belle Plain, Port Royal, White House and City Point; from the day the hospitals were started in this latter place until very late in the autumn, when December was spent as the preceding had been. William H. Holstein, at this time, and previously, engaged in the work of the United States Sanitary Commission, while Mrs. Holstein was absorbed in hospital duties. In January went to Annapolis, Maryland, occupied most fully there among the returned prisoners until July 3, 1866, when army hospitals were no longer needed.

Their home, with its country joys and pleasures, had never seemed to them more attractive than now in contrast with the sad and exciting scenes just ended.

Susan Holstein, born January 24, 1818; baptized by Rev. Dr. Collin; married William B. Roberts, son of Hon. Jonathan and Eliza Roberts, of Upper Merion, Montgomery county, Pennsylvania, 20th of October, 1841, by Rev. Jehu C. Clay. William B. Roberts died June 4, 1885, aged 67 years.

George Washington Holstein, born October 30, 1820; baptized by Rev. Nicholas Collin. George W. Holstein graduated in the medical department of the University of Pennsylvania, March 31, 1843; practiced medicine but a few years, when ill health compelled him to discontinue it. Married Abby Turner Brower, daughter of Daniel and Anna Farmer Brower, at Phœnixville, Chester county, Pennsylvania, October 19, 1847, by Rev. Edwin N. Lightner. Doctor Holstein went with the "emergency men" when called out by the Governor in 1862, and afterwards spent some weeks in hospitals, assisting the Christian Commission in their work of caring for the sick and wounded. His residence is Bridgeport, Montgomery county, Pennsylvania.

Isaac Wayne Holstein, born January 25, 1823; baptized by Rev. Nicholas Collin; married Alice Hallowell, daughter of William R. and Debora Hallowell, of Upper Merion, Montgomery county, Pennsylvania, at the parsonage of Swedes (Christ) Church, Upper Merion, December 27, 1854, by Rev. Edwin N. Lightner. Isaac W. Holstein died April 8, 1884, in the 62d year of his age, and is interred in the cemetery of Christ (Swedes) Church, Upper Merion.

It is a noteworthy fact, that of the eleven children of Colonel George W. and Elizabeth Wayne Holstein, ten were married, and all settled within an hour's ride of the old homestead. The grandchildren, thirty-one in number, following the example of their parents, are, with three exceptions, living within the same radius; two of the brothers, William H. and Isaac W. reside on farms that are part of the original tract, as the deed declares: "From John Justis to Matthias Holstein, made the 18th day of the month called February, in the 8th year of the reign of Queen Ann over Great Brittain, 1709," &c. The Matthias to whom this deed was made is the second of the name in this country, and the third son of "Matts Hollsten," was born July 1, 1681. This property seems to have been purchased previous to the year 1706, at which date his father's will was written. It is reasonable to suppose that Matthias was living there at the time of his marriage to Brita Rambo, which was October 10, 1705, and would account for his father having furnished him at that period with his share of his estate.

Children of John Hughes and Hannah Bartholomew—eight:

Rachel Bartholomew Hughes, born at "Walnut Grove," August 2, 1801; married Jacob Dewees, M. D., son of David and Catharine Dewees, of Trappe, Upper Providence township, Montgomery county, Pennsylvania, by Rev. Jehu C. Clay, November 9, 1826. Mrs. Rachel Dewees died August 24, 1862, and is interred in the ——— Cemetery, at Pottsville,

BENJAMIN B. HUGHES.

Pennsylvania. Dr. Jacob Dewees, born March 29, 1792; died January 23, 1872.

Isaac Wayne Hughes, born in Montgomery county, February 14, 1804; graduated in medical department of University of Pennsylvania in 1825; moved to Newbern, North Carolina, June 1, 1825; married in 1829 Eliza A. McLin, daughter of Thomas and Eliza McLin, of Newbern, North Carolina. The ceremony was performed by Rev. Lemuel Hatch (Presbyterian). Mrs. Hughes died in Newbern, in 1842, in the 33d year of age. She was celebrated for her beauty.

Dr. Hughes continued actively engaged in the practice of his profession at Newbern, except a short time during the late war. He went to Goldsboro the day after the capture of Newbern, and moved from there to Charlotte, North Carolina, where he continued the practice of medicine; returned to Newbern in 1865, where he resided the remainder of his life. His success was brilliant and substantial. Dr. Isaac W. Hughes married again at Newbern, North Carolina, Annie M. Smallwood of that place, on May 5, 1853, Rev. William N. Hawks (Episcopal) officiating.

Benjamin Bartholomew Hughes married Mary, daughter of Jonas and Nancy Rambo, of Upper Merion, Montgomery county, Pennsylvania, in 1829, by Rev. Jehu C. Clay. Mrs. Hughes died August 20, 1856, aged forty-seven years. Benjamin B. Hughes married the second time Mary J., daughter of David and Hannah Brooke, of "The Gulf," Upper Merion, Pennsylvania, August 17, 1858.

Benjamin B. Hughes, died March 11, 1892, aged 84, and was interred in the cemetery of Christ-Swedes Church on the 16th of March.

Slator Clay Hughes, married Susan, daughter of Joseph and Elizabeth Jarrett, of Upper Merion, August 4, 1836, by Rev. Jehu C. Clay. He died December 20, 1841, aged 31 years.

Francis Wade Hughes, born August 20, 1817, in Upper Merion township, Montgomery county, Pennsylvania.

He commenced the study of law 1834, in the office of the late George W. Farquahar, of Pottsville, Pennsylvania, and the following winter entered the office of John B. Wallace, of Philadelphia. In August, 1837, he was admitted as a member of Schuylkill county bar, and commenced the practice of his profession in Pottsville, Pennsylvania, where he passed his life. His success was immediate, brilliant and continuous; his practice extended to all branches of the profession, and his cases were important.

He married Elizabeth, daughter of Thomas and Sarah Silliman, of Pottsville, Pennsylvania, April, 1839, the ceremony by Rev. A. A. Miller.

He was appointed Deputy Attorney-General by Hon. Ovid F. Johnson, then Attorney-General. He resigned three times, but was subsequently re-appointed, and held the position altogether eleven years; his knowledge of criminal law was consequently thorough, but the great bulk of his practice had always been in the civil courts. He ranked among the first of the few great land-lawyers; was a fine equity practitioner, and understood patent and commercial law.

At no period of his life was he willingly concerned for the prosecution in homicide cases, and for twenty-five years refused such engagements. He had, however, very frequent engagements for the defense, with invariable success to the extent of preventing a conviction of murder in the first degree. He gave the subject of criminal jurisprudence a great deal of thought, and whilst he could not be said to be opposed to capital punishment to the extent, or for the same reasons, which influenced its opponents generally, yet he doubted the efficacy of capital punishment in any point of view. Nevertheless, when what are known as "Molly Maguire" cases came on for trial, he took an active part in the prosecution in Carbon, Schuylkill and Columbia counties. Through the efforts of Mr. Franklin B. Gowen, and the instrumentality of the Pinkerton detective agency, the requisite proofs and knowledge of the criminals was obtained. Capital punishment in their case seemed the only remedy for the ills under

FRANCIS W. HUGHES.

which the community suffered. Acting under this belief, Mr. Hughes actively, earnestly and successfully took part in the prosecutions. The result justified the efforts made; the lesson had been taught that punishment, if delayed for years, will follow crime, and life and property in the coal regions are again under the protection of the law. In 1843 he was elected to the State Senate in Schuylkill county. After serving in the Legislature one year he resigned his position, and returned to the practice of law. In 1851 he was appointed by Governor Bigler Secretary of the Commonwealth. This office he filled until 1853, when he succeeded Judge James Campbell as Attorney-General.

As Secretary of the Commonwealth, he was superintendent of common schools, and took great interest in the organization of the common school system of Pennsylvania, which, with slight modifications, is still maintained. He was the author of the Common School Act of 1854, and his decisions as superintendent of common schools, relative to the construction of the law, are regarded as authority.

He was earnest in his advocacy of the rights of women; he did not advocate their right to vote, but always claimed that the sphere of their employment should be enlarged, and their pay made commensurate with their services.

He regarded a civil war with dread, and hoped until the last to avert it; when, however, the resort to arms was inevitable, his support of the Union was prompt, energetic and valuable. He denied utterly any right of secession; he claimed that the government was one of the whole people, not a confederation of States.

He aided in fitting out two of the first five companies that reached Washington. He maintained with voice and pen the legal right of the government to put down rebellion with force of arms; he aided in the raising of regiments when the invasion of Pennsylvania was threatened by the forces of Lee, and one regiment was familiarly known as his regiment. Mr. Hughes also maintained that the right of a nation to defend and maintain its own existence is a right inherent in the fact of the existence of such nation, and in the case of our Federal Government exists, in the words of Thaddeus Stevens, "outside of the Constitution."

In politics, as in law, he was ever recognized as a power, brilliant, frequently irresistible. Mr. Hughes was always very active as a business man outside of his profession; he originated and aided in many enterprises, in the purchase and improvement of lands, in the opening and improvement of coal and iron mines, and in the establishment of iron works and other factories. He was of fine personal appearance, dignity of manners and character, pleasing address and amiable disposition; he was universally respected, and popular with political opponents as well as personal friends. He died October 22, 1885, aged 68 years.

Theodore Jones Hughes, married Caroline, daughter of Brice and Helen Oliver Fonville, of Onslow, North Carolina, 19th of November, 1844, by Rev. N. Collin Hughes.

Nicholas Collin Hughes, born in Montgomery county, Pennsylvania; ordained to the Diaconate in old St. Thomas' Church, New York City, June 30, 1844, by Bishop B. T. Onderdonk; moved South August, 1844; ordained priest in old Christ Church, Raleigh, North Carolina, May, 1846, by Bishop Ives; married Adaline Edmonds, daughter of Dr. Robert and Elizabeth Ellis Williams, of Pitt county, North Carolina, October 17, 1848, by Rev. J. B. Cheshire, of Tarboro, North Carolina.

Dr. Williams, the grandfather of Mrs. N. C. Hughes, was a surgeon in the war of the Revolution, filled many offices of public trust, and was greatly honored and beloved by all who knew him.

Jehu Curtis Clay Hughes, married March 13, 1851, to Mrs. Emma R. Heebner, daughter of Benjamin and Sarah Coombe, of Pottsville, Pennsylvania.

Children of Rachel Hughes and William Lukens Potts—seven:

Harriet Provost Potts, unmarried.

ROBT. B. POTTS.

THOMAS ISAAC POTTS.

Rachel Hughes Potts, married Francis S. Hubley, son of Jacob Hubley and Margaret Burd (of the well-known Burd family, of Philadelphia), January 27, 1829, by Rev. John C. Clay.

Thomas Isaac Potts, married Mary Frances, daughter of William Hamilton Johnson and Ann Wilson, of England, by Rev. J. C. Clay, Tuesday evening, April 25, 1837. (Mr. and Mrs. Johnson were married in Philadelphia by Rev. Dr. Stoughton, a well-known Baptist minister.) Thomas Isaac Potts, died March 16, 1885.

Charles Clay Potts, married Mary Joy, daughter of Thomas Shinn Ridgway and Mary Joy, his wife, by Rev. R. A. Henderson, in Pottsville, Pennsylvania.

Mr. Ridgway was a resident of Pottsville, Pennsylvania; the latter part of his life was spent in Philadelphia.

(Hannah) Elizabeth Potts, unmarried; resides in Philadelphia.

William Francis Potts, married Caroline, daughter of George Washington Tryon and Maria Christiana Kunkel, his wife, by Rev. John C. Clay, April 25, 1837. Mr. Tryon was one of the oldest and best known gunsmiths in Philadelphia.

Robert Barnhill Potts, married Sarah Page, daughter of John Grew (merchant of Boston) and Margaret Sarah Page, his wife, of Philadelphia, October 26, 1820, by Rev. Dr. Abercrombie, of Christ Church, Philadelphia. Mrs. Potts was born in Boston, where her parents resided a short time after their marriage.

The family of Grew was anciently of Warwickshire, England. R. B. Potts, manufacturing chemist of the firm of Potts and Klett, established in business many years in Camden, New Jersey, was an active member and vestryman of St. Paul's Episcopal Church. Mr. Potts was always true to the principles of his ancestors as an earnest supporter of his country during the late Rebellion, and a useful member of society. His public spirit and benevolence won for him the respect of the community in which he lived.

Mrs. Rachel Hughes Potts, died aged 92 years.

Children of Ruth Hughes and David Jones—three:
Charles Jones.
Theodore Jones, married Laura Rutter; lived in Missouri.
Harriet Jones, married Benjamin Evans, a lawyer, of Montgomery county, and son of Owen Evans and Ellen Lane, his wife.

Children of Sarah Hughes and David Rittenhouse—ten; four dead.

Hannah Hughes Rittenhouse, married Alexander Jordan, Judge of the Eighth Judicial District of Pennsylvania, October 13, 1858; resided in Sunbury, Pennsylvania; the marriage ceremony by Rev. William Simonton, Presbyterian. Judge Jordan died in Sunbury, October 5, 1878.

Benjamin Franklin Rittenhouse, married Isabel Laurie, daughter of Dr. James and Elizabeth Scott Laurie, both natives of Scotland, residing in Washington, by Rev. James Laurie, of Washington, District of Columbia. Mrs. Isobel Laurie Rittenhouse, died February, 1833. Mr. B. F. Rittenhouse married the second time, Henrietta Warring, daughter of James Davidson and Mary neé Higinbothom, by Rev. Mr. Hawley (Episcopal), of Washington, District of Columbia.

Mary Elizabeth Rittenhouse married A. B. Shuman, son of Jacob and Barbara (Brower) Shuman, of Maryland, November 1, 1837, by Rev. William R. Smith, Presbyterian. Mr. Shuman died in the City of David, in the Province of Chiriqua, New Granada, on the 10th of April, 1851. Mrs. Shuman died in Sunbury, Pennsylvania, March 20, 1890.

Emily Josepha Rittenhouse married Rev. David Hull, son of William Hull and Susan Marr, his wife, of Milton, Pennsylvania, by Rev. John B. Patterson.

Charles Edwin Rittenhouse married Sarah M., daughter of Samuel and Lydia (Newbold) Whittall, of Georgetown, October, 1840, by Rev. Mr. Hoff, Episcopal.

Rev. John Hughes Rittenhouse, a Presbyterian clergyman, married Jane L. Simonton, daughter of Hon. William L.

Simonton, M. D., and Martha Snodgrass Simonton, by Rev. Dr. DeWitt, of Harrisburg, Pennsylvania, September, 1847.

Children of Hannah Hughes and Francis Wade—nine—three died:

Sarah Wade.
Susan Wade.
Francis Wade.
Hannah Clay Wade.
Emily Wade.

George Wade married Sophia, daughter of Jacob DePuthron and Sophia Baker, his wife, by Rev. John Coleman. Mrs. Wade's parents were married in Philadelphia by Rev. Dr. Collin. Mr. Jacob DePuthron was from the Island of Guernsey, and his wife, Sophia Baker, from the Island of Sark.

Children of Ana Clay and Samuel Hepburn, of Milton, Pennsylvania:

Hannah Maria Hepburn, born in Milton, Pennsylvania, December 25, 1812; baptized October 24 by Rev. J. C. Clay; married in Milton to William Henry Blackiston, of Kent county, Maryland, son of James and Jemima Foard Blackiston, by Rev. William Wilson, June 8, 1855.

James Curtis Hepburn, born in Milton, Pennsylvania, March 13, 1815; baptized May 24 by Rev. Slator Clay. He graduated at Princeton College in 1832; studied medicine and graduated at the medical department of the University of Pennsylvania. Married Clara M. Leet, of Fayetteville, North Carolina, by Rev. Mr. Simon, October 27, 1840, and with his wife left his home in Milton on the 5th of January, 1841, for Siam, as a missionary physician, under the General Assembly's Board of Foreign Missions (Presbyterian). He was afterwards removed to Macao, in China, where he remained until his wife's health failing he returned to this country with their son, Samuel Dyer Hepburn. Dr. Hepburn then settled in New

York City and commenced the practice of medicine. He was rapidly securing a good practice at the time Japan was opened by treaty to foreigners. He felt it his duty to give up all worldly considerations and again offer himself as a missionary.

The Presbyterian Board of Foreign Missions were, at the same time, deliberating on whom they should send to possess the field. They unanimously came to the conclusion that Dr. Hepburn was the man. He at once closed up his business and with his wife again left their native land and sailed for Japan.

They were the first missionaries of the Presbyterian Board to occupy the field; he, opened a medical dispensary at once, as the only way of reaching the people, engaged a teacher and soon made himself acquainted with the language. He has compiled a Japanese and English dictionary and has completed the translation of the entire Bible, and is engaged in translating other religious books. He still resides there.

In an article in Williamsport *Bulletin* of August 12, 1889, copied from the Lock Haven *Democrat*, this notice of Dr. James Curtis Hepburn is given—that he arrived from Japan a few weeks ago, and is now visiting his sisters, Mrs. L. A. Mackey and Mrs. E. C. McClure, of that city.

Dr. Hepburn has been a resident of Japan for forty years, and is connected religiously, educationally, industrially and scientifically with the reformation and improvement of the Japanese.

He has, as it were, become one of them, and is deeply interested in their national progress toward the civilization of the West. He is the author of a Japanese dictionary with Chinese equivalent; that is, with Chinese words corresponding with the meaning of the Japanese verbs, nouns, adjectives, etc., etc., if that is what they call them over there.

This dictionary being too large and costly for common use, the doctor then made an abbreviated and condensed copy for the use of the schools, and afterwards translated the New Testament into the Japanese language, using both the Japanese characters and the Roman letters, the idea being, that if the Japanese could be gotten to use the Roman letters in spelling their language it would be much easier to educate them in their own or the English language. The doctor has for a long time been president of the college at Tokio, the royal city, and has many interesting things to relate. Sixteen years ago he was here on a visit, the occasion being the marriage of his son to Miss Annie, daughter of the late Wheeler Shaw.

The doctor is accompanied by his wife, and will remain here for some time. His son is in Japan, not in good health, and will probably return to this country and settle in or near San Francisco, California.

Dr. Hepburn is a native of Milton, Pennsylvania, and he comes once more to visit the familiar scenes of his youth in the West Branch Valley. He finds that its progress has been wonderful since his last visit. His native town passed through a baptism of fire since he saw it last, but he finds it rebuilt more beautiful than it was before, and now one of the most progressive places on the river.

He arrived just in time to witness the ruin wrought by the great flood of June 1, 1889, and will bear away with him to his eastern home vivid recollections of the damage caused in the land of his birth by the scourge of water.

Sarah Ann Hepburn, born in Milton, Pennsylvania, June 2, 1817; baptized by Rev. Thomas Hood; married James Pollock, a lawyer, of Milton, son of William and Sarah Wilson Pollock, by the Rev. John Curtis Clay, December 19, 1837.

The ancestors of James Pollock emigrated to America from the north of Ireland about 1760, his parents were born in Chester county, Pennsylvania; he was born in Milton, Northumberland county, Pennsylvania; graduated at Princeton College, New Jersey, 1831; has held a number of important and civil offices; was a Whig in politics; but notwithstanding this was twice elected a member of Congress from the Thirteenth District, then strongly Democratic, holding the office for six years. In 1850 he was appointed President Judge of the Eighth Judicial District, composed of the counties of Northumberland, Montour, Columbia, Lycoming and Sullivan. He held the office until the amendment of the Constitution required the election of judges by the people, when he declined a nomination for the position, and on leaving the bench resumed the practice of law. In 1854 he was nominated and elected by a large majority Governor of Pennsylvania. He held the office for one term, refusing to permit his name to be used for re-nomination. At the expiration of his official term Governor Pollock resumed the practice of his profession in the place of his nativity. In May, 1861, he was appointed by President Lincoln Director of the United States Mint at Philadelphia, and held the office until October, 1866, when, on the accession of Andrew Johnson to power, he resigned. By his efforts, with the approval of the Secretary of the Treasury, the motto, "In God We Trust," was placed upon the national coin. In 1869 he was reinstated by President Grant in his former position as Director of the Mint, which office he held for eight years. He was also naval officer under President Hayes four years.

Mrs. James Pollock, died in Philadelphia, April 24, 1886, aged 69, and was buried at Milton, Pennsylvania. Ex-Governor James Pollock, died at Lock Haven, Pennsylvania, April 19, 1890, and was buried at Milton, Pennsylvania, April 22, 1890. Rev. Joseph Hemphill, D. D., of the West Arch Street Presbyterian Church, Philadelphia, conducted the services; he paid a glowing tribute to the deceased, as he followed an official life, building up a character of spotless integrity and worth, and then added: "He was the undoubted and undoubting servant of Jesus Christ." One of the many notices of his death in the papers of that day says: "Here, in Milton, he began that life so fruitful in deeds and good works; here was the home with its careful ministries; here the friends who rejoiced at his conquests and victories, and again here to-day came numbers of those who knew him well, to pay their tribute of remembrance and tearful farewell in this life's closing scene. Yonder, in 'God's acre,' he rests by the side of the life partner, whom death claimed five years ago, and for whom there was an unending grief; for near half a century they trod a common and happy pathway together; then came a brief separation before the time of that other union, whose seal is not for this world's sight."

Slator Clay Hepburn, born in Milton, Pennsylvania, October 19, 1819; married Anna M., daughter of Samuel and Anna Maria Bayard Boyd, of New York city, 12th of September, 1849, by Rev. John C. Lowrie, of New York. Samuel Boyd, the father of Mrs. Hepburn, was a lawyer, native of Windsor, Orange county, New York. Mr. S. C. Hepburn, first graduated at Princeton College, afterwards studied for the ministry and graduated at Princeton Theological Seminary. He was called to the Great Island Presbyterian Church, where he remained five years as their pastor. He was then called to Hamptonberg Presbyterian Church, New York, and installed pastor, July 2, 1850, and has now, on the 2d of July, 1890, completed a pastorate of forty years.

Mary Hepburn, born in Milton, May 1, 1822; married L. A. Mackey, of Lock Haven, son of Thomas L. and Catharine Anastatt Mackey, formerly of Berks county, Pennsylvania, 22d of July, 1847, by Rev. Slator C. Hepburn, in Milton. Mr. Mackey was elected to Congress in 1875, from the Twentieth Congressional District. Mr. Mackey died February 8, 1889.

Emma Hepburn, born in Milton, Pennsylvania, July 22, 1825; married Lieutenant J. Hogan Brown, U. S. N., January 18th, 1849, by Rev. J. C. Hepburn. Both are deceased. Mrs. Brown died October 5, 1860.

Louisa Harriet Hepburn, born in Milton, March 7, 1828; married at Milton, January 25, 1855, to Edwin C., son of Robert and Mary Hepburn McClure, of Williamsport, Pennsylvania, by Rev. Slator C. Hepburn. No children. Edwin C. McClure died January 17, 1890.

Jane Hepburn, born in Milton, December 2, 1830; married at Milton, May 24, to Dr. Henry A., son of Griffith Lichtenthaler, of Juniata county, Pennsylvania, by Rev. Slator C.

Hepburn. Mr. Lichtenthaler died August 15, 1872. Both are now deceased.

Children of Rev. Dr. Jehu Curtis Clay and Margaret Annan—three:

Emily Clay, married William, son of Thomas Pollock and Mary Wilson Pollock, of Milton Pennsylvania, by Rev. Jehu C. Clay, October 5, 1841.

Ann Clay married Joseph, son of Joseph and Isabella Potts, of Pottstown, Pennsylvania, March 5, 1845, by Rev. Jehu C. Clay.

Julia Frances Clay married Dr. John T., son of Mark and Susan Evans, of East Coventry township, Chester county, Pennsylvania, July, 1847, by Rev. Jehu C. Clay.

(Mr. and Mrs. Mark Evans, the parents of Dr. John T. Evans, died the same day, October 11, 1843).

Mrs. Julia F. Evans died at Downingtown, Pennsylvania, March 20, 1884.

Children of Rev. Dr. Jehu Curtis Clay and second wife, Simmons Edy:

George Bolton Lownes Clay, M. D., married Clara J. Tiers, daughter of Arundius and Anna Tiers, of Germantown, Pennsylvania, April 16, 1855, by Rev. Dr. J. C. Clay, at Germantown, Pennsylvania.

Richard Edy Clay married Louisa Ann, daughter of Hon. James and Sarah Ann Pollock, of Philadelphia, February 5, 1863, by Rev. Dr. J. C. Clay.

Children of Charles H. Clay and Maria Evans Clay—five:

Harriet P. Clay married Rev. Edmund Leaf, son of George and Elizabeth Leonard Leaf, of Pottstown, Pennsylvania, October 26, 1848, by Rev. Dr. J. C. Clay.

Rev. Edmund Leaf was rector of the Episcopal church at Birdsboro and for thirty years rector of Douglassville, formerly Morlattan.

Ellen Lane Clay, deceased.

Hannah Maria Clay, deceased.

George Henry Clay married Amelia, daughter of Judge Charles and Elizabeth Donnel, of Sunbury, Pennsylvania, February 2, 1853, by Rev. William White Montgomery.

Mary Evans Clay, deceased.

Children of Rachel Coates and Nathaniel Smith—two.

Nathaniel Smith, died in infancy.

Charles Moore Smith, born February 29, 1816, in Montgomery county, Pennsylvania; married Mrs. Rebecca Grant, daughter of Charles and Mary Moore, of Batavia, Clermont county, Ohio, September 6, 1837, by Rev. George W. Maley.

Mrs. Rebecca Smith died in Batavia, aged forty-two years, in hope of a glorious immortality.

Charles M. Smith married the second time Adaline, daughter of James and Leah O'Conner, in Hamilton, Butler county, Ohio, by Rev. Arthur W. Elliott, in 1849.

Children of Matthias Coates and Sophia Hayman—nine:

Lindsay Coates, born in Chester county, Pennsylvania November 2, 1806; baptized by Rev. Dr. Collin, died December 30, 1830, aged 24 years.

Levi Pawling Coates, born in Upper Merion, Montgomery county, June 14, 1808; baptized August 1, 1813, by Rev. Dr. Collin; married Mary, daughter Abraham and Mary Yerkes, of Whitemarsh township, Montgomery county, Pennsylvania, September 28, 1837, at Philadelphia, by John Swift, Mayor of the city; he died September 9, 1874, in his 67th year.

William Hayman Coates, born in Philadelphia May 22, 1812; baptized August 1, 1813, by Rev. Dr. Collin; died August 11, 1834; unmarried.

Ann Hayman Coates, born in Upper Merion, Montgomery county, April 8, 1810; died December 26, 1824.

Matthew Henderson Coates, born in Norristown, Pennsylvania, October 15, 1814. Left Philadelphia September, 1834, and went to Cincinnati, Ohio; married Beulah W., daughter of William and Rachel Allen, of Upper Greenwich, New Jersey, April 10, 1836, in Cincinnati, Ohio, by Rev. William Burke. No children.

N. Collin Coates, born in Penn township, Philadelphia, May 17, 1817; baptized August 30, 1817; married Elizabeth, daughter of William and Margaret Stewart, of Philadelphia, March 4, 1841, by Rev. Thomas H. Stockton.

John Hughes Coates, born in Philadelphia, December 8, 1819; baptized July 1, 1820; died September 24, 1822.

Mary Moore Coates, born in Philadelphia, March 13, 1822; baptized by Rev. Dr. Collin, September 29, 1822; married John Smiley April 26, 1846, by Rev. John L. Grant, of Philadelphia. John Smiley died June 20, 1879, aged 62 years.

Charles Coates, born in Philadelphia, 16th of September, 1824; baptized May 21, 1825; died October 29, 1841, aged 17 years.

Children of Magdalena Roberts and Edward Lane—three:

Rebecca Roberts Lane, unmarried; resides in Bridgeport, Pennsylvania.

Samuel Lane, unmarried; died December 28, 1891; interred in cemetery of Christ-Swedes Church, Upper Merion, December 31, 1891.

Phoebe Lane, died in infancy.

Children of Peter DeHaven and Sarah Atlee DeHaven—six:

Sarah Rawle DeHaven, died; unmarried.

Atlee Augustus DeHaven, married Anna Courtney.

CAPTAIN JOSEPH EDWIN DeHAVEN.

Augusta Julianna DeHaven, married Richard Henry Ranson, of Jefferson county, Virginia, at Cannonsburg, Pennsylvania.

Samuel John DeHaven, died; unmarried.

William Niell DeHaven, born in Philadelphia, August 24, 1820; married Miss Warmsley, of Missouri; second wife, Miss Dodge, and removed to Caldwell county, Mississippi, in 1840; in 1852 crossed the plains to California; settled first near Marysville, from thence to Plumas county, where he engaged in mercantile and mining pursuits. While there was elected clerk of the county; afterwards removed to Lanson county, engaged in agriculture and filled the office of deputy sheriff. In 1856 settled in Chico, Butte county, California. In the spring of 1869 he purchased the material of "The Courant" (Republican) and "The Caucasian" (Democratic) papers, and uniting them, established the "Northern Enterprise," an independent paper, which he edited until his death, with the exception of one year in the Legislature of California. William Niell DeHaven, married Lizzie Regina, daughter of Louis Ansart and Barbara K. Hildreth, of Chico, California, April 14, 1870.

Joseph Edwin DeHaven, born March 4, 1828; married April 8, 1856, to Amelia Louisa, daughter of Commodore Bigelow, of Brooklyn, New York. Mrs. DeHaven died in 1867. During the late war Captain DeHaven was in the navy, principally engaged in the blockading service; was engaged in numerous skirmishes with the enemy; made a number of prizes; resigned in 1865. Captain J. E. DeHaven married a second wife, Miss Augusta W. Borek, by Rev. Mr. Draper, before the United States Consul Mr. Upton, in Geneva, Switzerland, March 21, 1874. Captain DeHaven died 3d of April, 1879.

Children of Amelia DeHaven and Joseph A. Atlee— three:

Juliana DeHaven Atlee, born May 2, 1814; baptized by Bishop White, of Philadelphia. Her grandmother, Sarah

Holstein DeHaven, sponsor; married December 27, 1836, to Robert Lewis, son of James and Priscilla Williams, of Bellefonte, Centre county, Pennsylvania, by Rev. William Stewart. He was an elder in the Presbyterian Church of Pine Grove Mills, Centre county, filling that position until his removal to Altoona, Pennsylvania, March 29, 1871; entered into rest December 2, 1886, aged 79; buried at Graysville, Huntingdon county, Pennsylvania.

Samuel John Atlee, born 21st of May, 1821; married Jane Stewart, of Stone Valley, Huntingdon county, Pennsylvania, January 27, 1847.

Emma Maria Atlee, born August 13, 1825; married Hiram Hendrixon, January, 1866.

Mr. Edwin A. Barber, of Philadelphia, gives me this account of the name of Atlee. It is written with one capital, as used by the family who have sent it to me, and also with two, AtLee. This latter he thinks the older and correct form, and says the name was originally "At-the-Lea," Sir Richard At-the-Lea being probably one of the ancestors of the name in the thirteenth century. The Lea was the name of a place. Some branches of the family have always used the capital L, while others prefer to write it Atlee. He uses the former, as being more correct and attractive.

Children of Holstein DeHaven and Sophia Elliott—four:

Charles Elliott DeHaven, married Mary Anna Carman, of Camden, New Jersey, by Rev. Dr. Dorr, December 15, 1846.

Hugh DeHaven, married Mary J., daughter of William Cleaver and Jane Thomas Cleaver, of Upper Merion, Montgomery county, Pennsylvania, September 13, 1842, by Rev. Jehu C. Clay. Mrs. Mary DeHaven died June 16, 1888; was interred in Montgomery Cemetery, Norristown, June 19, 1888.

Emma C. DeHaven, married William H. Hampton, May 27, 1844, by Bishop Odenheimer.

John DeHaven, died; unmarried.

Children of Hugh DeHaven and Christianna Lyng Bunting:

Susannah Shober DeHaven, baptized in St. Stephen's Church, Philadelphia, by Rev. G. T. Bedell; married July 8, 1847, to Samuel White (merchant), by Rev. Joseph Castle. Mr. White was a member of the firm of James, Kent, Santee and Company.

Mrs. White died November 27, 1859, aged 33 years and 7 months.

Charles Bunting DeHaven, baptized in Grace Church, Philadelphia, by Rev. B. B. Smith; died September 20, 1832, aged three years and 3 months.

Children of Hugh DeHaven and second wife, Zipporah Dill White:

Samuel White DeHaven, baptized by Rev. J. Lewis, at Frankford, Pennsylvania; married November 9, 1859, to Emma, daughter of Joseph H. Thompson, by Rev. Franklin Moore. Samuel White DeHaven died January 9, 1877, aged 43 years and 5 months.

Hugh DeHaven, baptized by Rev. Mr. Lippincott, at Frankford, Pennsylvania; married April 28, 1862, to Clara Boyd, daughter of Hill and Sarah Banton, near Cheyney Station, Media R. R., Pennsylvania.

Alexander Henry DeHaven, baptized by Rev. L. L. James; married Clara, daughter of R. R. Robinson, of Wilmington, Delaware, December 31, 1860, by Rev. Wesley Kenney. Mrs. Clara Robinson DeHaven died October 16, 1864, aged 24 years and 6 months.

Alexander H. DeHaven married the second time Mary A., daughter of Zadock Townsend, of Wilmington, Delaware, October 12, 1864. Mrs. Mary DeHaven died October 31, 1872.

Alexander H. DeHaven married the third time Rebecca Virginia, daughter of Zadock Townsend, of Wilmington, Delaware.

John White DeHaven and Joseph DeHaven, twins, born June 20, 1838.

John W. DeHaven baptized by Rev. John Henry, September, 1839. Joseph died June 20, 1838.

Sallie Letitia DeHaven baptized by Rev. Joseph Castle; married April 5, 1876, in London, to David T. Boyd, shipbuilder, of Glasgow, Scotland, where they have since resided.

Caleb DeHaven.

George Clay DeHaven, baptized by Rev. Mr. Hagany; died July 31, 1881; unmarried.

Children of Sarah Coates and Ebenezer Rambo:

William Rambo, married Mary Ann, daughter of Zimmerman and Hannah Henderson Supplee. Mrs. Rambo died February 13, 1840, in her 26th year.

William Rambo died April 27, 1839, aged 30 years.

Children of John Coates and Martha Pugh—four:

Henry Coates, born November 19, 1830; died April 15, 1847, aged 17 years.

Davis P. Coates, born July 5, 1832; married Anne, daughter of Elisha and Margaret Worrall, of Morgan's Corner, Delaware county, Pennsylvania, March 19, 1857.

John Coates, married Serapta, daughter of John and Mary Stringfield, of Philadelphia, March 5, 1865.

Louisa Coates, married Jacob Shainline, Jr., son of George W. and Hannah Moore Shainline, of Upper Merion, Montgomery county, Pennsylvania, April 9, 1857.

Children of Ann Coates and William Holloway:

Septimus Holloway, born January 12, 1822; died February 17, 1822.

Thomas Holloway, married Mary Ann, daughter of Samuel and Mary Eastburn, of Upper Merion, Montgomery county, Pennsylvania, December 15, 1844, by Rev. Samuel

Aaron. Thomas Holloway died November 7, 1887, in his 69th year.

Children of Samuel Holstein Coates and Margaret Owens—eleven:

Mary Holstein Coates, married George, son of Joseph and Elizabeth Saunders, of Rising Sun, Philadelphia, August 18, 1850, by Rev. E. N. Lightner. Mrs. Saunders died.

Jane Coates, married William, son of Thomas and Ann Knight, of Lancaster, Pennsylvania, September 9, 1841, by Rev. Nathan Stem, of Norristown, Pa. He died.

Sarah Coates, married Henry, son of John and Mary Bush, of Whitpain township, Montgomery county, Pennsylvania, by Rev. J. C. Clay.

Septimus Coates, died in infancy.

Susan Coates, married Jacob, son of Henry and Mary Hurst, of Whitpain township, Montgomery county, December 16, 1846, by Rev. E. N. Lightner.

Ann E. Coates, married Thomas, son of Alexander and Martha Maitland, of Reading, Pennsylvania, July 3, 1853, by Rev. J. C. Clay.

Matilda P. Coates and William Holstein Coates, twins; Matilda married Alexander, son of John and Anne McCurdy, of Philadelphia, November 11, 1856, by Rev. Mr. Jones. William died in infancy.

Margaret Coates, married Francis A., son of Abbott and Elizabeth Drew, of Plymouth, Massachusetts, August 15, 1852.

Samuel Coates, died in infancy.

Caroline P. Coates, married Abner, son of Thomas and Phœbe Brown, of Tredyffrin township, Chester county, Pennsylvania, by Rev. R. R. Graham.

Children of John Jonse Holstein and Elizabeth Williamson:

Ellen Douglass Holstein, born March 15, 1812; died September 15, 1815.

Linnaeus Holstein, born February 25, 1814; died August 28, 1815.

Louis Ducurdree Holstein, born February 12, 1816; married November 14, 1843, to Sarah Klingaman; he died December 10, 1852.

Mary Ann Jones Holstein, born May 18, 1818; unmarried; resided in Philadelphia; died February 9, 1885.

Children of Samuel Holstein (of Westmoreland county) and Mary Henderson:

Mary Holstein, married John, son of William and Sarah McDoo, of Indiana county, Pennsylvania, 25th of November, 1845, by Rev. Mr. Donalson.

Jane Holstein, married James, son of William and Ann Keir, of Indiana county, Pennsylvania, 23d of April, 1841, by Rev. Mr. Donalson.

Margaret Holstein, born October 22, 1820; married John, son of Thomas and Hannah Ellwood, 16th of June, 1843, by Rev. Mr. Donalson. Mrs. Margaret Ellwood died 8th of March, 1872, beloved and respected by the community where she resided.

Andrew Johnston Holstein, born January 14, 1823; married Margaret H., daughter of Robert and Ruth Fulton, of Indiana county, Pennsylvania, March 7, 1843, by Rev. Mr. Donalson, of Elder's Ridge, Indiana county.

James Holstein, born October 12, 1825; died 12th of April, 1828.

Robert Holstein, born October 2, 1830; unmarried; he studied medicine, and was about ready to commence practice when an affection of the lungs terminated his life 26th of October, 1855.

Annabell Holstein, born August 2, 1836; married Alexander, son of William and Mary Armstrong, of Indiana county, Pennsylvania, by Rev. Mr. Donalson, 31st of January, 1856. Mrs. Annabell Armstrong died 27th of April, 1875.

Joseph Holstein, born March 9, 1839; died February 23, 1842.

Children of Sarah Holstein and Robert Love, of Butler county, Pennsylvania:

Martha Jane Love, born October 13, 1829; married James McCafferty, 1st of April, 1851, by Rev. Ephraim Ogden, Presbyterian minister.

J. Holstein Love, born 10th of August, 1832; married Jane Love, 31st of March, 1859, by Rev. Ephraim Ogden. J. Holstein Love died 6th of February, 1870.

Elizabeth Love, born 24th of September, 1835; unmarried.

Sarah Ann Love, born 26th of November, 1837; married Robert Love, November, 1859, by Rev. Mr. Miller.

John Serron Love, born 7th of June, 1840; married Jane R. Harvey, April 1, 1864, by Rev. Mr. Shaffer. John Serron Love enlisted as a private in One Hundred and Thirty-Seventh Pennsylvania Volunteers, 7th of August, 1862. From Harrisburg his regiment was sent to one of the forts near Washington, District of Columbia, and thence to Antietam; was at Crampton's Gap, Maryland, South Mountain, Platt's Plantation, below Fredericksburg, and Chancellorsville; at Antietam they were placed to guard a large wagon train, and afterwards buried the Confederate dead near the meeting-house. They were then sent to Hagerstown with ambulances filled with wounded, and on to Washington, District of Columbia, Acquia Creek and Belle Plain; was in General Burnside's march through the mud, crossed the Rappahannock on the pontoon bridge, then back to Falmouth, and again crossed the river; was in the Wilderness fight, where his regiment was engaged. It was soon afterwards mustered out of service.

Rebecca Love and Rachel Love, twins. Rebecca Love, married David F. Norris, 19th of September, 1871, by Rev. J. McPherrin. Rachel Love, unmarried.

Sharp Serron Love, born 31st of July, 1847; died 11th of March, 1851.

Children of John Holstein, of Darby, Pennsylvania, and Jane Parkinson:

John Parkinson Holstein, died July 14, 1819, in his 5th year.

Elizabeth Holstein, died May 10, 1820, in her 4th year.

Eliza J. Holstein, died February 4, 1815, in her 4th year.

Peter Blake Holstein, born June 27, 1817; married Eliza Ann, daughter of Anthony and Rachel Farrel, of Kingsessing township, December 15, 1842. Peter B. Holstein died March 15, 1886, in his 69th year. Mrs. P. B. Holstein, died January 29, 1887.

Children of Christiana Holstein, of Darby, Pennsylvania, and Henry Makemson:

George Makemson, married Margaret Fullerton (two children, William and Frederick, died in infancy).

Mary Makemson, married Jonathan Urid, of Delaware.

Henry Makemson, married Susan Myers.

Peter Makemson, married Hannah, daughter of Edward and Susan Fadden, of New Jersey.

William Makemson, married Margaret, daughter of Wm. and Mary Simpson, of Philadelphia.

James Makemson.

Catharine Makemson, married Benjamin Yerkes, and second, John, son of John and Betty Schofield, of England.

Children of Sarah Holstein, of Darby, Pennsylvania, and George Brandt:

Catharine Brandt, married David, son of Elijah and Joanna Walton, of New Hampshire.

Mary Brandt, unmarried.

John Brandt, married Ann Eliza Helins.

Maria Brandt, married John, son of George and Phoebe Lincoln, of Upper Darby, Delaware county, Pennsylvania.

Georgianna Brandt, married Louis Lyman Albee, November, 1859.

PETER BLAKE HOLSTEIN.

SEVENTH GENERATION

Children of Magdalena Holstein, of Darby, and Abel Lodge—ten:

Elizabeth Lodge, married John Hoopes.

Catharine Lodge, married Azariah Bane.

Frances Lodge.

John Lodge, married Caroline, daughter of Abel and Mary Green, of Delaware county, Pennsylvania.

Abel Lodge, married his cousin Mary Margaret DeHart, March, 1851.

Phoebe Lodge.

Jane Holstein Lodge.

Henry Lodge, married Elizabeth McClellan.

Mary M. Lodge, married Alexander, son of John and Elizabeth Crozier, of Upper Darby.

Susan Lodge.

Children of Catharine B. Holstein, of Darby, and John DeHart:

Mrs. Catharine DeHart, died June, 1848.

Mary Margaret DeHart, married her cousin Abel, son of Abel and Mary Magdalena Lodge, of Delaware county, Pennsylvania.

Jane Gaul DeHart, married William Wilson Harvey, son of William and Margaret Stuart Harvey, of Ireland, May 25, 1853, by Rev. Mr. Hunter.

William Henry DeHart, unmarried.

Christiana G. DeHart, died aged 3 years.

Rachel DeHart, died in infancy.

SEVENTH GENERATION.

Children of Elizabeth Branton Holstein and John Henderson—three:

A daughter born August 14, 1820, died in infancy.

Samuel Holstein Henderson, born October 15, 1821; married Jane, daughter of Thomas S. and Matilda Cook Cunningham, of Mercer, Pennsylvania, February 4, 1845, by Rev. John Findley. Mrs. Jane Henderson died December 3, 1845.

Samuel H. Henderson married the second time Emeline W., daughter of Elijah and Sarah Ann Satterfield, of Mercer, Pennsylvania, January 11, 1849.

Branton Holstein Henderson, born December 24, 1823; unmarried; resides at Sharon, Mercer county, Pennsylvania.

Children of Rachel Moore Holstein and Thomas M. Jolly:

Elizabeth Jolly.
John Jolly.
Rebecca Jolly.

These three children died in infancy and are buried at Swedes Church Cemetery, Upper Merion, Pennsylvania.

Matthias Holstein Jolly, born at Norristown, Pennsylvania, March 20, 1828; married Anna Ashton, daughter of John and Amanda Ashton Squire, of Philadelphia, October 23, 1856, by Rev. Albert Barnes. Matthias H. Jolly died at Phillipsburg, Centre county, Pennsylvania, October 16, 1871, aged 43 years and 7 months.

Thomas Craig Jolly, born at Norristown, Pennsylvania, October 24, 1829; died at Vicksburg, 1858; unmarried.

Mary Anna Jolly, married Henry P., son of John Potts and Emily P. Rutter, of Pottstown, Montgomery county, Pennsylvania, December 23, 1851, by Rev. Dr. J. C. Clay. She died at Louisville, Kentucky, December 28, 1856, aged 25 years.

Children of Samuel Holstein and Anna Prichett—three:

Josephine Cora Holstein, born 31st of January, 1831; died at Bellevue, Lancaster county, Pennsylvania, 6th of November, 1846.

George Wolf Holstein, born 6th of November, 1842; married 31st of January, 1871, to Emma Hand, daughter of

daughter of Conrad and Mary Emery, of Pine Grove, Mercer county, Pennsylvania, 19th of August, 1876.

Constance Holstein, baptized by Rev. Mr. Hilton, at Kittanning, June, 1858; married D. M. Hadley, June, 1888, by Rev. Dr. Williams, of Sharon, Pennsylvania.

Children of Ann Sophia Holstein and Captain Andrew Shainline:

Elizabeth Holstein Shainline, married George W., son of William and Maria Bisbing, of Upper Merion, Montgomery county, Pennsylvania, December 13, 1849, by Rev. A. F. Auspach. During the late war, George W. Bisbing entered the army as lieutenant in Company I, Fifty-first Pennsylvania volunteers, Col. John F. Hartranft (afterwards Governor of Pennsylvania) commanding; was in the battles of Roanoke Island, Camden, second Bull Run, Chantilly, South Mountain, Antietam, Fredericksburg, Vicksburg, Jackson (Mississippi), Campbell's Station, siege of Knoxville, Wilderness and Spotsylvania. At the battle of Antietam his regiment, with the Fifty-first New York, held the bridge over the creek of that name, under a terrific fire of artillery; while on the bridge Lieutenant Bisbing's sword was struck by a piece of shell and broken in half, though he escaped serious injury. He was promoted to the rank of captain at Camp Reno, Newbern, North Carolina, in June, 1862; was wounded at Jackson, Mississippi, 16th of July, 1863; after recovering from his wound, participated in all the battles in which his regiment was engaged, until the 12th of May, 1864, when he was fatally wounded by musket shots in the thigh and arm, carried from the field into Fredericksburg, and placed in the upper story of a factory, where he remained four days; from thence moved to the officers' hospital, Georgetown, District of Columbia, where he lingered until the 7th of June, 1864, when death ended the sufferings of this noble officer. His body was brought home and interred in the cemetery of old Swedes (Christ) Church, Upper Merion, 12th of June, 1864.

> "Never truer soul
> From his speed to his goal,
> Whose legend marked our roll of him at his duty."

In connection with his death is an incident so singular, that though familiar to those who knew him could not have been heard by all into whose hands this record may chance to come.

Sunday, 7th of June, Captain Bisbing lay dying in the officers' hospital, Georgetown, District of Columbia. His wife, sitting by him, was watching the ebbing away of a life so precious. As the things of earth receded and another world dawned upon his gaze, the lamp of life flickered and flashed in this its closing scene. Suddenly rousing up, his voice, which had previously been faint and feeble, rang out in a startlingly clear, loud tone, "Lieutenant! Lieutenant!" A wounded lieutenant lying near him answered, "What is it, Captain?" He replied, "I am not calling you, it is Lieutenant-Colonel Schall. I saw him fall, and thought the way he was lying perhaps he was dead." His wife tried to soothe him by saying, "The colonel was all right," and the captain sank back exhausted on his pillow. But a few moments passed, and the same words were repeated in the like clear tone, "Lieutenant! Lieutenant!" that he had seen him fall, etc. Again he was soothed to quietness. Now fully conscious that death was near, the brave soldier, in a few earnest, never-to-be-forgotten words, sent home the message, that "he gave his life freely for his country." Then commending wife and children to God's loving care, in two hours peacefully passed to that land "where there is no more sorrow, or sickness, or pain."

In Captain Bisbing's death two homes were made desolate, he was an only child.

When Mrs. Bisbing returned with her husband's body to their home, she first learned that Lieutenant-Colonel Schall had fallen as the Captain described two days previously, shot through the neck at Cold Harbor. His body also was brought home for burial, and interred in Montgomery Cemetery, Norristown, the day preceding the captain's funeral.

DeWitt Clinton Shainline married Catharine, daughter of William and Elizabeth Davis, from Wales, then resident in Conshohocken, Pennsylvania, 1856, by Rev. Mr. Owen.

George Holstein Shainline, married Sarah, daughter of John and Sarah Forsythe, of Columbia county, Pennsylvania, by Rev. George Parsons, at Muncy, Pennsylvania, 1864.

William Holstein Shainline, married Mary Emily, daughter of Henry and Harriet Potter, of Tredyffrin township, Chester county, Pennsylvania, May 9, 1866, by Rev. R. M. Patterson, of Tredyffrin.

James Yocom Shainline, enlisted in the civil war, in Company I, Fifty-First Pennsylvania Volunteers; mustered in September 28, 1861, at Harrisburg, Pennsylvania, and with his regiment participated in all the battles in which they were engaged, ten in number, from Roanoke Island, North Carolina, to Fredericksburg, Virginia, where, on December 13, he was dangerously wounded in the forehead by a fragment of shell, which fractured the skull; taken to Washington, D. C., he was placed in the hospital, where his recovery, under the circumstances, was considered most remarkable. From thence, when sufficiently recovered, he was transferred to the Veteran Reserve Corps, doing garrison duty at Washington, D. C., and marching with the corps in defence of the Capital at the time of Early's invasion; remained with the corps until mustered out of service at the close of the war.

Rebecca Emily Shainline, unmarried.

Henry Harrison Shainline, married Abbie S., daughter of Mordecai and Elizabeth DeHaven, of Upper Merion, Montgomery county, September 18, 1866, by Rev. J. F. Halsey, pastor of the First Presbyterian Church of Norristown, Pennsylvania.

Henry H. Shainline entered the army with the first call for troops during the civil war; enlisted in the Fourth Regiment Pennsylvania Volunteers, Colonel John F. Hartranft, of Norristown, commanding; remained with the regiment until

MRS. EMILY W. THOMAS

mustered out of service, when he re-enlisted in the One Hundred and Thirty-Eighth Pennsylvania Volunteers, company C, and was with his regiment until the close of war in the following battles: Cedar Creek, Monocacy, Wilderness, Brandy Station, Cold Harbor, Mine Run, Pine Grove, Wappen Heights, Spottsylvania Court House, Petersburg, Ann Harbor, Weldon Railroad, Kelly's Ford, Winchester, Fisher's Hill and Sailor's Creek.

Mary Louisa Shainline, unmarried.

Anne Sophia Shainline, died in infancy.

Child of Rachel Moore Holstein and Thomas J. Molony:

George Holstein Molony, unmarried; went to San Francisco, California, where he died in November, 1855, after a short illness.

Children of Mary Atlee Holstein and William Amies:

Joseph Washington Amies, died in infancy.

Elizabeth Holstein Amies, married Charles Ellis Morris, son of Samuel W. and Anna Ellis Morris, of Wellsboro, Tioga county, Pennsylvania, in Bridgeport, Montgomery county, Pennsylvania, by Rev. E. N. Lightner, October 7, 1851. Charles E. Morris died December 28, 1883, aged 59 years.

Charles Thompson Amies, unmarried; died in United States army, San Antonia, Texas, March 20, 1859.

Emily Thomas Amies, married Abram Walker, of Philadelphia, May 29, 1879, by Rev. A. A. Marple; ceremony at the residence of her uncle, William H. Holstein, Upper Merion, Montgomery county, Pennsylvania.

Children of Emily Wilson Holstein and William B. Thomas—four:

Anna Elizabeth Thomas, married Nathan, son of Hugh Jones and Jemima Brooke, of Media, Delaware county, Pennsylvania, February 3, 1858, by Rev. Mr. Furness. Mr. Nathan Brooke died May 5, 1885, in his 53d year.

Benjamin Thomas, died in infancy.

Rebecca Brooke Thomas, married George Hamilton Colket, son of Coffin and Mary Walker Colket, of Philadelphia, November 20, 1867, by Rev. Mr. Furness.

Mary Amies Thomas, married Hunter, son of Hugh Jones and Jemima Brooke, of Media, Delaware county, Pennsylvania, February 25, 1874, by Rev. Mr. Furness.

Children of Louisa Brooke Holstein and George W. Dewees:

Eva Amelia Dewees, unmarried.

George Holstein Dewees, died in infancy.

William Holstein Dewees, died in infancy.

Isaac Holstein Dewees, married Olivia Camilla, daughter of Dennison and Olivia S. Ledyard, June 15, 1892, in St. John's Episcopal Church, Montgomery, Alabama.

Mary Hughes Dewees, unmarried.

Children of Susan Holstein and William B. Roberts, of Upper Merion, Pennsylvania:

Eliza Ann Roberts, married David Connard, son of Reese and Catharine Connard, of Whitemarsh township, Montgomery county, Pennsylvania, January 20, 1866, by Rev. Thomas S. Yocom; reside near Richmond, Virginia.

Sarah Louisa Roberts, married William Wills, son of William and Elizabeth Wills, of Plymouth township, Montgomery county, Pennsylvania, March 21, 1866, by Rev. T. S. Yocom, rector of Old Swedes Christ Church, Upper Merion, Pennsylvania.

Matthew Roberts, married Clara, daughter of Reese and Catharine Connard, of Whitemarsh township, Montgomery county, Pennsylvania, December 14, 1869, by Rev. Dr. D. C. Millett, of St. Thomas' Church, Whitemarsh.

GEORGE W. HOLSTEIN, M. D.

Matthew Roberts died in Virginia, July 8, 1883, aged 36 years.

William Holstein Roberts, married Laura, daughter of Isaac R. and Margaret Massey, of Tredyffrin township, Chester county, Pennsylvania, December 20, 1876, by Rev. O. Perinchief.

Jonathan John Roberts, married Sarah Louisa Beidler, daughter of Abram and Sarah Beidler, Chester county, Pennsylvania, May 17, 1882.

George Holstein Roberts and Edward Roberts, twins; George H. married Clara Fries, February 13, 1884, and second wife Mrs. Jennie Bowman, of Atlantic City, New Jersey, October 7, 1888. Edward, unmarried.

John Roberts, unmarried; resides at Pittsburg, Pennsylvania.

Children of Dr. George W. Holstein and Abby Turner Brower—four.

Charles Elliott Holstein and Elwood Harvey Holstein, twins; Charles E., druggist, in Bridgeport, Pennsylvania; Elwood H., died, aged 3 months.

Ella Holstein, married William W. Potts, son of Robert T. and Elizabeth Potts, of Upper Merion, Montgomery county, Pennsylvania, November 9, 1870, by Rev. Octavius Perinchief, rector of Christ Swede Church.

George Meade Holstein, married Sarah Corson, daughter of Felix Francis and Susan Highley, of Norristown, Pennsylvania, April 24, 1869, by Rev. A. A. Marple, assisted by Rev. G. G. Smeade, of Holy Trinity Church, Pulaski City, Virginia, where they reside.

Children of Isaac Wayne Holstein and Alice Hallowell:

Elizabeth Brookfield Holstein, married David M. Ellis, son of B. Morris and Elizabeth Masters Ellis, of Muncy, Pennsylvania, November 22, 1882, by Rev. A. A. Marple, at " Peach Park," Upper Merion.

William Hallowell Holstein, unmarried.

Mary Alice Holstein, married William A. Armstrong, Jr., son of Dr. William and Lillie P. Armstrong, of Philadelphia, March 11, 1886, by Rev. Isaac C. Winn, Camden, New Jersey.

Children of Rachel B. Hughes and Dr. Jacob Dewees:

Mary Catharine Dewees, born 16th of September, 1828; baptized by Rev. J. C. Clay; died 13th of March, 1837.

John Hughes Dewees, born 26th of February, 1831, at Trappe, Montgomery county, Pennsylvania; baptized by Rev. J. C. Clay; married Sarah Hammer, 20th of June, 1861, at Shamokin, Pennsylvania, by Rev. Abraham D. Hawn. Mrs. J. H. Dewees, died at Shamokin, 13th of July, 1866. John H. Dewees, married the second time Emily J. Milliken, daughter of Joseph Milliken and Elizabeth Moore Patton, of Lewistown, Pennsylvania, April 5, 1887.

John Hughes Dewees was educated at the boarding school of Rev. Henry J. Raudenbaugh in Trappe village, and ended his school days with Rev. Samuel Aaron, at Norristown, Pennsylvania. He commenced his profession as a civil engineer on the survey of the Chester Valley Railroad, between Downingtown and Bridgeport, Pennsylvania. He then went to Shamokin, where he became assistant to Kimber Cleaver, chief engineer of the Philadelphia and Sunbury Railroad, between Sunbury and Mt. Carmel. After the completion of the railroad he located in Shamokin as a mining engineer, and became agent of the New York and Middle Coalfield Railroad, the Green Ridge Improvement Company and the Northern Central Railroad Company. At this time, whilst yet a very young man, his natural inclination for geological studies developed itself. From that time forward, through all the vicissitudes of business changes in life, and suffering from continued ill health, the practical and scientific study of the earth and how it is formed was his occupation. Modest in his estimate of himself, unassuming and unobtrusive in his manners, by reason of real knowledge and the con-

RACHEL B. HUGHES DEWEES.

fidence in him that knowledge inspired, he was enabled to do much towards the proper development of the middle anthracite coal basin. Although at that time not a professional geologist, his opinion as to the quality of coal lands and the location of collieries was highly regarded. He became largely interested in the mining of coal at the Lambert, Excelsior and other collieries. After going out of the coal business, he naturally, and perhaps without serious intention on his part, drifted into his natural profession of a geologist, and very soon acquired reputation among those who knew him. When the State Geological Survey was organized he was appointed to a position under Professor Leslie, in which position he won and retained the confidence of those with whom he was associated, and rendered good service to the State.

He was subject, however, to severe attacks of inflammatory rheumatism, by which he was confined to his bed weeks, and even months, at a time. He became satisfied that he could not undergo the rigors of the northern winter, and consequently retiring from the State survey entered into the general practice of his profession, and visited professionally the gold fields of Arizona, where he remained some months, but with occasional examinations north. The field of his operations was in Virginia and North Carolina, up to the time of his death, in which last named State he died, on the 7th of December, 1883. Without being demonstrative in religious profession, he was a religious man, a member of the Episcopal Church. He helped to form the congregation at Shamokin, and was a large contributor to the building of the church. In all places he was afterwards located, he was a member of the vestry and active in church affairs.

Francis Percival Dewees, born 21st of December, 1837, in Pottsville, Schuylkill county, Pennsylvania; baptized by Rev. J. C. Clay; married Emma, daughter of Christopher and Louisa A. Loeser, of Pottsville, Pennsylvania, 20th of

October, 1862, in Gloria Dei Church, Philadelphia, by Rev. J. C. Clay, D. D.

He received his primary education at Washington Hall, Trappe, Pennsylvania, and in the public schools of Philadelphia. In 1844 he was sent to the Academy in Norristown, then in charge of Rev. Samuel Aaron, for whom he has always entertained the highest regard as a man and a pedagogue, especially as an instructor in the elements of elocution and English literature. He entered Marshall College, Mercersburg, Pennsylvania, John W. Nevin, D. D., LL. D., president, in 1849, when between 16 and 17 years old.

In 1850 he went to Union College, Schenectady, New York, and entered the sophomore class along with the late General John F. Hartranft, who had been a classmate at Marshall, and graduated with credit in 1853. He taught in the public school of Bridgeport, Pennsylvania, during the winter of 1853-4, and studied law under the instruction of Hon. B. Markley Boyer, of Norristown, Pennsylvania. In the spring of 1855 he went to Pottsville, where he entered the office of his uncle, Hon. Francis W. Hughes; was admitted to practice law in Schuylkill county, Pennsylvania, June, 1855. He continued to reside in Pottsville and practice law there, always taking an active part in politics as a Democrat, but was never an aspirant for any office. In 1861 he enlisted as a private in the Washington Artillerists, the services of which company were tendered to the government before the President had issued his proclamation calling for 75,000 men, and as one of the "first defenders," was among that distinguished body of men who were first to arrive at the National Capital. Shortly afterwards he was offered a commission as first lieutenant in the regular army by Hon. Simon Cameron, then Secretary of War, but preferring to remain with the comrades with whom he had enlisted the offer was declined. His term of enlistment expiring in July, he returned home. In the spring of 1868 he moved his family to Kentucky, where for three years he was engaged in making charcoal iron at Belmont and Nelson furnaces, first as the managing partner of F. P. Dewees and Company, and afterwards as the president of the Belmont and Nelson Iron Company. In the spring of 1874 he returned to Pottsville and resumed the practice of law. During the latter part of the year 1876 he wrote " The Molly Maguires," published by J. B. Lippincott and Company. This book met with a very favorable reception, and became the recognized authority concerning that band of outlaws in the anthracite coal region.

In 1877 he became chairman of the Executive Committee of the National Greenback Party of Pennsylvania. He acted with that party for several years, being at one time chairman of the Executive Committee of the United States. In 1880 he was the nominee of the party for Judge of the Supreme Court, in Pennsylvania, but during the campaign an issue arose between him and Weaver, the nominee for President, which resulted in his withdrawing from the contest, and entering vigorously into the support of Hancock, the candidate of the Democratic party.

It was while he was the executive officer of the National Greenback Party that it attained its greatest power and numerical strength.

In 1885 he received the appointment of assistant attorney under Attorney-General Garland, which position he retains under the present Harrison administration. He is regarded as an able lawyer, a polished writer and a logical and forcible speaker.

Theodore Lyng Dewees, born 21st of December, 1837, at Trappe, Montgomery county, Pennsylvania; married Ardelia Louisa, daughter of Alfred R. and Phoebe James Fiske, of Rhode Island, 20th of January, 1869, at Shamokin, Pennsylvania, by Rev. Daniel Washburne.

William Henry Dewees, born 28th of August, at Trappe, Montgomery county, Pennsylvania; baptized by Rev. J. C. Clay; unmarried; resides in Philadelphia.

James Collin Dewees, born 16th of September, 1843, at Philadelphia; baptized by Rev. J. C. Clay; married Charity

Bye, daughter of John P. and Sarah H. Packer, of Lock Haven, Pennsylvania, 9th of October, 1872, by Rev. Nathan J. Mitchell.

Children of Dr. Isaac Wayne Hughes (of North Carolina) and Eliza McLinn:

John Hughes, born 30th of March, 1830, graduated at the University of Pennsylvania (Literary Department) in 1848, at the age of 18 years; went to Pottsville, Pennsylvania, and read law in the office of his uncle, Francis W. Hughes; was licensed in 1851; practiced law in Pottsville, at first alone, next as partner of William B. Wells, and lastly as partner of F. W. Hughes. In 1860 was Democratic nominee for Congress in the district composed of Northumberland and Schuylkill counties. In 1861 (July 8th), left Pottsville and returned to his native State. In April, 1862, entered the Confederate army with the rank of Captain, in Seventh Regiment, North Carolina State Troops, Colonel Campbell. Subsequently was promoted to the staff of Major-General R. F. Hoke, with rank of Major, where he remained until the surrender of General Joseph E. Johnston's army at High Point, North Carolina, in 1865; was present at the battles around Richmond in 1862, capture of Harper's Ferry by the Confederates, Fredericksburg, Chancellorsville, Gettysburg, Fort Fisher, Bentonville, etc.; was never wounded, but had two horses captured on the occasion of the famous mine explosion at Petersburg, Virginia. Returned to Newbern in 1865; was admitted to the bar in North Carolina in that year, and commenced the practice of law in Newbern, which he continued; was elected to the Senate of North Carolina in the fall of 1867, and was the first person in the Senate ever voted for by the negroes under the Reconstruction Acts; was a candidate for elector on the Seymour and Blair ticket in 1868. In 1869 was elected president of the National Bank of Newbern; was the Democratic candidate for Lieutenant-Governor of North Carolina in 1872. John Hughes married Jane, daughter of

JOHN HUGHES.
N. C.

John P. and Elizabeth B. Daves, of Newbern, North Carolina, in Christ Church (Episcopal), January 24, 1854, Rev. Henry F. Green officiating. By the will of his grandfather, John Hughes, of Montgomery county, Pennsylvania, John Hughes, of North Carolina, came into possession of a fine old English upright clock, which is still loyal enough to the land from which it came to play every hour, " God Save the King." It stands in the hallway of his house, a splendid time-keeper, and a superb piece of mechanism, and is, according to tradition, two hundred years old. It is highly prized, both for its intrinsic value and the association connected with it. John Hughes died at Beaufort, North Carolina, of paralysis, September 9, 1889.

Among old papers in the possession of Benjamin B. Hughes, deceased, was found this bill, which gives the history of the clock:

" John Hughes, Esq.,
     Bought of Downs and Lee,
 June 4, 1770,   One Musical Clock,
       £112. 10.
Received at same time, the above in full.
             Stephen Lee."

Hannah Hughes, born 1851; died in infancy.

James Bettnor Hughes, born 9th of June, 1833; graduated at the University of North Carolina (Chapel Hill), in 1853; graduated in medicine in the University of Pennsylvania in 1856; was resident physician at St. Joseph's Hospital, Philadelphia, in 1855-6; then went to Europe where he spent two years perfecting himself in his profession; returned to Newbern in 1858, where he associated himself with his father in the practice of medicine. He has been eminently successful; he entered the Confederate army as a surgeon at the very beginning of the war; was with the Second Regiment of North Carolina State Troops. Dr. James B. Hughes, married January 6, 1859, Laura A. W., daughter of James W. and Ann M. Bryan, of Newbern, North Carolina, Rev. Mr. Crogan (Roman Catholic) officiating. In May, 1868, Mrs. Laura A. W.

Hughes died at Newbern. Dr. James B. Hughes married the second time, Eliza W., daughter of Dr. Reuben and Eliza H. Knox, of Kinston, North Carolina, June 6, 1871, Rev. William Gordon (Episcopal) officiating.

Theodore Jones Hughes, born October 16, 1834; received a good education, and early developed a marked taste and talent for business pursuits. He became an extensive shipping and commission merchant at Newbern, before the war, and was highly successful. At the breaking out of the war he entered as staff officer the Second Regiment of North Carolina Cavalry, with rank of captain. Remained in the army for some time and was then, at his own request, transferred to the "State Navy," and was, until nearly the close of the war, the purser of the steamer "Advance" (a vessel belonging to the State of North Carolina), in which he ran the blockade with great success many times without accident, between Nassau, New Providence, and Wilmington, North Carolina. He was at the same time purchasing agent for the State of North Carolina for the purpose of procuring supplies for her troops. This vessel enabled North Carolina to keep her soldiers in the field better clothed than those from any other state in the south.

Theodore J. Hughes was never wounded. After the war he settled again in Newbern, but very soon removed to Mobile, Alabama, where he successfully carried on the business of a commission merchant.

He married in Newbern, North Carolina, October 3, 1855, Clara Filman, daughter of James Chapman and Elizabeth Stevenson, Rev. N. Collin Hughes officiating. March 22, 1870, Mrs. Clara Hughes died at Point Clear, Baldwin county, Alabama. Theodore J. Hughes married the second time Isabella Hunter, daughter of Thomas Storm and Eliza M. King, October 21, 1871, by Rev. Dr. Massey. Mrs. Theodore J. Hughes, neé King, died January 26, 1885, and is buried at Mobile, Alabama.

Nicholas Collin Hughes, born March 10, 1840; unmarried. He graduated at the University of North Carolina,

(Chapel Hill), in 1860; went to Pottsville in that year and read law in the office of Francis W. and J. Hughes, returned to North Carolina in the winter of 1860, and read law in Newbern with Hon. J. H. Haughton. In 1861 was appointed aid to Governor Ellis, of North Carolina, with the rank of Colonel, but, being anxious to go to the field, resigned in that year, and was appointed first lieutenant in the Second Regiment of North Carolina State Troops (Colonel Few). He was immediately appointed adjutant of the regiment, in which position he served with distinguished courage and great satisfaction to his superior officers. He participated in all the earlier battles of Virginia, including the celebrated battles around Richmond in 1862.

He was badly wounded in a skirmish in sight of his native town in the winter of 1862 by the explosion of a shell fired from a Federal gun-boat in the Neuse river. Prior to this he had been appointed Assistant Adjutant-General on the staff of General J. Pettigrew, in which position he was serving at the time he was wounded. He went to Raleigh (where all the family were then and had been living since the capture of Newbern, March 14, 1862), and as soon as he recovered from his wounds returned to Virginia and went with Lee's army to Gettysburg. He passed successfully through the battles of the 1st and 2d of July at that place, but late in the afternoon of the 3d, while gallantly leading a column in a charge up Cemetery Hill, he fell, mortally wounded. But such was his coolness and courage, that even while he lay bleeding and agonized with pain on the field he directed the attention of an officer to a portion of the line that was wavering under the fearful fire to which it was exposed and had them rallied. When they finally fell back he was carried from the field by some of his soldiers, who were devoted to him, and who were unwilling to abandon him, although they greatly imperilled their own lives by the exposure to which they thus voluntarily subjected themselves. He was conveyed in an ambulance to Martinsburg, Virginia, where he died on the 15th of July, 1863, after having received the tender nursing of the accomplished ladies of a family named Buchanan and the medical attendance of his brother, Dr. James B. Hughes.

He was remarkable for his talent, wit, chivalry and great beauty of person. He was admired by his superior officers, and beloved by his subordinates.

Children of Dr. Isaac Wayne Hughes, of Newbern, North Carolina, and second wife, Anne Smallwood:

Isaac W. Hughes, died in boyhood, in Newbern, North Carolina.

Francis Wade Hughes, born in Newbern, 9th of September, 1856.

Edward S. Hughes and Annie M. Hughes, twins; born at Raleigh, North Carolina, 16th of January, 1863; Annie died in infancy at Charlotte, North Carolina.

Children of Benjamin Bartholomew Hughes and Mary Rambo—ten:

John J. Hughes, married Hannah, daughter of Hunter and Hannah Adams Brooke, of Lower Merion, Montgomery county, Pennsylvania, 1851.

Isaac Wayne Hughes, graduated in medical department of University of Pennsylvania in 1852; located in Sunbury, Pennsylvania, same year; married Alice E., daughter of Judge Charles and Elizabeth Donnel, of Sunbury, Pennsylvania, 11th of April, 1855, Rev. William White Montgomery (Episcopal) officiating. In the autumn of 1854 removed to West Philadelphia, where he still continues the practice of medicine, in which he has been eminently successful. Dr. Isaac W. Hughes was a volunteer surgeon during the late war. Mrs. Alice E. Hughes died.

Dr. I. W. Hughes married the second time Emilie Baker, daughter of John C. and Almira Baker, of Philadelphia, January 24, 1878, by Rev. Dr. A. A. Willets.

Nathan Rambo Hughes, married Amanda E., daughter of David M. and Emily H. Stacker, of Lower Merion township,

JOHN J. HUGHES.

Montgomery county, Pennsylvania, 19th of April, 1864, by Mayor Henry, of Philadelphia.

Nathan R. Hughes died 28th of November, 1880.

Charles Collin Hughes, married Emily, daughter of George and Mary Pechin, of Bridgeport, Pennsylvania, February 21, 1860. Mrs. Emily Hughes died January 21, 1883. Charles Collin Hughes died December 4, 1888.

Mary Ann Hughes, married Hubert O., son of Dr. Joseph and Hannah Blackfan, of Radnor, Delaware county, Pennsylvania, December 18, 1872, by Rev. O. Perinchief.

Henry Clay Hughes, entered the service as a private of Company B, Fourth Pennsylvania Volunteer Infantry, April 20, 1861; occupation of Perryville, Maryland, April 21st; duty in Washington, District of Columbia, May 8th to June 24th; skirmish near Shuster's Hill, Virginia, June 30th; assigned to the First Brigade (Franklin), Third Division (Heintzelman), Army of Northeast Virginia, July 2d; moved to Shangster's Station, Virginia, July 18th, and to Centreville, July 19th; mustered out at Harrisburg, Pennsylvania, July 27, 1861, expiration of term.

Re-entered the service as a corporal of Company F, Fifty-First Pennsylvania Volunteers, September 13, 1861; served in the Second Brigade, First Division North Carolina Expeditionary Corps, December, 1861, March, 1862; moved to Annapolis, Maryland, November 16-17, 1861; sailed to Hatteras Inlet, North Carolina, January 9-26, 1862; moved to Roanoke Island, February 7th; battle of Roanoke Island, February 7-8; expedition to Newbern, March 11-13; battle of Newbern, March 13-14; discharged on surgeon's certificate at Newbern, North Carolina, May 21, 1862.

This was General Hartranft's old regiment that fought seventeen battles.

First Lieutenant Company G, Seventeenth Pennsylvania Volunteer Militia, September 17, 1862; served in General J. F. Reynolds' command during the invasion of Maryland by the Army of Northern Virginia; mustered out with company, September 28, 1862.

Second Lieutenant Company A, One Hundred and Seventy-Fifth Pennsylvania Infantry, November 4, 1862; resigned on account of ill health January 16, 1863, at Newbern, North Carolina.

Fifth and last enlistment, First Lieutenant Company I, Thirty-Fourth Pennsylvania Volunteer Militia, June 3, 1863; served in the army corps of the Susquehanna and the district of the Lehigh during the invasion of the North by the Army of Northern Virginia. This regiment was held in reserve at the time of the battle of Gettysburg.

Mustered out with the company, August 24, 1863, expiration of term.

Henry Clay Hughes was married to Kate A. Longacre, at the residence of her brother, at West Philadelphia, December 25, 1871, by N. B. Durell. Kate A. Longacre was the daughter of John and Mary Watts Longacre, of Norristown, Pennsylvania.

Hannah Hughes, unmarried; died March 8, 1884. The report of the superintendent of the Sunday school of Swedes (Christ) Church, Upper Merion, Pennsylvania, in which she was a teacher, has this notice of her death: "Regard for the living and respect for the dead alike demand that we should pay tribute to the memory of one of our most efficient teachers, Miss Hannah Hughes. Her place in the Sunday school can with difficulty be supplied; her long experience as a teacher peculiarly qualified her for the position she so acceptably filled. Her eminent virtues and her elevated character as a Christian were surpassed by none. Her remains lie in the sacred ground which surrounds this edifice, along with those of her forefathers, there to await the blessedness which comes with the first resurrection. Of her we say in truth, 'None knew her but to love her, none named her but to praise.'"

Catharine Dewees Hughes, married April 19, 1877, Edmund M. Evans, son of David and Lavinia Evans, by Rev. J. P. Tustin.

William Corson Hughes, unmarried.

FIRST LIEUT. HENRY C. HUGHES.

Francis Wade Hughes, died aged 5 years, May 7, 1860.

Children of Slaytor Clay Hughes and Susan Jarrett—two:

John Jarrett Hughes, married Mary E. Clark, of Philadelphia, October 3, 1858, by Rev. Louis P. Hornberger; died January 13, 1874, in his 37th year.

Jane Augusta Hughes, married Robert Carmer, son of Charles M. and Caroline G. Hill, of Pottsville, Pennsylvania, by Rev. Daniel Washburn, of Pottsville, October 28, 1862.

Children of Francis Wade Hughes and Elizabeth Silliman—four:

Thomas Silliman Hughes, died June 15, 1855, aged 17 years.

Frances Hughes, married Guy E. Farquhar, son of George Wildman Farquhar, formerly of Philadelphia, and Amelia von Schrader (from Prussia), of Pottsville, Pennsylvania, 15th of November, 1864, by Rev. William P. Lewis.

Annette Hughes, married George Ringgold Kaercher, son of Franklin B. and Susannah H. Kaercher, of Pottsville, Pennsylvania, August 3, 1883, by Rev. James E. Powers.

Lucy Hughes, unmarried.

Children of Theodore J. Hughes and Caroline Fonville:

Isaac Wayne Hughes, born in Newbern, North Carolina, 15th of October, 1845. He entered the Confederate service in 1861, at the age of fifteen years, in the Fifth North Carolina Cavalry, Company D, Captain Galloway. Fought in twenty-six battles and engagements; was killed on the 1st of June, 1864, at Ashland, Virginia, fourteen miles north of Richmond. He, with six others under him, were sent to capture a party of Federal soldiers. The Federals retreating, drew them into an ambush, where all were killed. Wayne fell, and his body was found under the others.

Edward Hall Hughes, born 29th of January, 1848, in Pottsville, Pennsylvania; died in Philadelphia, March 30, 1885.

Benjamin Francis Hughes, born in Fairfax county, Virginia, 28th of March, 1851; died in Pottsville, Pennsylvania, September 3, 1853.

Louis Curtis Hughes, born in Pottsville, Pennsylvania, 9th of January, 1854, married Charlotte Tritle, January 26, 1882, by Rev. J. Q. Waters, Pittsburg, Pa.

Helen May Hughes, born in Pottsville, Pennsylvania, January 26, 1856; died in Newbern, North Carolina, February 21, 1869.

Children of Rev. N. Collin Hughes and Adaline Williams Hughes:

Mary Elizabeth Hughes, born 16th of November, 1849; baptized in St. Paul's Church, Greenville, Pitt county; married Rev. Nathaniel Harding, rector of St. Peter's Church, Washington, North Carolina. The marriage ceremony was performed by her father, Rev. N. Collin Hughes, assisted by Rev. J. Harding, in Greenville, North Carolina, February 3, 1874. The parents of Rev. N. Harding were Nathaniel and Elizabeth Harding, residing near Washington, North Carolina. Both died during the civil war at their home. Rev. N. Harding served for some time in the Confederate army as a private soldier, though only about 17, when the war ended. Mrs. Mary Elizabeth Harding died January 5, 1887.

Hannah Hughes, born 15th of November, 1851; baptized by immersion in Trinity Chapel, Beaufort county, North Carolina, July 20, 1852; married Charles Cottingham Calvert, son of William and Alice Calvert, of North Carolina, February 7, 1878, by her father, Rev. N. Collin Hughes, assisted by his son-in-law, Rev. Nathaniel Harding. The service was performed in Trinity Church. Mr. and Mrs. Charles C. Calvert reside in Denison, Texas.

John Robert Hughes, born 26th of November, 1854; baptized in Trinity Chapel, Beaufort county, North Carolina, 13th of April, 1855; married Sallie Nelson, daughter of

Benjamin Franklin and Winifred Harding, of Beaufort county, North Carolina, February 27, 1889, his father, Rev. N. Collin Hughes, officiating; reside in Norfolk.

Nicholas Collin Hughes, born June 20, 1856; baptized in Trinity Chapel, Beaufort county, August, 1856; married April 27th, 1880, in Trinity Church, Beaufort county, North Carolina, to Martha Elizabeth, daughter of Rev. Israel and Caroline Virginia Harding, his father, Rev. N. Collin Hughes, assisted by Rev. Israel Harding, performed the ceremony.

N. Collin Hughes, Jr., was ordained to the Diaconate, in Newbern, North Carolina, in July, 1880. Bishop Atkinson officiating. From that time he has entered earnestly and successfully into the plans of his father, Rev. N. Collin Hughes, in carrying on the Trinity school at Chocowinity; in connection with it, he has always been engaged in church mission work.

Isaac Wayne Hughes, born at Hendersonville, North Carolina, 17th of July, 1864; baptized by his father, Rev. N. C. Hughes, in St. James Church, Henderson county, North Carolina.

Children of Rachel Hughes Potts and Francis S. Hubley—five:

Julia Harriet Hubley.

William Potts Hubley.

Anna Elizabeth Hubley.

Edward Burd Hubley, married (his second cousin) Mary Louisa, daughter of William and Emily Clay Pollock, of Pottsville, Pennsylvania.

Louisa Harriet Hubley, married Edward Burd Peale, of Schuylkill county, Pennsylvania, 6th of November, 1859. He was the son of Rubens Peale and Eliza Patterson, his wife, of Philadelphia. Rubens Peale was a brother of Rembrandt Peale, the artist. Rubens and Rembrandt Peale were sons of Charles Wilson Peale, of Peale's museum. Rubens Peale possessed the same artistic talent as his brother, but did not find out his ability to paint until he was 75 years of age, and continued to practice his art until his death, which took place when above 80.

Children of Thomas Isaac Potts and Mary Frances Johnston Potts:

Anna Frances Potts.

Harriet Potts, married William Potts Rockhill (her cousin), son of Edward Augustus and Eliza Potts Rockhill, of Pittstown, Hunterdon county, New Jersey, October 10, 1866, by Rev. W. H. Furness.

William Potts Rockhill entered the army as a private 14th of August, 1862; served with distinction in several battles; enlisted in the Fifteenth Pennsylvania Cavalry, known as the "Anderson Troop." Many of the private soldiers in this troop were young men of good family. It was considered one of the most superior of the Pennsylvania cavalry regiments. He was in the battle of Antietam, September 17, 1862, and was wounded at the battle of Murfreesboro, December 29, 1862, while charging a brigade of rebel infantry. Was appointed First Lieutenant of Company L, by special field order No. 57, by General Rosecrans. Promoted to the Captaincy of Company C by special field order No. 127. He was engaged with his regiment in the battles of Honer's Gap, Chickamauga, Mossy Creek, Dandridge and others. It was at the battle of Murfreesboro that many of the men refused to fight, giving as an excuse that the regiment was not properly officered. About two hundred and eighty went into the fight, of whom Mr. Rockhill was one. He was there wounded in the thigh, a musket ball passing entirely through his leg. Seeing his superior officer fall wounded he was dismounting to go to his assistance when the bullet struck him as he was throwing his leg over the saddle. He resigned on account of physical disability July 29, 1864. As his health was much impaired by his wound he retired, after his resignation, to the estate of his ancestors, near Pittstown, New Jersey.

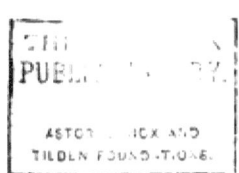

Horace Turley Potts, married Annie, daughter of Isaac Harrison O'Harra and Elizabeth Miles, of Philadelphia, by Rev. Dr. Boardman, Baptist.

Kate B. Potts, married Captain Charles Hobbs (of the regular army), son of George W. and Sarah W. Hobbs, by Rev. W. H. Furness. Captain Hobbs served through the war of the Rebellion; was in many battles and was severely wounded.

Mary Potts.

Children of Charles Clay Potts and Mary Joy Ridgway:

Julia H. Potts, married Samuel H. Gray, son of Philip James and Sarah Woolston Gray, September 25, 1862, in Christ Church, Philadelphia, by Rev. Benjamin Dorr, D. D.

Mr. Gray is a leading and accomplished lawyer, practicing in all the courts of New Jersey, and is constantly retained in important cases before the several Superior Courts sitting at Trenton, where his reputation is deservedly high.

Children of William Francis Potts and Caroline Tryon—four:

Sarah Potts.

Mary Potts.

Ellen Potts, married Jacob M., son of Peter and Emalie Stokes Armbruster, of Philadelphia, by Rev. J. C. Clay.

Charles W. Tryon Potts, married Adelaide, daughter of George W. Kelly and Mary Carey Watson, of Philadelphia, by Rev. J. A. Sisso.

Children of Robert Barnhill Potts and Sarah Page Grew—three:

William John Potts, unmarried; resides in Camden, New Jersey.

Robert B. Potts, unmarried; resides in Camden, New Jersey.

Sallie Hughes Potts, unmarried; resides in Camden, New Jersey.

Children of Theodore Jones and Laura Rutter—three:
Laura Jones.
Marion Jones.
Theodore Jones.

Children of Harriet Jones and Benjamin Evans:
Ellen Evans.
Harriet Evans.

Children of Benjamin Franklin Rittenhouse and Isobel Laurie:

Elizabeth Scott Rittenhouse, married William Henry Fitzhugh, son of Rev. R. R. and Eliza M. Gurley, by Rev. Dr. Eckard (formerly missionary to India), on January 30, 1854. The father, Rev. R. R. Gurley, was born in Connecticut, the mother, Eliza, in Portland, Maine; were married in Portland. Mr. W. H. F. Gurley died July 7, 1866.

S. Emily Rittenhouse, unmarried.

Isobel L. Rittenhouse, married Joseph Harvey Nourse, son of James and Sarah Harvey Nourse, March, 1853. The ceremony was performed by Dr. Laurie, the grandfather of Isabel, who died a month afterwards, having preached in the city of Washington fifty years. Mrs. Isobel L. Rittenhouse died February, 1883.

Children of Benjamin Franklin Rittenhouse and second wife, Henrietta Davidson:

Mary D. Rittenhouse, married Rev. A. Miller Woods, son of Rev. Dr. James Woods, of Lewisburg, and Miss Witherspoon (who was the daughter of Dr. Witherspoon, of Princeton, of the eminent family of that name, one of whom signed the Declaration of Independence). The marriage ceremony was performed by Rev. Dr. Woods.

Henrietta W. Rittenhouse, married Captain Thomas Wilson (U. S. A.), a graduate of West Point, in Georgetown, District of Columbia, by Rev. Dr. Bocock (Presbyterian), May 6, 1858.

J. H. RITTENHOUSE
SCRANTON, PENNA.

Benjamin Franklin Rittenhouse, married Elizabeth Shapter, of Brooklyn, New York, by Rev. William Sandford, March 4th; resides in Baltimore; during the late war was Major United States Artillery, and wounded by a sharpshooter in front of Petersburg, Virginia; retired from the service on account of the severe wound.

David Rittenhouse, married Mary Tilghman Earle, May 24, 1887, is receiving teller in Riggs and Company's Bank, Washington, District of Columbia.

Clementina Crawford Rittenhouse, married R. S. T. Cissel, of New York, by Rev. A. A. E. Taylor (Presbyterian), May, 1868.

James Delosier Rittenhouse, married Dolores Casillas; resides in Arizona.

Helen Murray Rittenhouse, unmarried.

James Hall Rittenhouse, civil engineer and chemist in Scranton; married Ida R. Cole, daughter of Rev. Leonard Cole, and granddaughter of Nancy Morse, of the old Morse family, April 10, 1878.

Charles Edwin Rittenhouse, married Helen S. Goode.

John D. Rittenhouse, died in infancy.

Children of Mary Elizabeth Rittenhouse and A. B. Shuman:

David R. Shuman, unmarried.
Sarah Shuman, died in infancy.
Helen M. Shuman, died February 14, 1866.
Emily A. Shuman, unmarried.
Mary R. Shuman.
Charles F. Shuman, died May 20, 1859.

———

Children of Emily Josepha Rittenhouse and Rev. David Hall:

William R. Hall, married Jerusha Willard, by Rev. Dr. Hall.

Joseph Hull, married Elizabeth Mahaffey, by Rev. Dr. Hall; no children.

Children of Charles Edwin Rittenhouse and Sarah M. Whitall:

Fannie Rittenhouse, married Thomas Hyde, of Riggs and Company, bankers, October, 1864, by Rev. Dr. C. Butler, Episcopal.

Sarah Louisa Rittenhouse, unmarried.

Mary W. Rittenhouse, married Leonard Gunnel, October, 1868, by Rev. Pelham Williams, of Boston, Episcopal. Mrs. M. Gunnel died February 18, 1872.

Samuel White Rittenhouse, married Caroline, daughter of Professor H. Lockwood, of the navy, September, 1874, by Rev. Dr. Alexander Shiras.

Charles Edwin Rittenhouse, died in his 14th year.

Anna Rittenhouse, died in infancy.

Emily Rittenhouse, unmarried.

Children of John Hughes Rittenhouse and Jane L. Simonton:

Martha L. Rittenhouse, married Joshua Williams by Rev. F. T. Brown, of St. Paul, Presbyterian.

Charles Edwin Rittenhouse, married Grace Hubbell, daughter of James B. Hubbell and Catharine Tew, December 24, 1883, by Rev. M. McG. Dana.

Mary F. Rittenhouse married D. D. Lambie, by Rev. William McKibbon, assisted by Rev. D. R. Breed.

Children of George Wade and Sophie DePathorn:
Francis Wade.
Sophia Wade.
George Wade.

Children of Hannah Maria Hepburn and William H. Blackiston, of Maryland:

Samuel Hepburn Blackiston, born at Head of Sassafras, Kent county, Maryland; married Mrs. Sarah T. Brooke, nee Raisin, 17th of September, 1868, at Christ Church, Kent county, Maryland, by Rev. Morton Wattson.

Henry Curtis Blackiston, Lieutenant Company B, First Maryland cavalry; killed in a skirmish at Bunker Hill, Virginia, September 3, 1864.

Josephine Blackiston, married Henry Augustus Newland (second wife), October 20, 1885.

Anne Blackiston, died.

Emma Blackiston.

Rev. Slator Clay Blackiston, married Margaret Monroe, of Mississippi.

Rev. Slator Clay Blackiston is a graduate of Nashotah Theological Seminary, Wisconsin, Episcopal, and rector of a church at Austin, Nevada.

Clara Blackiston.

Lizzie Blackiston, married Henry Augustus Newland, October 25, 1876; died December 1, 1883.

Mary Eugenia Blackiston, married J. Woodbridge Patton, of Philadelphia, by Rev. Dr. Patton, of Middleton, Delaware county, 8th of July, 1873.

Child of Dr. James Curtis Hepburn and Clara M. Leet:

Samuel Dyer Hepburn, married Clara Shaw, of Lock Haven, Pennsylvania, 16th of October, 1873, by Rev. Joseph Nesbit.

Children of Sarah Ann Hepburn and Hon. James Pollock, of Milton:

Samuel Hepburn Pollock, born in Milton, Pennsylvania, 23d of October, 1838. In 1862 he entered the Union army as Adjutant of the One Hundred and Thirty-First Regiment of Pennsylvania Volunteers, Colonel Allebach commanding. General Humphrey's division. He was with his regiment in all the battles in which they were engaged from Antietam to Fredericksburg and Chancellorsville, and died 25th of October, 1865, from disease contracted in the army.

William Curtis Pollock was born in Milton, Pennsylvania, August 30, 1840; married Ella M. Burr, of Philadelphia, 21st of April, 1868, by Rev. Slator Clay Hepburn.

Louisa Ann Pollock, born in Milton, Pennsylvania, 11th of August, 1842, married Richard Edy Clay, son of Rev. Jehu C. Clay and Simmons Edy, 5th of February, 1863, by Rev. Dr. J. C. Clay, rector of Gloria Dei Church, Philadelphia.

Emily Clara Pollock, born in Milton, Pennsylvania, February 22, 1845; died July 5, 1846.

James Crawford Pollock, born in Milton, Pennsylvania, November 29, 1847; married Mary Agnes Kelsey, in Chicago, Illinois, November 18, 1879, by Rev. Slator Clay Hepburn; resides in Buffalo, New York.

Sarah Margaret Pollock, born in Milton, 20th of March 1850; married, in Philadelphia, to Henry T. Harvey, of Lock Haven, Pennsylvania, son of George C. and Roxanna S. Attwood Harvey, of Salona, Clinton county, Pennsylvania, 18th of April, 1872, by Rev. Slaytor Clay Hepburn.

Emma Pollock, born in Milton, Pennsylvania, March 22, 1853; married Charles Corss, a lawyer of Lock Haven, June 5, 1889.

Child of Rev. Slator Clay Hepburn and Anna Boyd:

Samuel Boyd Hepburn, married Sarah R. Booth, October 24, 1882, by Rev. Slator Clay Hepburn. S. B. Hepburn resides in New York city.

Children of Mary Hepburn and L. A. Mackey, of Lock Haven—three:

Annie Hepburn Mackey, born in Milton, April 23, 1848; married Dr. Joseph Hayes, son of William and Sarah Reader Hayes, of Lock Haven, Pennsylvania, 28th of October, 1869, by Rev. Slator Clay Hepburn.

Samuel Hepburn Mackey, died in infancy.

Mary Louisa Mackey, born in Lock Haven, 18th of April, 1858; married Dr. Frank P. Ball, June 6, 1883, by Rev. Slator C. Hepburn.

Children of Emma Hepburn and J. Hogan Brown, United States Navy:

Annie Louisa Brown, born in Milton, Pennsylvania, 29th of November, 1849; married Albert S. son of John Shuman and Elizabeth H. Furst, November 11, 1869, by Rev. Joseph Nesbit, in Lock Haven.

Samuel Curtis Brown, born August 29, 1853; died in Philadelphia, February 12, 1865.

Gertrude Mary Brown, born in Lock Haven, March 7, 1858; married Thomas Hilton, a druggist, by Rev. Slator C. Hepburn, June 5, 1879.

Children of Jane Hepburn and Dr. Lichtenthaler:

Annie Mary Lichtenthaler, born in Lock Haven, 10th of July, 1856; married Thomas R. Mann, owner of axe factory at Mill Hall, Pennsylvania, November 26, 1876.

Dr. Henry Curtis Lichtenthaler, born in Lock Haven, Pennsylvania, 27th of July, 1860; married Annie Keeser, May 1886, by Rev. Joseph Nesbit.

Children of Emily Clay and William Pollock, of Pottsville — even:

Curtis Clay Pollock was among the first to respond to the call at the very beginning of the war for troops for three months and arrived in Washington, D. C., April 18, 1861. In the fall of that year he enlisted as a private in the Forty-Eighth Regiment Pennsylvania Volunteers, Company G, Second Division, Ninth Army Corps, under General Burnside; he was in every engagement of the Division, except Newbern; was in the battles of Antietam, South Mountain, Fredericksburg, second Bull Run, siege of Knoxville, etc., and was with his regiment in all the battles of 1864, when General Grant was marching on Richmond. He was commissioned Second Lieutenant June, 1862, promoted to First Lieutenant two weeks later. He was commanding Company G, and was the only officer in his company when he received the wound in his shoulder, in front of Petersburg, January 17, 1864, which proved fatal. He was taken to the Officers' Hospital, Georgetown, D. C., where he died on the 23d of January of tetanus.

Mary Wilson Pollock, born November 22, 1844; married Edward Burd Hubley, March 30, 1875, by Rev. William P. Lewis, of Pottsville.

Margaret Annan Pollock, born February 16, 1847; married William Gould Meigs, April 20, 1869, by Rev. William P. Lewis, of Pottsville, Pennsylvania. Mr. Meigs died February 13, 1888.

Juliet Campbell Pollock, born May 24, 1849; married Lewis L., son of Lewis Walker and Sarah Hubley, in Philadelphia, June 22, 1885, by Rev. Edmund Leaf.

James Pollock, born 1851; married October, 1882, in Mauch Chunk, Pennsylvania, Mary Douglas, daughter of Alexander and Anna Ruddell Leisenring.

Francis Hughes Pollock, born September, 1854; married Fannie McGinnes, daughter of E. W. and Ann S. McGinnes, of Pottsville, Pennsylvania.

Ann Clay Pollock, born July 12, 1858; married in Trinity Church, Pottsville, Pennsylvania, October 12, 1881, to Samuel M., son of Rev. Henry A. and Blendina Muller Riley, formerly of Montrose, Pennsylvania.

Children of Ann Clay and Joseph Potts, of Pottstown, Pennsylvania:

Henry W. Potts, married Eleanor S. Powell, daughter of John and Ellen Lee Powell, September, 1881, in Trinity Church, Shepardstown, West Virginia, by Rev. Dr. Landon

Mason. Mrs. Ellen Lee Powell is a near relative of General Robert E. Lee.

Emily Frances Potts, married Edward Kneass Landis, son of Henry and Katharine Reynolds Landis, February, 1882, in Christ Church, Pottstown, by Rev. Dr. Warren. Mrs. Katharine Reynolds Landis is a sister of General John F. Reynolds, who lost his life in the first day's fight at Gettysburg.

Child of Julia Frances Clay and Dr. J. T. Evans:
Eva Frances Evans, died in her 20th year.

Children of Dr. George Bolton Lownes Clay and Clara Tiers:
Clara Isabel T. Clay, born August 4, 1856.
Annie A. Clay, born September 18, 1858.
Henry Clay, born March 4, 1860.

Child of Richard Edy Clay and Louisa Ann Pollock:
Richard Edy Clay.

Children of Harriet P. Clay and Rev. Edmund Leaf, of Pottstown, Pennsylvania:
Charles Clay Leaf.
Edmund Leonard Leaf, deceased.
Ellen Lane Leaf.
Samuel Bowman Leaf.
George Herbert Leaf.

Children of George Henry Clay and Amelia Donnel:
Charles H. Clay.
Lillie Clay.

Children of Charles Moore Smith and Mrs. Rebecca Grant—seven:

Henderson Coates Smith, born June 27, 1838, at Batavia, Clermont county, Ohio; married Flora C. Allison, of same county, 8th of October, 1873, by Rev. W. D. Unsler.

Collin Coates Smith, born October 11, 1840, married Emma Kennedy, of Batavia, Clermont county, Ohio, daughter of James C. Kennedy, ceremony by a Roman Catholic priest in Cincinnati, Ohio.

Thomas Lowrey Smith, born 21st of February, 1842.

Lindsay Coates Smith, born December 9, 1843; died August 30, 1860, aged 16 years 8 months.

Mary Emma Smith, born 20th of January, 1846.

Levi Coates Smith, born July 5, 1848; died same day.

William Wayland Smith, born July 20, 1849; died aged 1 month.

Children of Charles Moore Smith and second wife, Adaline O'Connor:

Charles Moore Smith, born September 3, 1855.

James O'Connor Smith, born August 29, 1859.

Albert Smith, born August 22, 1863.

Children of Levi Coates and Mary Yerkes—three:

Aaron Yerkes Coates, born December 18, 1838; married Margaret Ann, daughter of John and Mary Sheard, of Frankford, Pennsylvania, September 28, 1864, by Rev. John Childs, of Philadelphia.

Matthias Coates, born July 4, 1840; married Mary Augusta, daughter of John and Adelia McMullen, of Cheltenham, Montgomery county, Pennsylvania, March 19, 1866, by Rev. Dr. Alexander Reed, at Philadelphia. Matthias Coates was enrolled in Company A, Fortieth Pennsylvania Militia, for three months' service.

Susan Yerkes Coates, born June 4, 1844; married Charles Wilkinson, son of Hiram and Eveline Castor, of Philadelphia, September 21, 1865, by Rev. Richard Newton, in Philadelphia.

Children of Mary Coates and John Smylie:

Matthias Coates Smylie, born in Philadelphia, 25th of April, 1847; married Virginia Maria, daughter of John and Elizabeth F. Peters, August 22, 1870, at Alexander Presbyterian Church, by Rev. George F. Cain, Philadelphia.

John Smylie, born in Philadelphia, April 30, 1849; died August 30, 1852.

Ellen Morrison Smylie, born September 24, 1851; died May 6, 1852, in Philadelphia.

Ellen Smylie, born June 14, 1853; married Alfred Morris Herkness, son of Alfred Morris Herkness and Annie Dorothea Weaver, January 13, 1876, by Rev. Cortland Whitehead, of Bethlehem, Pennsylvania, assisted by Rev. William Suddards, of Philadelphia.

William Duff Smylie, born December 10, 1855, in Philadelphia; married Sarah Alice Keiser, January 5, 1844.

Mary Elizabeth Smylie, born March 1, 1858, at Easton, Pennsylvania; married Frank Dallett, January 1, 1883.

Robert Sayre Smylie, born May 5, 1861, in Philadelphia; married Virginia Wright Kiehl, September 14, 1882. Mrs. Virginia Smylie died May 29, 1889.

Children of N. Collin Coates and Elizabeth Stewart Coates:

Charles Coates, born 18th of June, 1843; baptized by Rev. P. S. Hanson, 1st of April, 1852. Enlisted for three years in the civil war on the 20th of September, 1861, in Company G, Ninety-First Pennsylvania Volunteers, Captain Peter M. Keyser; re-enlisted in December, 1863; promoted for gallantry to sergeant 18th of June, 1864; wounded at Fredericksburg 13th of December, 1861, and again at Chancellorsville 3d of May, 1863, from the effects of which he died on the 22d of November, 1864, aged 21 years. He was with his regiment in all the battles in which it participated.

Matthew Henderson Coates, born 16th of July, 1845; baptized by Rev. J. C. Clay 9th of January, 1851; married

Mary B., daughter of Conrad and Barbara Drum, of Philadelphia, 21st of May, 1873, by Rev. J. E. Meredith.

Mary Mumford Coates, born 10th of October, 1849; died January 7, 1851.

Annie Hayman Coates, born 26th of June, 1856; baptized by Rev. P. S. Henson, 7th of April, 1872; married William, son of Charles and Emmaline Mason, January 26, 1887, by Rev. Wayland Hoyt, D. D.

Sophia Louisa Coates, born January 29, 1862.

Children of Atlee Augusta DeHaven and Anna Courtney—four:

Mary DeHaven.
Augusta DeHaven.
Anna DeHaven.
Joseph DeHaven.

Child of Augusta Julianna DeHaven and Richard Henry Ransom:

Joseph Morgan Ransom, married Miss Smith, of Covington, Kentucky.

Child of William Niell DeHaven and Miss Wormsley, of Missouri:

Henry DeHaven.

Children of William Niell DeHaven and third wife, Lizzie Regina Hildreth, of California:

George Louis DeHaven, born February 8, 1871; died June 28, 1871.

Niell Montgomery DeHaven, born in California, September 19, 1873.

Children of Captain Joseph Edwin DeHaven and Amelia Louisa Bigelow:

BARONESS VON ALTEN,
née DeHAVEN.
DRESDEN, GERMANY.

Josephine Amelia DeHaven, baptized by Archbishop Hughes, in New York; married in 1874, to Mr. Towson Caldwell, grandson of General Towson, of Revolutionary fame.

Augusta Louisa DeHaven, born in New York 21st of October, 1861; baptized by Bishop McLaughlin, of Brooklyn, New York; married 21st of October, 1882, in Berlin, Germany, to Baron Eberhard Curd von Alten, son of Baron Herman von Alten, of Gross Gottern, Hanover, Germany, and Baronin Adelaide von Alten, née von Heimburg. Baron Eberhard was born the 4th of May, 1857, in Gross Gottern. The marriage ceremony was performed by pastor Sternow Dorotheen Kirche, in Berlin.

Sarah Elizabeth DeHaven, born 26th of December, 1863, in New York; baptized by Bishop Cummins, of New York; married the 22d of November, 1884, in Bucklburg, Germany, Hans Frederick Carl Moritz von Campe, Doctor of Medicine. The marriage ceremony was performed by pastor Dr. Kuhlgatz. Dr. von Campe was born 27th of July, 1856. His father's name was Carl Hemrick Siegfried von Campe (Geheimer Zustiz Kanylairath); his mother's name was Clara Sophie Friedericke, née von Ustar Gleichen.

Children of Captain Jos. E. DeHaven and second wife, Augusta W. Borek:

Holstein Joseph Atlee DeHaven, born in Geneva, Switzerland, November 20, 1874; baptized April 18, 1875, by Rev. Mr. Bacon, in Geneva, Switzerland.

Edwin Augustus DeHaven, born in Geneva, Switzerland, June 18, 1877; baptized July 3, 1877, by Rev. Mr. Muller, in Geneva, Switzerland.

Children of Julianna DeHaven Atlee and Robert Williams—ten:

Amelia A. Williams, born January 9, 1838; baptized by Rev. John McKinney; married David Sterrett Lightner, son of Benjamin and Jane Lightner, of Ferguson township, Centre county, Pennsylvania, December 27, 1859, by Rev. Samuel Moore. Mr. Lightner enlisted for the civil war in Company G, Forty-Fifth Pennsylvania Volunteers; was wounded at the battle of South Mountain, Virginia, September 14, 1862, in the right lung, and died at Middletown September 28, 1862. Mrs. Amelia A. W. Lightner married the second time, January 21, 1873, Casper Frederick, son of Conrad and Barbara Elizabeth Goodyear, of Middle Spring, Cumberland county, Pennsylvania, by Rev. Robert M. Wallace.

Susan Miles Williams, born November 2, 1839; married in 1861, William Martin Travis.

James Augustus Williams, born December 3, 1840; baptized by Rev. John McKinney; enlisted in the Union army September, 1861; during the following winter was sick for a long time; at the time of the battle of Fredericksburg, was guarding commissary stores. Many of his comrades were wounded in that engagement, while he, wearying of his position, asked permission to march with his regiment; the request was granted, and the next tidings of him was that he fell at Gettysburg, 2d of July, 1863, aged 22 years and 7 months. Some of his friends, passing over the field on Sunday after the battle, found in a cluster of six new made graves one marked with his cap; this was all they knew of his fate.

Sarah DeHaven Williams, born March 25, 1842; unmarried.

Priscilla Martin Williams, born December 31, 1843; married George Thompson, son of James and Nancy Travis, of Franklin township, Huntingdon county, Pennsylvania, July 12, 1866, by Rev. William J. Gibson, D. D. Mr. Travis died November 29, 1887.

Emma Clay Williams, born 28th of March, 1846; died 9th of February, 1847.

Ellen Harriet Williams, born November 21, 1847; married Claudius B. Hess, son of Lewis and Rebecca Hess, of Phillipsburg, Centre county, Pennsylvania. Mr. Hess was in

HOLSTEIN JOSEPH DE HAVEN.
GENEVA, SWITZERLAND.

EDWIN AUGUSTUS DeHAVEN.
GENEVA, SWITZERLAND.

the Union army all through the war; was in Libby Prison, Richmond, for several months.

Jos. Atlee Williams, born October 5, 1849, married in 1875, Mrs. Mary Reed, nee Goodyear, of Shippensburg, Pennsylvania.

Elizabeth Boal Williams, born March 22, 1852; baptized by Rev. Dr. L. Hughes. She has in her possession the engagement ring of Harriet DeHaven Barber (she was married April 20, 1809), which is pearls in the centre of a plait of hair of Mr. and Mrs. Barber, and the initials on it in gold under glass, " H. D. B."

Robert Lewis Williams, born 1853; married Mary Emma Wileman, May 17, 1889.

Julia DeHaven Williams, born 28th of November, 1857; died 1st of December, same year.

Children of Samuel John Atlee and Jane Stewart:

Hugh DeHaven Atlee, born October 7, 1848; married in 1878, Mary M. Carmany; she died September 1, 1883. Hugh DeHaven Atlee married the second time, Miss Lizzie Cary, of Stone Valley.

Mary Emma Atlee, born June 29, 1851; died July 30, 1853.

John Stewart Atlee, born October 22, 1855; married Elizabeth Stewart, January 26, 1882; she died March 15, 1882; he married the second time, Clara Funk.

Joseph Augustus Atlee, born September 7, 1858; married Mamie Harper, of Tyrone, Blair county, Pennsylvania, and resides in that place.

Thomas James Atlee, born May 9, 1864; died in infancy.

Jane Amelia Atlee, born March 9, 1867; died December 5, 1869.

Twin sons, born 1870; lived but a few hours.

Child of Emma Maria Atlee and Hiram Hendrixon:
William Hendrixon.

Childen of Charles Elliot DeHaven and Mary Anne Carman :

Sarah Carman DeHaven, married in Christ Church, Philadelphia, December 9, 1878, by Rev. Joseph H. Garrison, Richard Meade Bache, son of Hartman Bache and Marie del Carmen Meade.

Charles Elliott DeHaven, married Anne Traquair Henderson, daughter of Wallace Henderson and Mary Emily Bartholomew Henderson, of Upper Merion, Montgomery county, Pennsylvania, September 15, 1875, by Rev. O. Perinchief. Charles E. DeHaven died June 17, 1887. Mrs. Charles E. DeHaven died September 14, 1892.

Mary Anna DeHaven, married Malcolm W. Bryan, son of George and Anne White Bryan, by Rev. George C. Currie, in St. Luke's Church, Philadelphia, December 15, 1886.

Maria S. DeHaven, died, unmarried, aged 17.

Children of Hugh DeHaven, of Upper Merion, Montgomery county, Pennsylvania, and Mary J. Cleaver:

Holsten DeHaven, married Annah Colket Gallup, daughter of Coffin Colket and Mary Walker Colket, of Philadelphia, in St. Luke's Church, Philadelphia, November 13, 1891, by Rev. Mr. Bradley.

Jane Cleaver DeHaven, unmarried.

Sophia M. DeHaven, unmarried.

Emma DeHaven, married Francis, son of Michael and Margaret K. Bright, of Pottsville, Pennsylvania, December 28, 1875, by Rev. O. Perinchief. Reside in Philadelphia.

Children of Emma DeHaven and William H. Hampton :

Sophia M. Hampton, married S. D. Adams, September 18, 1867, by Rev. William Suddards.

Emma Hampton, married B. P. Sloan, December 21, 1869, by Rev. William Suddards.

William Henry Hampton, born December 4, 1850; died June 13, 1852.

HOLSTEIN DeHAVEN.

Children of Susan Shober DeHaven and Samuel White:
Hugh DeHaven White, born 1848.
Sarah White, born 1849.
Samuel White, born 1851.
Charles Gordon White, born 1852.
Christian Bunting White, born 1855; married Charles L. Bains, in Philadelphia, October 19, 1882, by Rev. O. H. Tiffany, D. D.
Lillie White, born August 20, 1856.
Emily Louisa White, born November, 1858; married Dr. E. H. Neall, January 5, 1889, by Rev. J. A. M. Chapman, in Philadelphia.
Mary Elizabeth White, born November 14, 1859.
Mrs. Susan Shober White, died in Philadelphia, November 27, 1859.
Samuel White, died in Philadelphia, July 12, 1889.

Children of Hugh DeHaven and Clara Boyd Brinton:
Hugh Hill DeHaven, deceased.
Mary Florence DeHaven, deceased.
Clara Brinton DeHaven, baptized by Rev. Richard Newton.
Sarah Cole DeHaven, baptized by Rev. William Newton.

Child of Alexander Henry DeHaven and Mary Townsend:
Walter T. DeHaven.

Children of Sallie Letitia DeHaven and David T. Boyd, of Glasgow, Scotland:
Harold DeHaven Boyd, born July 1, 1877.
Etheldreda Holstein Boyd, born August 8, 1879.
David Thompson Boyd, born October 26, 1880.
Helen Boyd, born June 4, 1883.
Children all born in Glasgow, Scotland.

Child of William Rambo and Mary Ann Supplee:
Hiram Rambo, born 1836; died January 24, 1854, aged 18 years.

Children of Davis Coates and Anne Worrall:
Joanna Potts Coates.
Katie Louisa Coates.

Children of John Coates and Sarepta Stringfield:
Sherman Coates, died January 13, 1886, aged 19 years.
Martha Louisa Coates, unmarried.

Child of Louisa Coates and Jacob Shainline, Jr.:
Martha Emily Shainline, died aged 18 months.

Children of Thomas Holloway and Mary Ann Eastburn:
William H. Holloway, born January 3, 1846; married Ida Virginia, daughter of John and Elizabeth Buzby, of Bridgeport, Montgomery county, Pennsylvania, January 21, 1869, by Rev. Mr. Weddell, of Norristown, Pennsylvania. William H. Holloway died in Dunwiddie county, Virginia, October 2, 1884, aged 38 years.
Anna Elizabeth Holloway, born January 14, 1848; died September 12, 1848.
Anna Mary Holloway, born 27th of August, 1849; married George M., son of George and Mary White, of Norristown, March 1, 1871, by Rev. Charles Collin.
Hannah Ella Holloway, born 1st of September, 1851; died August 23, 1854.
Samuel Eastburn Holloway, born 9th of April, 1853; married Sarah Hardcastle, of Norristown, Pennsylvania, 1873, by Rev. J. R. Halsey, of Norristown.
Ida Holloway, born September 11, 1855; married David M. Jarrett, son of Jesse and Ann Jarrett, of Lower Providence township, Montgomery county, October 30, 1877, by Rev. Mr. Collin.

Henry M. Holloway, born July 14, 1859; married Libby DuMont, of Larned, Kansas, December 1, 1886. Resides in Kansas.

Bertha Holloway, born October 18, 1861; married Joseph Oliver Burnett, son of James and Mary Ann Burnett, of Plymouth township, March 22, 1882, by Rev. Charles Collin.

George W. Holloway, born September 11, 1863; died August 21, 1864.

Children of Jane Coates and William Knight:

Margaret Ann Knight, married Joseph Frantz, March 26, 1872, by Rev. John K. Murphy.

Thomas Knight, died, aged 6 years.

Emily Jane Knight, married John R. Pugh, December 21, 1869, by Rev. T. S. Yocom.

Samuel Coates Knight, married E. J. McBride, June 17, 1873, by Rev. O. Perinchief.

William Thomas Knight, married E. P. McDowell, July 11, 1877, by Rev. G. Gibson.

Mary Bertha Knight, died, aged 3 years.

Kate Gertrude Knight, married Harry T. Walter, June 18, 1879, by Rev. James Halsey.

Grace Irene Knight, married Dr. T. L. Adams, September 23, 1879, by Rev. John K. Murphy.

Blanche Eva Knight, married T. R. Vernon, February 27, 1880, by Rev. J. R. Gray.

Paul Gardiner Knight, married E. J. Gotwaltz, June 25, 1890, by Rev. A. A. Marple.

Children of Sarah Coates and Henry Bush:

Samuel Holstein Coates Bush, died November, 1892.

Helen M. Bush.

Adelia A. Bush, died, aged 21 years.

Children of Susan P. Coates and Jacob Hurst:
Margaret A. Hurst, married John B. Sommers, October 23, 1879, by Rev. G. Gibson.
Harry H. Hurst.
Jacob M. Hurst.
Three died in infancy.

Children of Ann E. Coates and Thomas M. Maitland:
Margaret M. Maitland, married William Caldwell, April 30, 1872, by Rev. Mr. Newton.
Martha Maitland, married D. Kunkle.

Children of Matilda P. Coates and Alexander McCurdy:
Adelaide McCurdy, married Charles Hank, by Rev. A. A. Marple.
Herbert McCurdy, married Manerva Davis.
Havilah J. McCurdy.

Children of Margaret Coates and Francis Drew:
Laura J. Drew, married Charles Caldwell.
Samuel Drew, died in infancy.
Adelade Drew, died.
George Drew, married Ida Bittings, February 15, by Rev. William Bridenbaugh.
William Corson Drew.

Children of Caroline P. Coates and Abner H. Brown:
Mary Emily Brown.
Anna Brown.

Children of Louis Ducurdee Holstein, of Pennsylvania, and Sarah Klingman:
John Jones Holstein, born 27th of December, 1844; married Annie M. Pearl, in 1885; resides in Birdsboro, Berks county, Pennsylvania.

Elizabeth Mary Holstein, born 14th of November, 1846; died April 22, 1864, aged 17 years.

Anna Margaret Holstein, born 7th of August, 1849; died January 5, 1852.

Rebecca Ellen Holstein, born 10th of March, 1852; died July 5, 1852.

Children of Jane Holstein, of Westmoreland county, Pennsylvania, and James Keir:

Mary Ann Keir, died.

Rebecca Keir.

Margaret Keir.

Sarah Love Keir, married George A. McRacken, of Slate Rock, Armstrong county, Pennsylvania, October 11, 1876, by Rev. Dr. George Hill.

Isabel Keir, died.

William Keir, died.

Samuel Keir, died.

Children of Margaret Holstein, of Westmoreland county, and John Ellwood:

Alexander Donalson Ellwood, died 11th of August, 1844, aged 16 months.

Thomas Ellwood, born 27th of December, 1855; died in infancy.

Children of Andrew Johnson Holstein, of Westmoreland county, and Margaret H. Fulton:

Ruth C. Holstein, born January 30, 1844; died 31st.

Melinda Holstein, born 4th of September, 1845; married Thomas A., son of Andrew and Elizabeth Craft, of Armstrong county, Pennsylvania, 6th of October, 1872, by Rev. B. Y. Thomas, of Elderton, same county.

Robert Holstein, born 23d of December, 1846; married Mattie, daughter of Samuel and Sarah Coulter, of Indiana county, Pennsylvania, 31st of August, 1874, by Rev. J. Ansley, of Johnstown, Cambria county, Pennsylvania.

Alexander Holstein, born 6th of March, 1849; married Elinor E., daughter of John and Eliza Rosensteel, of Indiana county, Pennsylvania, 14th of September, 1872, by Rev. W. Coulter, of Hicksville, Ohio.

Samuel Holstein, born 7th of March, 1851; died 5th of September, 1852.

Lavinia Holstein, born 22d of May, 1853; died 3d of February, 1861.

Silas Holstein, born 14th of July, 1855; died January 6, 1863.

Jane Holstein, born 12th of February, 1857; died 7th of March, 1859.

Jemimma Holstein, born 16th of February, 1860; died 20th of December, 1874.

Sarah Holstein, born 1st of April, 1862.

Children of Martha Jane Love and James McCafferty:

James McCafferty, born 25th of December, 1851; married Eva Thompson.

Robert McCafferty, born 9th of April, 1853; married Ellie Elliott. A daughter born 18th of June, 1856, died 13th of August, same year.

John Andrew McCafferty, born 11th of May, 1858; married Emma Pames.

Sarah Ann McCafferty, born 16th of December, 1860.

Mary Jane McCafferty, born 17th of April, 1863.

Martha Ellen McCafferty, born 14th of February, 1865.

William McCafferty, born 31st of August, 1867.

Nannie Bell McCafferty, born 10th of August, 1874.

Children of J. Holstein Love and Jane Love:

Lelia Ada Love, born 7th of January, 1860; married Joseph Chesnut, November 19, 1885.

Anna Bell Love, born 23d of May, 1864; unmarried.

Child of Sarah Ann Love and Robert Love:
Annette Love, born in Allegheny city, 1864; married J. Calvin Elder, September 24, 1885.

Children of Rebecca Love and David T. Norris:
William Holstein Norris, born 14th of June, 1872.
Rachel Lucella Norris, born 17th of January, 1874.
Sadie Blanche Norris, born 30th of January, 1876.
Robert Blaine Norris, born November 5, 1879.
Pearl Norris, born January 24, 1881.
Nannie Lelia Norris, born May 25, 1884.

Children of Peter Blake Holstein, of Darby, Pennsylvania, and Eliza Ann Farrell:
Hannah Holstein, married Louis S., son of Henry and Emily Kochersperger, of Philadelphia county, February 14, 1861.
John Holstein, married Christiana, daughter of Frederick and Anna Riter, of Kingsessing, March 10, 1859. Mrs. John Holstein died April 13, 1883. John Holstein died December 10, 1885, aged 59 years.
William Simes Holstein, married Phoebe Urian. William Simes Holstein died June 13, 1890, in his 33d year.

Children of Margaret Holstein and William Hunter:
Jane Hunter, born in Philadelphia, February 26, 1843; married Robert Washington Ballenger, October 7, 1866.
Rachel Pocahontas Hunter, born in Tinnicum, Delaware county, Pennsylvania, in 1866; married James Benjamin Flinn, of Loudon county, Virginia.
Catharine Ann Hunter, born in Tinnicum; married Jesse Murray, of Fredericksburg, Virginia.
John Carson Hunter, married Maggie Littlefield, of Alexandria, Virginia; married second time, Emma Johnson, of Fairfax county, Virginia.

Benjamin Parkinson Hunter, born in Tinnicum, Pennsylvania; married Mary Dearborn, of Alexandria, Virginia.

James Blake Hunter, born in Tinnicum, Delaware county, Pennsylvania; married Annie Johnson, of Fairfax county, Virginia.

Children of Mary Makemson and Jonathan Urid:
John Makemson Urid.
Mary Ann M. Urid, died in infancy.
Kate M. Urid.
Susanna Urid, married William, son of Walter and Mary Bell, Venango, Pennsylvania.
Elizabeth Urid, married Robert, son of Robert and Catharine Egner, of Philadelphia.

Child of Henry Makemson and Susan Myers:
Christiana Makemson.

Children of Peter Makemson and Hannah Fadden:
Ella Makemson.
William Makemson.
Rachel Makemson.
Martha Makemson.
Susan Makemson.

Children of William Makemson and Margaret Simpson:
Mary Makemson, died aged 17.
George Makemson.
Charles Makemson.

Child of Catharine Makemson and Benjamin Yerkes:
Eugene Yerkes.

Child of Catharine Yerkes and John Schofield:
Elizabeth Schofield.

Children of John Brandt and Ann Eliza Helms:
George Brandt, married Susan Orr, November, 1862.
William Brandt, married Sarah Harman, May, 1869.
Sarah Brandt, married William Howard, December, 1866.
Henry Brandt, married Catharine Humphrey, March, 1865.
Frank Brandt.
Charles Brandt.
Mary Brandt, married James Groves, June, 1862.
Hannah Brandt, married Daniel Preston, May, 1868.
Ella Brandt.

Child of Georgiana Brandt and Louis Lyman Albee:
George B. Albee.

Children of Elizabeth Lodge and John Hoopes:
Pratt Hoopes, married Rebecca, daughter of George and Mary Dickinson, of Kingsessing.
Lydia Hoopes, married William Davidson, of Muscatine, Iowa.
Walker V. Hoopes, married Miss Thibet; no children.
Thomas J. M. Hoopes, married Mary Bomgardener.
Ellis S. Hoopes.

Children of Catharine Lodge and Azariah Bane:
Mary Bane, deceased.
Louis Bane.
Elton Bane, deceased.
Hannah Bane.
Abel Bane.

Children of John Lodge and Caroline Green:
Emmor Lodge, married Hannah Mary, daughter of Homer and Lydia Eachus, of Edgemont, Delaware county, Pennsylvania.
Matilda E. Lodge, married William, son of Homer and Lydia Eachus, of Delaware county, Pennsylvania.

Abel Lodge, married Anna Hall.
Elizabeth Lodge, married Frank Baldwin.
Thomas Lodge, married Hettie Hetson.
John Lodge.

Children of Abel Lodge and Mary Margaret DeHart:
Ida Lodge, married Homer E., son of Walker Y. and Hannah Hoopes, of Media.
Frank Lodge, married Lizzie Ewe.
Walter Lodge, married Annie Morgan.

Children of Henry Lodge and Elizabeth McClellan:
Sallie Lodge, married George Griswold.
Ella Lodge, married Andrew Ford.
Henry Lodge, unmarried.

Children of Mary M. Lodge and Alexander Crozier:
Susanna Crozier.
Helen Crozier.

Children of Jane DeHart and William Wilson Harvey, of Philadelphia:
John B. N. Harvey, died aged 2 years.
Newman Harvey, died aged 6 years.
Mary Margaret Harvey.

There is in the possession of Mrs. Jane DeHart Harvey one of the Swedish books sent by King Charles XI., of Sweden, to the Swedes in this country. These books are now very rare. The translation of contents, by the late Mr. Mickley, of Philadelphia, is as follows: Title page of first part. "The Swedish Psalm Book, with the parts belonging to it, which will be found in the index on the following leaf.

"Upon his Royal Majesty's gracious command, and the Worthy Consistory of the year 1693, revised with great care, improved and augmented. Printed in Stockholm, in the year 1694."

EIGHTH GENERATION

Then follows: Index of Catechism, with Confession of Faith; Prayer Book, with Psalms and Hymns. Second Part: The Epistles and Gospels for Sundays and holy days; as also a collection of prayers belonging thereto; printed in 1693. Then, Index of Psalms, morning and evening prayer. "A Little Prayer Book, with church prayers and psalms, to be read at meals, printed 1694."

In the book is written in English: "Peter Holstein. A gift from his father, January 12, 1788."

Children of Samuel Holstein Henderson, of Mercer county, Pennsylvania, and Jane Cunningham:

Matthias Holstein Henderson, married Lucy, daughter of John and Mary Bower, of New Castle, Pennsylvania, October 14, 1886, by Rev. Joseph D. Herron, rector of Trinity church, New Castle, Pennsylvania.

Children of Samuel H. Henderson and second wife Emmaline W. Satterfield:

Jane Henderson, married Charles W., son of Morris and Maria Kellogg, of Philadelphia, 10th of January, 1877, by Rev. Joseph R. Moore, of the church of the Resurrection, Philadelphia.

Elizabeth Branton Henderson, married Edwin Burrough Campion, son of Nathan Field and Eliza Campion, October 29, 1885, by Rev. Robert T. Innes, in St. Mary's Church, Hamilton Village, Philadelphia.

John Henderson, married Marian Agnes, daughter of James and Catharine Hagan, June 20, 1887, at the clergy house of St. Patrick's Cathedral, New York city, by Rev. Father McMahon. No children.

Children of Matthias Holstein Jolly and Anne Ashton Squires:

Mary Anna Jolly, born in Altoona, Pennsylvania; married Samuel W. Loomis, son of Capt. John B. and Rebecca W. Loomis, of Clarion county, Pennsylvania, September 4, 1879, by Rev. Isaac Heckman.

Rebecca Mayberry Jolly, born in Tyrone, Blair county, Pennsylvania.

Elizabeth Ashton Jolly, married Reuben D. Neff, son of Daniel and Emily Neff, September 4, 1879, by Rev. Isaac Heckman.

Charles Squires Jolly, born in Tyrone, Blair county, Pennsylvania.

Warner Jolly, born in Tyrone, Blair county, Pennsylvania.

Charlotte Reed Jolly, born at Bigler, Blair county, Pennsylvania.

Children of Mary Anna Jolly and Henry P. Rutter, of Pottstown, Pennsylvania:

Anne Rutter, born in Philadelphia, October 17, 1852.
Sally Saylor Rutter, born in Philadelphia, May 21, 1854.
James Leonard Rutter, born in Altoona, Pennsylvania, 1st of April, 1856.

Children of George Wolf Holstein and Emma Eagle:
Josephine Prichett Holstein, born January 29, 1873.
Elizabeth Branton Holstein, born March 20, 1875.
Edith Lawrence Holstein, born in Belvidere, New Jersey, May 7, 1879.

Children of Eliza Branton Holstein and Smith K. Campbell:

Elizabeth Anna Campbell, married Boyd Henry, of Kittaning, Pennsylvania, 5th of December, 1887, by Rev. DeWitt Benham.

Holstein Pritner Campbell, " died May 12, 1887, in his 22d year, was buried in the Kittaning cemetery. When a child of four years of age he met with an accident that lamed him for life, compelling him to use crutches to move about. He graduated from the high school with honor and began the study of law in the office of McCain and Leaso. He won the admiration and love of a large circle of acquaintances and friends; with his clear intellect and literary ability, they predicted for him a distinguished future. He was a consistent member of the Second Presbyterian Church, manifested a strong faith and died in blessed hope. He was an active member of a society known as the "White Cross," and took an active part in all its proceedings.

"At his funeral the young men of this society acted as a guard of honor, and at the grave each cast upon the coffin a small bouquet of flowers as an emblem of the resurrection, in which all believed. A touching incident of the funeral was the carrying of Holstein's crutches by two of his young friends, who placed them in the grave; thus burying with his decaying body the most important reminder of his sufferings.

"Holstein's earthly plans were not realized, and the hopes of his friends were not fulfilled here, but they bury with him all earthly disappointments and rest in a confident belief of the life beyond the grave."

> "Things of the earth, in the earth we lay;
> Ashes with ashes, the dust with the clay.
> Lift up the heart, and the eye, and the love,
> Lift up thyself, to the regions above;
> There, the pure mind from earth's trammels set free,
> All wisdom shall know, all glory shall see."

Alice Colwell Campbell, unmarried.

Children of Sarah Eastburn Holstein and James McDowell:

Charles Hamilton McDowell.
Constance McDowell.
Branton Holstein McDowell.

Children of Matthias Holstein (son of Branton Holstein) and Alice Emery:
  Alice Holstein.
  Jesse Holstein.
  Ralph Holstein.
  Anna Holstein.
  Branton Holstein.

Children of Elizabeth Holstein Shainline and George W. Bisbing:
  William Holstein Bisbing, born at Spring Mill, Montgomery county, Pennsylvania.
  Winfield Scott Bisbing, born at Spring Mill; died aged 5 years.
  Maria Streeper Bisbing, born at Spring Mill; died aged 3 years.
  Anna Holstein Bisbing, born in Upper Merion, Montgomery county, Pennsylvania.

Children of DeWitt Clinton Shainline and Catharine Davis:
  William Davis Shainline, died in infancy.
  Varina Thomas Shainline.
  William Henry Shainline, married Caddie, daughter of Charles and Isabella Ganer, July 4, 1882, by Rev. W. H. Smith.
  Ann Sophia Shainline, married Daniel S. Middleton, son of J. C. and Rebecca P. Middleton, September 14, 1886, by Rev. W. H. Smith.
  Andrew Shainline, died in infancy.
  Elizabeth Bisbing Shainline.
  Marianna Shainline.
  Sarah Shainline.
  Emily Rambo Shainline.

Children of William Holstein Shainline and Mary Emily Potter:

Joseph Potter Shainline.
Harriet Anna Shainline.
Isaac Holstein Shainline, died in infancy.
Ella Baker Shainline, died in infancy.
Helen Anderson Shainline, died in infancy.

Children of George Holstein Shainline and Sarah Forsyth:

Anna Elizabeth Shainline, born in Wolf township, Lycoming county, Pennsylvania; died October, 1881, aged 18 years.

George Bishop Shainline, born in Wolf township, Lycoming county, January 27, 1867.

Ella May Shainline, born in Wolf township, Lycoming county, May 1, 1870.

William Ellis Shainline, born in Wolf township, Lycoming county, March 6, 1873.

Andrew Lawrence Shainline, born in Wolf township, Lycoming county, October 17, 1876.

Children of Henry Harrison Shainline and Abbie S. DeHaven:

Sallie DeHaven Shainline, born in Montgomery county, Pennsylvania, July 31, 1868.

Ernest Manning Shainline, born in Montgomery county, July 2, 1870.

Florence Ella Shainline, daughter of Harry H. and Abbie S. Shainline, of Chester Valley, Pennsylvania, born in Montgomery county, February 20, 1872; married Harvey H. Smith, son of Isaac and Sarah Smith, formerly of Mobile, Alabama, now of Malvern, Pennsylvania, April 19, 1892, at Salem M. E. parsonage, by Rev. Lewis Parcels.

Elizabeth DeHaven Shainline, born in Montgomery county, February 19, 1874.

Franklin Howard Shainline, born in Montgomery county, October 29, 1875.

Burton Tolen Shainline, born in Montgomery county, February 1, 1878.

George Henry Shainline, born in Chester county, Pennsylvania, September 28, 1879.

Charles R. Shainline, born in Chester county, May 21, 1882.

Beulah May Shainline, born in Chester county, May 20, 1854.

Children of Elizabeth Holstein Amies and Charles Ellis Morris:

Mary Amies, died in Bridgeport, Pennsylvania, aged 20 months.

Anna Ellis Morris, died near Lewisburg, Pennsylvania, aged 4 years.

John Roberts Morris, born near Lewisburg, Pennsylvania; married, 1881, to Nellie, daughter of Alfred and Mary Henderson Woolston, of Upper Merion, Montgomery county, Pennsylvania.

Emily Amies Morris, aged 7 years. William Ellis Morris, aged 4 years. Buried together the same day.

Charles Wells Morris.

Herbert Holstein Morris.

Elizabeth Rooke Morris, died in Norristown, aged 18 months.

Virginia Morris.

George Holstein Morris.

Children of Anna Elizabeth Thomas and Nathan Brooke:

William Thomas Brooke, married Rebecca H. Chapman, daughter of Joseph and Sarah G. Chapman, May 11, 1881, by Rev. Thomas F. Milly. William Thomas Brooke died March 10, 1889.

Ida Longmire Brooke, married J. Howard Lewis, Jr., son of J. Howard and Malvina Lewis, December 14, 1881, by Rev. William H. Furness.

Hugh Jones Brooke.
Hunter Brooke.
Emily Thomas Brooke.

Children of Rebecca Brooke Thomas and George H. Colket:
Emily Thomas Colket, married Harrison Koons Caner, 30th of October, 1890, in St. Luke's Church, Philadelphia, by Rev. Mr. Bradley.
Mary Walker Colket.
Tristram Coffin Colket.
George Hamilton Colket.

Children of Mary Annes Thomas and Hunter Brooke:
Helen Brooke, born September 10, 1878.
Mary Thomas Brooke, born June 5, 1882.

Children of Eliza Ann Roberts and David Connard:
Elizabeth Styer Connard, born March 27, 1868.
Susan Holstein Connard, born June 21, 1870.
Catharine Styer Connard, born December 2, 1872.
Sarah Louisa Connard and Clara Virginia Connard, twins, born October 17, 1874.
Mary Schlater Connard, died in infancy.
Laura Roberts Connard, born July 14, 1877.
Reese Connard, born near Richmond, Virginia, April, 1880; died in Virginia, aged 2 years.

Children of Sarah Louisa Roberts and William Wills:
Susan Roberts Wills, born June 14, 1868, in Plymouth township, Pennsylvania; married Harry Stoner Welsh, son of James Harry and Sue F. Welsh, at Woodbury, New Jersey, August 20, 1890, by Rev. Edward Dillon. Mr. and Mrs. James Harry Welsh were from Waynesboro, Franklin county, Pennsylvania.

Elizabeth Marple Wills, born November 13, 1869, in Plymouth township, Pennsylvania; married Charles Collin Hughes, son of John J. and Hannah Hughes, of Upper Merion township, April 19, 1892, in Norristown, by Rev. A. B. Atkins, of Calvary Episcopal Church, Conshohocken, Pennsylvania.

Anna Gorgas Wills, born May 2, 1871.
Jonathan Roberts Wills, born February 21, 1873.
George Edward Wills, born June 11, 1874.
Sarah Tyson Wills, born October 19, 1875.
Mary Hannah Wills, born August 19, 1879.
Louis Andrew Wills, born August 21, 1882.
Eleanora Wayne Wills, born December 4, 1883; died in infancy.
William Wayne Wills, born June 24, 1887, in Plymouth township, Montgomery county, Pennsylvania.

Children of Matthew Roberts and Clara Connard:
Reese Connard Roberts.
Catharine Connard Roberts, died in infancy.
William B. Roberts, died in infancy.
Susan H. Roberts, died in infancy.
David C. Roberts.
Clara Virginia Roberts.

Children of William Holstein Roberts and Laura S. Massey:

Emma R. Dunwoody Roberts, born 27th of September, 1877, in Chester county, Pennsylvania.
Greta Massey Roberts, born 2d of January, 1879, in Upper Merion, Pennsylvania.
Susan Holstein Roberts, born 1st of June, 1881, in Upper Merion, Pennsylvania.
Anna Ellis Roberts, born 12th of December, 1886.

ALICE HOLSTEIN ELLIS.

Children of Jonathan John Roberts and Sarah Louisa Bodler:
Mary Davis Roberts, born February 12, 1883.
Edith May Roberts, born January 28, 1886.
Walter Jonathan Roberts, born January 24, 1890.

Child of George H. Roberts and Jennie Bowman:
William B. Roberts, died in infancy.

Children of Ella Holstein and William W. Potts, of Swedeland, Upper Merion, Pennsylvania:
Brita Holstein Potts.
Helen Potts.
Carrie Potts.
Abbie Holstein Potts, "daughter of William W. and Ella H. Potts, died January 17, 1886, aged six years and one month. She was truly a loving, lovely child, full of those winning ways that so attract the fond affections of other hearts, making the pathway of life seem brighter and shedding a halo of love on all around her. In the beautiful home circle where all heretofore has been a continuous stream of peace and quiet affection she was a very sunbeam, the pet of the household, and now that the light of her presence has passed away we almost murmur at the decree, and feel that it is a cruel blow. The lesson of these little lives should not be lost upon us; they are here for a purpose, first to add a charm to existence and then to draw our hearts and affections after them heavenward. We are all conscious of being better because this dear child has been permitted to dwell amongst us, even for so brief a period, and as time passes away may this consciousness deepen, until the purpose of her mission be fully attained."
Ella Holstein Potts, born July, 1892.

Children of Elizabeth Brookfield Holstein and David Ellis:
Holstein Ellis, born at Muncy, Lycoming county,

Pennsylvania, February 25, 1884; died in Philadelphia, of diphtheria, on Sunday, November 29, 1891. This notice of her death is from the Norristown *Herald*:

"The hearts of loving kindred are shrouded in gloom at the loss of this darling child, whose gentle and loving disposition and confiding nature made friends of all who knew her.

"Gifted beyond her years with a keen perception of the beautiful life beyond the river, and knowing, as we all do, that the change to her is one of unspeakable bliss, yet it is so hard for us to still the unbidden murmurings that well up within, because we could not keep the precious jewel longer to shed its lustre on our pathway here.

"But, oh! let us remember that she is with the angels now, and will bid us welcome when we, too, shall have crossed over to the other shore."

William Holstein Ellis, born in Upper Merion, Montgomery county, Pennsylvania, October 31, 1886.

Children of Mary Alice Holstein and William A. Armstrong, Jr.:

Lillie Etta Armstrong, born in Philadelphia, August 22, 1889.

William A. Armstrong, third, born in Wilkesbarre.

Isaac Wayne Holstein Armstrong, born in Wilkesbarre, 1892.

Children of Francis Percival Dewees and Emma Loeser:

Percival Dewees, born in Pottsville, Pennsylvania, August 5, 1863; died in infancy.

Louis Loeser Dewees, born January 3, 1865, in Pottsville, Pennsylvania.

Emma Loeser Dewees, born at Nelson Furnace, Nelson county, Kentucky.

Ethel Hughes Dewees, born at Belmont, Bullitt county, Kentucky.

FRANCIS P. DEWEES

Children of Lyne Starling (Theodore) Dewees and Ardelia Louisa Fiske:

Catharine Alliene Dewees, born at Shamokin, Pennsylvania.
Louisa Fiske Dewees, born February 18, 1872.
Phoebe James Dewees, born February 5, 1875, at Pottsville, Pennsylvania; died April 12, 1875.
Rachel Hughes Dewees, born at Pottsville, Pennsylvania.
Alfred Rollin Dewees, born March 28, 1879.
Theodore John Dewees, born December 12, 1883.
Frances Farquhar Dewees, born April 25, 1885.
James Collin Dewees, born March 3, 1890.

Child of James Collin Dewees and Charity Bye Packer:

Lennis Dewees, born September 22, 1873, in Lock Haven, Pennsylvania; died in infancy.

Children of John Hughes (of North Carolina) and Jane G. Daves:

John Daves Hughes.
Elizabeth G. Hughes, born at Pottsville, Pennsylvania, July 7, 1858; died at Pottsville August 28, 1859.
Jane Daves Hughes, born at Raleigh, North Carolina, December 30, 1862.
Ann C. Hughes, born at Raleigh, North Carolina, January 1, 1865; married Edmund Strudwick, son of Dr. William and Caroline J. Strudwick, of Norfolk, Virginia, June 5, 1890, ceremony at the residence of her parents in Newbern, North Carolina, by Rev. T. M. N. George.
Eliza A. Hughes, born at Newbern, North Carolina, October 25, 1866; died at Beaufort, North Carolina, August 8, 1867.
Mary Alice Hughes, born at Newbern, May 5, 1868; died at Newbern, July 31, 1869.
Isaac Wayne Hughes, born at Newbern, North Carolina, March 20, 1870.

Children of Dr. James Bettnor Hughes and wife Laura A. W. Bryan:

Ann Bryan Hughes, born August 5, 1860, at Newbern, North Carolina; baptized by Rev. A. A. Watson, of Christ's Church; married Basil Manley, son of Matthias E. and Sarah Louisa Manley, October 22, 1882, by Rev. Van Winder Shields.

Isaac Wayne Hughes, born August 24, 1861, Newbern, North Carolina; baptized by Rev. Mr. Wetmore, Christ Church.

James Bryan Hughes, born May 17, 1863, at Goldsboro, North Carolina; baptized by Rev. William C. Hunter.

Laura Hughes, born January 5, 1866, at Newbern, North Carolina; baptized by Rev. Mr. Forbes, Christ Church.

Nicholas Collin Hughes, born May 7, 1868, at Newbern, North Carolina; baptized by Rev. Mr. Forbes.

Mabel Hughes, born July 27, 1878, at Newbern, North Carolina; baptized by Rev. Charles L. Hale, Christ Church.

Ethel Hughes, born February 4, 1883, at Newbern, North Carolina; baptized by Rev. E. M. Forbes.

Hugh Hughes, born February 5, 1886, at Newbern, North Carolina; baptized by Rev. Rev. V. W. Shields.

Children of Dr. James Bettnor Hughes and second wife, Eliza W. Knox:

Eliza Knox Hughes, died in infancy.

Julia Washington Hughes, died in infancy.

Children of Theodore Jones Hughes, 2d, and Clara Filman Stevenson:

Eliza McLinn Hughes, born August 30, 1857, Newbern, North Carolina; baptized by Rev. Mr. Mumford; married Thomas Forbes, of Texas, March 29, 1875, by Rev. Dr. Massey, in Mobile, Alabama.

Susan Taylor Hughes, born October 19, 1858, Newbern, North Carolina; died in infancy.

Clara Stevenson Hughes, born March 6, 1860, Newbern, North Carolina; baptized by Rev. Dr. Massey, Trinity Church, Mobile, Alabama; married Walter Parker Williamson, September 24, 1884.

George Stevenson Hughes, born September 9, 1861, Newbern, North Carolina; died June 7, 1862.

Theodore Jones Hughes, 3d, born February 7, 1863, Chapel Hill, North Carolina; baptized by Rev. Dr. Massey, Trinity Church, Mobile, Alabama.

Kathleen Cawthorne Hughes, born October 11, 1864, at Raleigh, North Carolina; baptized by Rev. Dr. Massey, Trinity Church, Mobile, Alabama; married William Lightfoot Ross, December 1, 1884, by Rev. D. J. L. Tucker, of Mobile, Alabama.

Annie Smallwood Hughes, born December 31, 1865, Newbern, North Carolina; baptized by Rev. Dr. Massey, Trinity Church, Mobile, Alabama; married Harry Allen Lowe, November 17, 1886, by Rev. Mr. Tucker.

Collina Hughes, born November 12, 1867, at Point Clear, Baldwin county, Alabama; baptized by Mr. Stephen Forbes, Christ Church, Newbern, North Carolina.

Cordelia Vass Hughes, born January 14, 1869, at Point Clear, Baldwin county, Alabama; baptized by Rev. Dr. Massey, Trinity Church, Mobile, Alabama.

Child of Theodore Jones Hughes, 2d, and second wife, Isabella Hunter Knox:

Zophar Mills Hughes, born May 16, 1873, Mobile, Alabama; baptized by Rev. Dr. Massey, Trinity Church, Mobile, Alabama.

Children of John Jones Hughes (of Upper Merion, Pennsylvania) and Hannah Brooke:

John Hunter Hughes.

Mary Rambo Hughes, married Winfield Scott Stacker, son of David and Emily H. Stacker, of Lower Merion, Pennsylvania, January 26, 1881.

Nathan Brooke Hughes.

Benjamin Bartholomew Hughes, died aged 2 years.

Anna Brooke Hughes.

Benjamin B. Hughes, 2d.

Fanny Farquhar Hughes, married Mr. J. Cloude Smith, son of Mary Blackfan and Joseph Cloude Smith, 9th of October, 1890, by Rev. A. A. Marple, of Swede's (Christ) Church, Upper Merion.

Charles Collin Hughes, married Elizabeth Marple Wills, daughter of Sarah Louisa Roberts and William Wills, in Norristown, Pennsylvania, 19th of April, 1892, by Rev. Dr. Atkins.

Child of Dr. Isaac W. Hughes, of West Philadelphia, and Alice E. Donnel.

Donnel Hughes, born March 1, 1858; married November 19, 1884, to Sarah Summers, daughter of Rev. Gideon James and Helen C. Burton. Rev. G. J. Burton, Rev. T. C. Yarnall and Rev. Robert Innis, officiated.

Donnel Hughes graduated in the Medical Department of the University of Pennsylvania, March 14, 1879.

Bertram Hughes, born October 23, 1860; married Caroline Cordelia Love, daughter of James Stewart Love and Amanda Bate, January 19, 1882.

Bertram Hughes, died December 22, 1888.

Benjamin Raymond Hughes, born May 2, 1864; died September 30, 1872.

Children of Dr. Isaac W. Hughes, of West Philadelphia, and second wife, Emilie Baker:

Wayne Baker Hughes, born March 21, 1880.

David Porter Hughes, born September 27, 1885.

Julia Diefendorf Hughes, born December 24, 1887.

Children of Nathan Rambo Hughes, of Bridgeport, Pennsylvania, and Amanda Stacker:

ISAAC WAYNE HUGHES, M. D.
PHILADELPHIA.

Emily Irene Hughes, married November 26, 1884, to William Harrison Yerkes, of Norristown, Pennsylvania, by Rev. A. A. Marple, rector of Christ (Swedes) Church, Upper Merion.

Frank Stacker Hughes, druggist.

Children of Catharine Dewees Hughes and Edmund M. Evans:

Benjamin Hughes Evans, born May 10, 1880, in Norristown, Pennsylvania.

Ray Wright Evans, born July 20, 1882, in Norristown, Pennsylvania.

Mary Hughes Evans, born September 18, 1883, died October 11, 1883.

Children of Frances Hughes, of Pottsville, Pennsylvania, and Guy E. Farquhar:

Elizabeth Hughes Farquhar, died aged 4 years.
Francis Hughes Farquhar.
George Wildman Farquhar.
Annette Farquhar.
Otto Edward Farquhar.
Marion Amelia Farquhar.

Children of Annette Hughes, of Pottsville, Pennsylvania, and George Ringgold Kaercher:

Francis Kaercher.
George Hughes Kaercher.

Child of Louis Curtis Hughes and Charlotte Tritle, of Pittsburg, Pennsylvania:

Wayne Hughes, born March 27, 1886, at East Liberty, Pittsburg; baptized by Rev. T. C. Yarnall, in St. Mary's Church, West Philadelphia.

Children of Mary Elizabeth Hughes, of North Carolina, and Rev. Nathaniel Harding:

Collin Hughes Harding, born December 26, 1874, at Washington, North Carolina; baptized by Rev. N. Collin Hughes, February 24, 1875.

Frederick Harriman Harding, born September 12, 1876; baptized by his father, Rev. N. Harding, November 12, 1876.

Adaline Williams Harding, born October 22, 1877, died July 6, 1881.

Mary Elizabeth Harding, born December 4, 1879.

Nathaniel Harding, born November 18, 1881, died August 2, 1883.

Martha Harding, born November 13, 1882, died August 2, 1883.

William Blount Harding, born January 24, 1884.

Robert Harding, born December 29, 1886, died May 29, 1887.

Children of Hannah Hughes and Charles Cottingham Calvert, of Texas:

Nicholas Collin Hughes Calvert, born October 30, 1879.

Charles Cottingham Calvert, born May 4, 1882.

Lalla Calvert, born March 21, 1884.

Adaline Calvert, born November 13, 1885.

Zoe Frost Calvert, born October 8, 1887, died October 23, 1888.

Zoe Ella Calvert, born May 14, 1889.

Child of John Robert Hughes, of North Carolina, and Sallie Nelson Harding:

Lucretia Nash Hughes, born February 19, 1890.

Children of Rev. N. Collin Hughes, Jr., of North Carolina, and Martha Eliza Harding:

Caroline Virginia Hughes, born April 27, 1881.

Nicholas Collin Hughes, 3d, born January 29, 1883.

Israel Harding Hughes, born July 5, 1884.
Addaline Williams Hughes, born April 7, 1886, died October 29, 1888.
Baby, lived but a few hours, born April 29, 1887.
Susan Mary Hughes, born September 20, 1888, died July 29, 1889.
Paul Hughes, born September 12, 1889, died January 26, 1890.

Children of Edward Burd Hubley and Mary Louisa Pollock, of Pottsville:
Mary Louisa Hubley, born December 21, 1880.
Francis Curtis Hubley, born July 9, 1883.
Jennette Schuyler Hubley, born August 5, 1885.

Children of Louisa Harriet Hubley and Edward Burd Peale, of Schuylkill county:
Francis Peale, born August 10, 1860.
Reubens Peale, born August 10, 1872.

Children of Harriet Potts and William Potts Rockhill, of Pittstown, New Jersey:
Edward Potts Rockhill.
Anna Potts Rockhill.

Children of Horace Turley Potts and Annie O'Harra, of Philadelphia, Pennsylvania:
Harrison Isaac Potts.
Thomas Charles Potts.
Helen Potts.
Horace Potts.

Child of Kate B. Potts and Capt. Charles Hobbs, United States Navy:
Horace Potts Hobbs.

Children of Julia H. Potts and Samuel H. Grey, Esq.:
Julia Ridgway Grey.
Charles Philip Grey.
Mary Joy Grey.
Ethel Grey.
Alice Croasdale Grey.

Child of Ellen Potts and Jacob H. Armbruster:
Carrie Tryon Armbruster.

Children of Elizabeth L. Rittenhouse and William Henry Fitzhugh Gurley:
Ralph R. Gurley, married Ella A. Gibbon.
Franklin R. Gurley.
William Fitzhugh Gurley, married Elizabeth S. Buckeye.
George Hull Gurley.
Five died in infancy.

Children of Isabel L. Rittenhouse and Joseph H. Nourse:
Isabel Nourse.
Emily Nourse.
Edward Nourse.
Harvey Nourse.
Laurie Nourse.
Louisa Nourse.
Bessie Nourse.
Two died in infancy.

Children of Mary D. Rittenhouse and Rev. A. Miller Woods:
Henrietta R. Woods.
James S. Woods.
Franklin R. Woods.
Two died in infancy.

Children of Henrietta Waring Rittenhouse and Captain Thomas Wilson, U. S. A.:

William Lowe Wilson, died in infancy.

Mary D. Wilson, married Warren Switzler, son of William F. and Mary J. Royal Switzler, at Omaha, Nebraska, by Rev. W. J. Harsha, pastor of the First Presbyterian Church, November 15, 1882.

Henrietta Rittenhouse Wilson married Lieutenant Daniel Hall Boughton, a graduate of West Point, son of Nelson Boughton and Mary Fisher, June 30, 1887, at Fort Levenworth, Kansas, by Chaplain Barry, of the army.

Margaret Stevens Wilson, unmarried.

Children of Major Benjamin Franklin Rittenhouse and Elizabeth Shapter:

B. Franklin Rittenhouse.
Elizabeth Rittenhouse.
Norris Rittenhouse.
One died in infancy.

Children of Clementina Rittenhouse and R. S. T. Cissel, of New York:

Mary C. Cissel, married Samuel Berry.
Helen M. Cissel.
Henrietta D. Cissel.
Clementina S. Cissel.
Margaret S. Cissel.
Katharine B. Cissel.
Atkinson Cissel.

Child of William R. Hull and Jerusha Willard:
J. Frampton Hull.

Children of Fannie Rittenhouse and Thomas Hyde, D. C.
Thomas Hyde, married Nellie Augur.
Emily Rowland Hyde, married Barry Buckley.

Child of Mary N. Rittenhouse and Leonard Gunnel:
Leonard Gunnel.

Children of Samuel Whitall Rittenhouse and Caroline Lockwood:
Carolyn Rittenhouse.
Mary W. Rittenhouse.
Henry Rittenhouse.
Charles Edwin Rittenhouse.
Paul Rittenhouse.

Children of Mary F. Rittenhouse and D. D. Lambie:
D. Dale Lambie.
Helen Rittenhouse Lambie.
Ethel Lambie.

Child of James Delozier Rittenhouse and Dolores Cassillars:
Zen Delozier Rittenhouse.

Children of James Hall Rittenhouse and Ida R. Cole:
Lucia Morse Rittenhouse, born May 3, 1879.
Ralp Davidson Rittenhouse, born January 14, 1881.
Leonard Cole Rittenhouse, born October 31, 1884.
Howard Rittenhouse, born ; died January 4, 1886.
Karl David Rittenhouse, born March 2, 1888.

Children of Charles E. Rittenhouse and Ellen S. Goode:
Sadie Rittenhouse.
Arthur Rittenhouse.

Children of Martha L. Rittenhouse and Joshua Williams:
Alice Jane Williams.
Louis Hudson Williams.
Charles Rittenhouse Williams.
Rachel Louise Williams.

MARTHA L. RITTENHOUSE WILLIAMS.

Children of Charles E. Rittenhouse and Grace Hubbell:
John Hugh Rittenhouse, born February 5, 1885; died April 26, 1886.
Catharine Rittenhouse, born May 31, 1886.

Children of Samuel Hepburn Blackiston and Mrs. Sarah L. Brooke:
Helen Hepburn Blackiston, died in infancy.
Henry Curtis Blackiston.
Josephine Blackiston.

Children of Rev. Slator Clay Blackiston and Margaret Monroe:
Martha M. Blackiston.
Annie J. Blackiston.
Alice Medford Blackiston, born February 15, 1876.
McCall Blackiston, born February 17, 1878.
Helen Blackiston, born August 10, 1882.
Slator Clay Blackiston, born May 10, 1884.

Children of Lizzie Blackiston and Henry Augustus Newland:
Maria Hepburn Newland, born November 20, 1878.
Augustus James Newland, born July 5, 1881.
Mary Blackiston Newland, born May 31, 1883.

Children of Mary Eugenia Blackiston and J. W. Patton:
J. Woodbridge Patton.
Helen Patton.
Agnes Patton, born September 13, 1877.
Henry Blackiston Patton, born September 1, 1879.

Children of William Curtis Pollock and Ella M. Burr:
James Hepburn Pollock.
William Curtis Pollock.

Mary Louisa Pollock, died in infancy.
Walter Pollock.

Child of Louisa Ann Pollock and Richard Edy Clay:
Richard E. Clay, Jr.

Children of James Crawford Pollock and Mary Agnes Kelsey:
Ethel Hepburn Pollock, born in New York, September 29, 1880.
Mabel Kelsey Pollock, born in New York, January 24, 1883.

Children of Sarah Margaret Pollock and Henry F. Harvey:
Sallie Hepburn Harvey and James Pollock Harvey, twins. James died December 12, 1888.
Henry Thomas Harvey, born July 12, 1882.

Children of Samuel Boyd Hepburn and Sarah Reese Booth:
Anna Bayard Hepburn, born in New York City, September 23, 1886.
Amy Louisa Hepburn, born in New York City, September 23, 1888.

Children of Annie Hepburn Mackey and Dr. Joseph Hayes:
L. A. Mackey Hayes.
William Bruce Hayes.

Child of Mary Louisa Mackey and Dr. F. P. Ball:
Mary Hepburn Ball, born February 1, 1886.

Children of Annie Louisa Brown and Albert Furst:
J. Hogan Furst.
Richard Clay Furst.

Children of Gertrude Mary Brown and Thomas C. Hilton:
Edwin Norris Hilton, born July 18, 1882, died May 29, 1884.
Norris Hepburn Hilton, born August 5, 1885.

Child of Anna Mary Lichtenthaler and Thomas R. Mann, of Mill Hall, Pennsylvania:
Jennie Hepburn Mann.

Child of Dr. Henry Curtis Lichtenthaler and Anne Reeser:
Mary Elizabeth Lichtenthaler, born in Larned, Kansas, October 1, 1889.

Children of Mary Wilson Pollock, of Pottsville, Pennsylvania, and Edward Burd Hubley:
Mary Louisa Hubley, born December 21, 1880.
Francis Curtis Hubley, born July 9, 1883.
Jennette Schuyler Hubley, born August 5, 1885.

Children of Margaret Annan Pollock and William Gould Meigs:
William Pollock Meigs.
Curtis Clay Meigs.

Children of James Pollock, of Pottsville, Pennsylvania, and Mary Douglas Leisenring:
Laura Leisenring Pollock, born January 10, 1884.
Emily Clay Pollock, born July 14, 1885.

Children of Francis Hughes Pollock, of Pottsville, Pennsylvania, and Frances McGinness:
Henry Clay Pollock, born August 5, 1880.
Enoch Walton Pollock, born 14th of February, 1883.
William Pollock, born June 3, 1888.

Children of Ann Clay Pollock, of Pottsville, Pennsylvania, and Samuel M. Riley:
Louis Adams Riley, born May 10, 1883.
Emily Clay Riley, born June 25, 1885.
Robert Annan Riley, born November 17, 1887.

Children of Henry W. Potts, of Pottstown, Pennsylvania, and Eleanor S. Powell:
Eleanor Lee Potts.
Joseph Henry Potts.
Margaret Annan Potts.

Child of Emily Frances Potts, of Pottstown, Pennsylvania, and Edward Kneass Landis:
Isabel Potts Landis.

Children of Aaron Yerkes Coates, of Philadelphia, and Margaret Ann Sheard:
Roland Coates, born 5th of February, 1867, at Frankford, Pennsylvania.
Levi Pawling Coates, born 5th of February, 1875, at Frankford, Pennsylvania.

Child of Matthias Coates, of Philadelphia, and Mary Augusta McMullen:
Frank Raymond Coates, born June 20, 1869, in Philadelphia.

Children of Susan Yerkes Coates, of Philadelphia, and Charles Wilkinson Castor:
Levi Coates Castor, born July 5, 1866, at Frankford, Pennsylvania.
Lewis David Castor, born June 19, 1868.
Mary Coates Castor, born March 6, 1870.

ADELAIDE AUGUSTA NINA EDWINA
AND
FORNGARD STELLA VON ALTEN.
DRESDEN, GERMANY.

Child of Matthew Coates Smylie and Virginia Maria Peters:
    Ellen Smylie, born May 27, 1873.

Children of Ellen Smylie and Alfred Morris Herkness, of Philadelphia:
    John Smylie Herkness, born September 30, 1878.
    Alfred Morris Herkness, born December 24, 1879.
    Wayne Herkness, born November 2, 1882.
    Walter Lindsay Herkness, born September 23, 1884.
    Gilbert Herkness, born July 6, 1887.
    Malcolm Herkness, born August 3, 1889.
    Sydney Herkness, born April 23, 1891.

Children of William Duff Smylie and Sarah Alice Kaiser:
    John Smylie, born January 21, 1888.
    William M. Smylie, born August, 1890.

Children of Robert Sayre Smylie and Virginia Wright Kiehl:
    Virginia Wright Smylie, born June 30, 1883.
    Dorothy Smylie, born March 24, 1888.

Child of Matthew Henderson Coates, of Philadelphia, and Mary B. Drum:
    Collin Coates, born 25th of April, 1874; baptized by Rev. William Frick, March 2, 1875.

Child of Josephine Amelia DeHaven and Towson Caldwell, of New York:
    Mackey Caldwell.

Children of Augusta Louisa DeHaven and Baron Eberhard Curd von Alten, of Gross Gottern, Germany:
    Adelaide Augusta Nina Edwina von Alten, born 31st of

October, 1883, in Berlin, Germany; baptized by Pastor Sternon Dorotheen Kirche, in Berlin.

Fomgard Stella von Alten, born 7th of March, 1886, in Langhermsdorf; baptized by Pastor Wehl, in Niebusch.

Children of Sarah Elizabeth DeHaven and Dr. Hans Friedrick Carl Moritz von Campe, of Germany:

Hans Ustar Bigelow von Campe, born in Dresden, Germany, October 6, 1885.

Otto Joseph Carl Herman von Campe, born January 26, 1887, in Hanover, Germany.

Edwin Gothard Edmund Hans von Campe and Alice Hedwig Clara Marie von Campe, twins, born December 19, 1889, in Hanover, Germany.

Children of Amelia Atlee Williams, of Centre county, Pennsylvania, and David Sterrett Lightner:

Julia Jane Lightner, born February 6, 1861; baptized by Rev. George Guyer, of the Methodist Church; married January 21, 1886, Willis A. Jolly, of Johnstown, Pennsylvania, by Rev. A. H. Jolly, of Alexandria, Pennsylvania.

Mrs. Jolly has in her possession the wedding ring of Sarah Holstein, who married Hugh DeHaven, April 27, 1775; from being a heavy band of gold it is worn to the size of a small cord. Mrs. Hugh DeHaven left it to her granddaughter, Juliana DeHaven Atlee; she, in turn, gave it to her granddaughter, Julia Jane Lightner, now Mrs. Willis A. Jolly, of Morristown, Tennessee.

Children of Amelia Atlee Williams Lightner and (second husband) Casper Frederick Goodyear:

Robert Conrad Goodyear, born January 27, 1874; baptized by Rev. Daniel H. Evans, October, 1874.

Joseph Atlee Goodyear, born December 8, 1876; died December 8, 1876.

Helen Louisa Goodyear, born February 10, 1878; died March 9, 1878.

Margaret Priscilla Goodyear, born October 17, 1879; died October 20, 1879.

Child of Susan Miles Williams and William Martin Travis:

Robert Williams Travis, born December 22, 1861; married in 1883, Miss Mary Singleton; she died in 1887. He is now in the United States Postal Service and resides in Dunkirk, New York.

Children of Priscilla Martin Williams and George Thompson Travis:

James Hunter Travis, born April 20, 1867.

Oscar Hills Travis, born August 25, 1868.

Lewis Williams Travis, born March 15, 1870; died May 3, 1871.

Clara Ellen Travis, born October 23, 1871; died May 10, 1872.

Charles Gardner Travis, born December 3, 1872; died August 28, 1873.

Claude Lineton Travis, born February 5, 1878.

Julia Atlee Travis, born March 28, 1887.

All baptized in infancy.

Children of Ellen Harriet Williams and Claudius Buchanan Hess:

Julia Elizabeth Hess, born March 25, 1873; died January 19, 1879.

Susan Rebecca Hess, born June, 1874; died January 10, 1879.

Sarah Bell Hess, born November, 1875.

Martha Lewis Hess, born 1877.

Joseph Atlee Hess, born 1879.

Agnes Amelia Hess, born May 31, 1882.

Lewis Claudius Hess, born 1883.
All baptized in infancy.

Children of Joseph Atlee Williams and Mrs. Mary B. Reed:

Robert Conrad Williams, born at Arch Spring, Blair county, Pennsylvania, October 30, 1876.

James Frederick Williams, born April 16, 1878, at Arch Spring, Blair county.

William Gibson Williams, born May 6, 1880, at Arch Spring, Blair county.

John T. Williams, born August 7, 1882, at Eldorado, Blair county, Pennsylvania.

Julia Elizabeth Williams and twin brother, born July 17, 1885. The boy lived a few hours.

Louisa May Williams, born at Martinsburg, Blair county, Pennsylvania, May, 1887.

Alice Mabel Williams, born at Oakton, near Altoona, August, 1889.

Children of Hugh DeHaven Atlee and Mary M. Carmany:

Mary Black Atlee, born January 38, 1879.
Stewart Lee Atlee, born September 10, 1881.
Margaret Gray Atlee, born August 31, 1883.

Children of Hugh DeHaven Atlee and second wife, Lizzie Carey:

Lizzie Atlee.
Eva Atlee.

Child of Sarah Carman DeHaven and Richard Meade Bache:

Edith Bache.

Children of Charles Elliott DeHaven and Anne Traquair Henderson:

Charles Elliott DeHaven, born December 8, 1877, died March 15, 1878.

Wallace Henderson DeHaven, born August 4, 1880.

Children of Anna C. DeHaven and Malcolm W. Bryan:

Guy Bryan.

Malcolm Guy Bryan.

Children of Emma DeHaven, of Upper Merion, and Francis D. Bright:

Mary DeHaven Bright, born November 20, 1876.

Holstein DeHaven Bright.

Children of Sophia Hampton, of Philadelphia, and S. D. Adams:

Clara Jessup Adams.

Emma H. Adams.

Douglas Adams.

S. Francis Adams.

Children of Emma Hampton, of Philadelphia, and B. P. Sloan:

Louis H. Sloan.

Elizabeth Worral Sloan.

Edward Holstein Sloan.

Kate Sloan, born October 28, 1873, died August 22, 1876.

Helen DeHaven Sloan.

Children of Christiana Bunting White and Charles L. Bains:

Otis Tiffany Bains.

Helen White Bains.

Charles Bains.

Children of William H. Holloway and Ida Virginia Buzby:

Egbert Benson Buzby Holloway and Ella May Holloway, twins, born August 10, 1869.
Anna Mary Holloway, born in 1871, in November.
Malvina Richards Holloway, born in August, 1873.
Thomas Holloway, born in 1875.
William P. Holloway.
Elizabeth H. Holloway.
James Garfield Holloway.
Walter Buzby Holloway.

Children of Anna Mary Holloway and George W. White:
Thomas Holloway White, born December 10, 1871.
Alice White, born March, 1875.
Bertha Holloway White, born February, 1878.
George W. White, born April, 1882.

Children of Samuel Eastburn Holloway and Sarah Hardcastle:
Harry Pauling Holloway.
Frank Eastburn Holloway.

Children of Ida Holloway and David M. Jarrett:
Mary Ann Jarrett, born August 17, 1878.
Irene B. Jarrett, born June 4, 1880.
Jessie Mabel Jarrett, born 22d of November, 1884.

Child of Henry M. Holloway and Libby DuMont:
Mabel Holloway, born 17th of April, 1890.

Child of Bertha Holloway and Joseph Oliver Burnett:
Don Silas Burnett, born in Kansas, December, 1885.

Ella May Holloway, married Roger Evants, of Dinwiddie county, Virginia, December 10, 1888.

Child of Margaret A. Knight and Joseph Frantz:
Jennie Coates Frantz.

Children of Emily J. Knight and John R. Pugh:
DeWitt P. Pugh.
Nina Knight Pugh.
Jennie W. Pugh.
Willie Knight Pugh, died aged 10 months.
Grace Frantz Pugh.
One died in infancy.

Children of William T. Knight and E. P. McDonnell:
Gertrude Beatrice Knight.
George McDowell Knight.

Children of Kate Gertrude Knight and Harry T. Walter:
Frances Knight Walter.
Meta Walter.

Children of Grace Irene Knight and Dr. T. L. Adams:
William Knight Adams.
Thomas Birdsal Adams.

Children of Blanche E. Knight and T. B. Vernon:
William Knight Vernon.
Jennie Coates Vernon.
Helen Rosamma Vernon.

Children of Adelaide McCurdy and Charles Hank, of Norristown:
Ida Hank, deceased.
Pearl Adelaide Hank.

Children of Margaret M. Maitland and William Caldwell:
Mary Coates Caldwell.

Anna Lillian Caldwell.
Thomas Caldwell.
H. W. Caldwell.
Barton Caldwell.

Child of Melinda Holstein, of Westmoreland county, and Thomas Craft, of Armstrong county, Pennsylvania:
Andrew Craft, born December 26, 1872.

Child of Robert Holstein, of Westmoreland county, and Mattie Coulter, of Indiana county, Pennsylvania:
Mina A. Holstein, born June 7, 1875.

Children of Alexander Holstein, of Westmoreland county, and Elinor E. Rosensteel, of Indiana county, Pennsylvania:
Will C. Holstein, born February 28, 1872.
Sadie B. Holstein, born February 8, 1874.
Earl R. Holstein, born December 30, 1876.

Children of James McCafferty and Eva Thompson:
Mary Love McCafferty, born December 26, 1884.
Mabel Grey McCafferty, born November 4, 1887.

Child of Robert McCafferty and Ellie Elliott:
Ethel McCafferty, born August 24, 1888.

Child of John Andrew McCafferty and Emma Pames:
Grace Bell McCafferty, born March 23, 1889.

Children of Lelia Ada Love and Joseph Chesnut:
Sarah Edith Chesnut, born July 19, 1886.
One died in infancy, October, 1888.

Child of Annette J. Love and J. Calvin Elder:
Robert Brown Elder, born December 22, 1889.

Child of Hannah Holstein, of Kingsessing and Louis S. Kochersperger:
    Henry Kochersperger.

Children of John Holstein, of Kingsessing, and Christiana Riter:
    Eliza Ann Holstein, died June 18, 1882, aged 12 years.
    Anna Fenner Holstein, died March 15, 1876, in her 10 year.
    Emma Gertrude Holstein, died June 8, 1882, aged 5 years.
    Louis Kochersperger Holstein, died June 11, 1882, aged 2 years.
    Frederick Riter Holstein, died June 30, 1882, aged 4 years.

Children of William Simes Holstein, of Kingsessing, and Phœbe Uriam:
    Henry Kochersperger Holstein.
    William Blake Holstein.
    John Holstein.
    George Washington Holstein.
    William Simes Holstein, died June, 1890.

Children of Jane E. Hunter and Robert Ballenger:
Clinton Summerfield Ballenger, born August 2, 1867.
Franklin Lee Ballenger, born October 25, 1872.
Peyton Rowe Ballenger, born February 20, 1874.
Nannie Hunter Ballenger, born December 20, 1875.
Jane Parkinson Ballenger, born March 17, 1887.

Child of George Brandt (Darby) and Susan Orr:
Sarah Brandt.

Children of William Brandt and Sarah Harman:
John Brandt.

Children of Sarah Brandt and William Howard:
Joseph Howard.
Harrison Howard.
Charles Howard.
John Howard.
Serena Howard.
Gertrude Howard.

Children of Henry Brandt (of Darby) and Catharine Humphrey:
George Brandt.
Annie Brandt.
Henry Brandt.
Daniel Brandt.

Children of Mary Brandt and James Groves, of Media, Pennsylvania:
Ida Brandt.
Edward Brandt.
William Brandt.

Children of Pratt Hoopes and Mary Dickinson:
Mary Hoopes.
John Hoopes.

Child of Thomas J. M. Hoopes, Media, and Mary Bombgardener:
Edith Bombgardener Hoopes.

NINTH GENERATION

Children of William Davidson, of Muscatine, Iowa, and Lydia Hoopes:
 Elizabeth Hoopes Davidson.
 Sidney Hoopes Davidson.

Children of Emmor Lodge and Hannah Mary Eachus:
 Correna Lodge.
 Ida Lodge.
 Caroline Lodge.

Children of Matilda Lodge and William Eachus:
 George Eachus.
 Walter Eachus.

NINTH GENERATION.

Child of Matthias Holstein Henderson, of Sharon, Pennsylvania, and Lucy Bower:
 Florence Henderson, born October 7, 1887.

Children of Jane Henderson and Charles W. Kellogg:
 Henderson Kellogg, born April 20, 1878.
 Charles Wetmore Kellogg, born February 27, 1880.
 Edith Kellogg, born November 27, 1882.
 Alfred Gilpin Kellogg, born February 2, 1887.
 Branton Holstein Kellogg, born May 11, 1889.

Children of Mary Anna Jolly and Samuel W. Loomis:
 Charlotte Jolly Loomis, born July 15, 1880, died June 11, 1883.
 Jennie Maffet Loomis, born September 4, 1883.
 John Braman Loomis, born April 3, 1885, died August 21, 1885.

Children of Elizabeth Ashton Jolly and Reuben D. Neff:
 Charles Jolly Neff, born August 18, 1880.

Edith Virginia Neff, born April 26, 1882.
Robert Bruce Neff, born June 28, 1884; died.
Joyce Holstein Neff, born May 24, 1888.

Children of William Henry Shainline, of Norristown, Pennsylvania, and Caddie Ganer:
DeWitt Clinton Shainline.
Joseph Brookfield Shainline.
Alda Bailey Shainline.
Thomas William Shainline.

Children of Ann Sophia Shainline, of Norristown, Pennsylvania, and Daniel S. Middleton:
Varina Shainline Middleton
William Shainline Middleton.

Children of John Roberts Morris and Nellie Woolston:
Emily Walker Morris.
Courtland Southworth Morris.
Russell DuPont Morris.
Charles Ellis Morris.

Children of William Thomas Brooke and Rebecca Hanna Chapman:
Ida Lewis Brooke, born 1st of March, 1882.
Josephine Atmore Brooke, born 15th of November, 1885.
Gertrude Chapman Brooke, born 29th of December, 1886.

Children of Ida L. Brooke and J. Howard Lewis, Jr.
Anna Brooke Lewis and infant son, twins, born December 25, 1882. Anna died 22d of November, 1886. The son died 25th of December, 1882.
Sarah Fallon Lewis, born 21st of January, 1883, died 26th of November, 1886.
Helen Brooke Lewis, born 23d of September, 1887.

Child of Emily Thomas Colket and Harrison Koons Caner, of Philadelphia.

Harrison Koons Caner, Jr., born in Philadelphia, 25th of April, 1892.

Child of Susan Roberts Wills and Mr. Welsh.

James Harold Welsh, born in Norristown, August 13, 1892.

Children of Van Bryan Hughes, of Newbern, North Carolina, and Basil Manley:

Matthias E. Manley, born October 25, 1885, Newbern, North Carolina; baptized by Rev. Father Riley, St. Paul's.

Basil Manley, Jr., born January 2, 1890, at Newbern, North Carolina.

Children of Eliza McLain Hughes, of North Carolina, and Thomas Forbes, of Texas:

Edward Ripley Forbes, born February 6, 1876, in Sherman, Texas; baptized by Rev. W. H. Crane, St. Stephen's Church.

Bessie Forbes, born May 19, 1877, Sherman, Texas; baptized by Rev. James Lytton, St. Stephen's Church, Sherman.

Gifford Thomas Forbes, born September 13, 1878, Sherman, Texas; baptized by Rev. James Lytton, St. Stephen's Church; died February 27, 1879.

Thomas Gifford Forbes, born December 23, 1879, Sherman, Texas; baptized by Rev. John Pemker, St. Stephen's Church, Sherman.

Randolph Hughes Forbes, born September 20, 1885, Mobile, Alabama; baptized by Rev. Gardiner Tucker, St. John's, Mobile; died November 9, 1888.

Frank Andrew Forbes, born April 25, 1887, Mobile, Alabama; baptized by Rev. Gardiner Tucker, St. John's, Mobile.

Children of Clara Stevenson, North Carolina, and Walter Parker Williamson:

Kathleen Hughes Williamson, born July 7, 1882, Tarboro, North Carolina; baptized by Rev. Joseph Cheshire, Calvary Church, Tarboro, North Carolina.

Theodore Williamson, born August 29, 1885, Mobile, Alabama; baptized by Rev. Mr. Spaulding, St. John's Church, San Francisco, California.

Children of Kathleen Cawthorne Hughes, of Mobile, Alabama, and William Lightfoot Ross:

Clara Hughes Ross, born October 29, 1885, Mobile, Alabama; baptized by Rev. J. L. Tucker, Christ Church, Mobile, Alabama.

Alfred Green Ross, born May 4, 1887, Mobile; baptized by Rev. J. L. Tucker, Christ Church, Mobile.

William Lightfoot Ross, 2d, born January 24, 1889, Mobile, Alabama; baptized by Rev. J. L. Tucker, Christ Church, Mobile.

Child of Mary Rambo Hughes, of Upper Merion, Pennsylvania, and Winfield Scott Stacker:

Hannah Hughes Stacker, born 14th of June, 1882.

Children of Dr. Donnel Hughes, of West Philadelphia, and Sarah Summers:

Burton Donnel Hughes, born September 15, 1888.

Sarah Summers Hughes, born February 2, 1890.

Children of Bertram Hughes, of Philadelphia, and Caroline Cordelia Love:

Alice Donnel Hughes, born March 19, 1883, died August 10, 1883.

Francis Wade Hughes, born July 30, 1884.

Bertram Hughes, Jr., born August 12, 1887, died April 7, 1888.

HANNAH HUGHES STACKER.

Child of Emily Irene Hughes and William Harrison Yerkes:

Beatrice Hughes Yerkes, born 19th of November, 1891, in Norristown, Pennsylvania, died August 27, 1892, aged 9 months and 17 days.

Children of Mary D. Wilson and Warren Switzler:
Thomas W. Switzler, born May 2, 1884.
Robinson M. Switzler, born November 19, 1885.
Alice R. Switzler, born November 26, 1886.

Child of Henrietta Rittenhouse Wilson and Lieut. Daniel Hall Boughton:
George Wilson Boughton.

Children of Julia Jane Lightner and Willis A. Jolly:
Thomas Hubert Jolly, born Denver, Colorado, May, 1887; baptized by Rev. Dr. Beal, at Johnstown, in 1887.
Charles Frederick Jolly, born July 23, 1889, at Altoona, Pennsylvania; baptized in Morristown, Tennessee.

Children of Robert Williams Travis and Mary Singleton:
Ethel Ray Travis, born September, 1884.
Clarence Williams Travis, born near Fort Scott, Kansas, 1885, died in Huntingdon county, Pennsylvania, 1887.
Laura Bell Travis, born near Fort Scott, Kansas, November, 1886.

Child of Ella May Holloway and Roger Evants:
Ida May Evants, born September 3, 1890.

WILL OF MATTS HOLSTEIN,

WHO WAS BORN JUNE 1644. DIED APRIL 9, 1708.

In the name of God. Amen. I, Matthias Holstein, of ——— ———, in the County of Philadelphia, Province of Pennsylvania, yeoman, being weak in body and antient in years, but of perfect sense, memory and understanding, do make, constitute and appoint this my last will and testament, in manner following, as to the settling and disposing of that estate which it hath pleased God to give me in this world. I bequeath and dispose of the same as followeth:

First, having already given unto my two sons, Lawrence and Matthias, their due part and portion out of my said estate, this my Will is, that they be therewith satisfied and contented, I not intending to give them any more than what is already given them.

Item. I give and bequeath to my son Andrew the sum of fifteen pounds, to be paid out of my clear estate by my executrix, hereinafter named.

Item. I give and bequeath to my son, Frederick, the sum of forty pounds and one cow, to be paid and given him by my said executrix, within two years after my decease.

Item. I give and bequeath to my well beloved wife, Katharine Holstein, the sum of fifty pounds out of my clear estate, for her use and behoof, immediately after my decease, to her and her heirs forever.

Item. I give unto my two sons, Peter and Henry, each of them the sum of thirty pounds, to be paid to them when they come to the age of twenty-one.

Item. If any of my said sons, Lawrence, Matthias, Andrew and Frederick, should chance to die without heirs, my will is that the part and portion already given them should be equally divided among the other survivors.

Item. If either of my two sons, Peter and Henry, should chance to die without heirs, my will is that the porcon of my estate already given them shall descend to the survivor.

Item. My said will is, that my said wife shall, and may, keep the respective proporcons and sums already given to my younger sons, Peter and Henry, in her hands until they come of age, to have the use thereof for their education, and all the rest and residue of my estate I give to my said wife, with power to her to sell and dispose of the same, if she think fitt, for the maintenance and education of my younger children, not herein before menconed, with power, also, to her, to give and dispose of the same remainder of my estate among my said younger children as she may think fitt.

And I do hereby make, constitute and appoint my said beloved wife the only executrix of this my last will and testament. Desiring my friends, William Carter and Peter Mound, to be assistants to my said executrix in the execucon of this my last will and testament.

In witness whereof, I have hereunto sett my hand and seal this fourteenth day of December, A. D. 1706.

      MATTHIAS HOLSTEIN. [L. S.]

 Signed, sealed, published and declared in presence of
  Andrew Sandel,
  Peter Cock,
  Thomas Makin.
Peter Evans, Register.

WILL OF MATTHIAS HOLSTEIN, 2D.

I, Matthias Holstein, 2d, of the Township of Upper Merion, in the County of Philadelphia, and the Province of Pensilvania, being weak in body, but of a perfect mind and memory, do make and ordain this my last Will and Testament. It is my Will, and I do order in the first place, all my just debts and funeral charges to be paid and satisfied.

Item. I give and bequeath unto Brichard, my dearly beloved wife, the third of my personal and real estate.

Item. I give and bequeath to my son Matthias, two hundred acres of land, and the tenements belonging thereunto, to him and his heirs forever, where they now dwell.

Item. I give and bequeath to my son Andrew, one hundred pounds, or the value of it in land.

Item. I give and bequeath to my son Frederick, the sum of eighty pounds.

Item. I give and bequeath to my daughter Catharine, the sum of twenty pounds.

Item. I give and bequeath to my daughter Debora, the sum of forty pounds.

Item. I give and bequeath to my daughter Mary, the sum of forty pounds, at age to be paid.

Item. I give and bequeath to my daughter Brichard, the sum of forty pounds, at age to be paid.

Item. I give and bequeath to my daughter Elizabeth, the sum of thirty pounds, to be paid when she is at age.

I do order as my Will and Testament, that my son Matthias Holstein, and my well beloved wife Brichard Holstein, to be my sole executors.

Dated the 17th day of March, 1736.

In witness whereof I have hereunto set my hand and seal.

MATTHIAS HOLSTEIN.

Signed, sealed, published, pronounced and declared by the said Matthias Holstein, as his last Will and Testament, in the presence of us the subscribers.

I do nominate and appoint Jeremiah Smith and Laurence Holstein to see my will performed.

Matthew Robert, Edward Robert, note the words that is in the seventeenth and in the twenty-ninth lines, that are interlined before signing.

Philadelphia, 11th of May, 1737. Then personally appeared Matthew Robert and Edward Robert, the witnesses to the within written Will, and on their solemn affirmation according to law did declare they saw and heard Matthias Holstein, the testator within named, sign and publish and declare the within written Will to be his last Will and Testament, and that at the doing thereof, he was of sound mind, memory and understanding, to the best of their knowledge.

CORAM, PETER EVANS,
Deputy Register.

Be it remembered, that on the 11th of May, 1737, the last Will and Testament of Matthias Holstein was proved in due form of law and probate, and letters testamentary were granted, well and truly to administer the said estate, to Brichard Holstein and Matthias Holstein, executors therein named.

Given under the seal of the said office.

PETER EVANS, Register General.

WILL OF ANDREW HOLSTEIN.

Andrew Holstein. In the name of God. Amen.

This 27th day of December, 1761, I, Andrew Holstein, of Upper Merion, County of Philadelphia, "inn-keeper," being weak in body but of sound mind and memory, do make this my last will and testament:

FIRST. I commend my soul to God who gave it, finally trusting for His favor and mercy through Jesus Christ.

I ordain that all my moveable effects be sold at public sale immediately after my decease. I further order that my tenement or plantation in Charlestown township, Chester county, adjoining William Moore, George Martin and Richard Jacobs' land, to be sold, as soon as the lease of one William Gunners is expired, who now lives on the premises.

Further, my will is that this plantation that I now live on, in Upper Merion, aforesaid, shall be leased out for the term of seven years after my decease, and when expired—

ITEM. I give to my son Peter, all the last mentioned land and plantation in Upper Merion, with all its appurtenances whatsoever thereunto belonging, to hold. To my son Peter, all my right to a library in the Great Valley.

ITEM. I give and bequeath to my daughter Martha, the sum of one hundred pounds, on sufficient bonds, when she arrives at the age of one and twenty years.

ITEM. I give and bequeath to my daughter Martha, the sum of one hundred pounds, on sufficient bonds, when she arrives at the age of one and twenty years.

ITEM. I give and bequeath to my daughter Amy, the sum of one hundred pounds, on sufficient bonds, when she arrives at the age of 21 years.

ITEM. I give to my daughter Magdalena, the sum of one hundred pounds in money, on sufficient bonds, when she arrive at the age of 21 years.

LASTLY. I do nominate, constitute and appoint Thomas George, of Upper Merion, and my son Peter, to be sole executors of this my last will and testament, and I desire that it may be fulfilled in every way according to the true intent and meaning thereof. And I do hereby revoke all other wills and testaments before this.

ANDREW HOLSTEIN. [L. S.]

Signed in presence of us.
    JOHN EASTBURN,
    GEORGE GEORGE.

Philadelphia, February 3, 1762.
        WILLIAM PLUMSTEAD, Register.

WILL OF MATTHIAS HOLSTEIN, 3D.

In the name of God. Amen.

This 10th day of December, 1768, I, Matthias Holstein, of Upper Merion, in the County of Philadelphia and Province of Pennsylvania, yeoman. Being sick and weak in body, but sound mind and memory—thanks be to God therefor,—and calling to mind the mortality of this my body, and knowing that it is appointed for all men once to die, do make and ordain this my last Will and Testament, in manner and form following, viz:

Principally and first, I commend my soul to God, who gave it, and my body to the earth, to be there buried in a Christian-like and decent manner, at the discretion of my executor hereinafter mentioned. And as to the worldly estate, it hath pleased God to bless me with in this world, I give and demise and dispose thereof as follows; that is to say: Imprimis, my will is, that all my just debts and funeral expenses be justly paid and defrayed.

ITEM. I give and bequeath unto my three eldest daughters, viz: Hannah, Rebecca and Rachel, that piece or parcel of land the north side of the Swedes' Ford road, whereon Martin Waters now resides, to them and their heirs and assigns forever, to be equally divided between them, share and share alike. Also a new side-saddle for each of them, to be delivered as soon as possible after my decease by my executor.

ITEM. I give and bequeath unto my daughters Sarah and Magdalena, the sum of one hundred pounds, lawful money of Pennsylvania, to be paid to each of them out of my estate by my executor, when they arrive at the age of eighteen years. But if either of them, or both of them, shall die before they arrive at the aforesaid age of eighteen years, their aforesaid legacy and legacies shall be equally divided between my daughters living, share and share alike.

ITEM. I give and bequeath unto my beloved wife Magdalena, the sum of fifteen pounds, lawful money of Pennsylvania, a year, and year by year, during her natural life, to be paid to her out of my estate by my executor, quarterly, viz: three pounds and fifteen shillings each quarter of a year. I give her also one good feather bed, and complete furniture fitting for it. Also my best looking-glass and one of my best cows, as she shall choose, to be delivered to her immediately after my decease, for her own use and at her disposal. It is also my Will, that my executor do keep one cow for my wife in the best manner, winter and summer, during her natural life, or during the time she shall live in the room I shall allot for her. And also provide her a good horse for her use, when she pleases. I also give for her the room in the kitchen (wing) for her own use during her natural life, and sufficient firewood brought to her room door, ready cut, fitting for use, with free and full privilege to and from said room through any part of the house, or kitchen, or anybody in her employ; with free and full privilege of any part of the kitchen, or cellar or milk-house for her use as she shall judge she has occasion for. But if my said wife shall choose to live elsewhere, that she shall not put anybody to live in said room, and my executor shall be exempt from the keeping of the cow and horse, except she return.

ITEM. I give and bequeath unto my son Samuel, all my estate, real and personal, moveable and immoveable, excepting the before-mentioned legacies, in consideration of his paying the before-mentioned legacies, and bringing up my younger children to the age of eighteen years, and giving my two youngest daughters each six months' schooling, to him and his heirs and assigns forever. I also nominate, constitute and appoint my said son Samuel whole and sole executor of this my last Will and Testament. I also appoint my trusted friends John Hughes and Peter Holstein overseers, and desiring they will see this my will accomplished.

And I do disannul and revoke all other Wills and Testaments, legacies and executors, at any time before this was made, by word or writing, ratifying and confirming this, and no other, to be my last Will and Testament.

In witness whereof, I have hereunto set my hand and seal.

MATTHIAS HOLSTEIN. [L. S.]

Signed in presence of us.

>TOBIAS RAMBO.
>JONATHAN ROBERTS.

WILL OF PETER HOLSTEIN.

In the name of God. Amen.

I, Peter Holstein, of Upper Merion township, in Montgomery county, Pennsylvania, being weak in body but of sound mind and memory (blessed be God), do, this 2d day of September, A. D. 1785, make and publish this my last will and testament in manner following, to wit:

IMPRIMIS. I commend my soul to the disposal of Almighty God who gave it, and my body to the earth from whence it came, to be buried in a decent manner at the discretion of my executors hereinafter named. And as to that worldly estate wherewith God hath been pleased to bless me I dispose of them as follows:

FIRST. That all my just debts and funeral expenses be fully paid and satisfied.

ITEM. I give and devise unto my only and beloved daughter Mary Holstein, all my estate and inheritance, both real and personal, after payment of my just debts and funeral expenses, aforesaid. The real estate to be kept or retained entire, and without sale, if possible or reasonably it can be done, for her and her heirs for ever. Which, however, I leave to the discretion of my executors hereinafter mentioned, who I do hereby empower to make sale of and convey such part as shall be deemed absolutely necessary for discharging my just debts (if need be), but if she, my said daughter Mary Holstein, should die before she arrives at the age of twenty-one years and without lawful issue, then to be equally divided between my three sisters, or their heirs, as the law in that case directs. And I do make, constitute and appoint my good friends and kinsmen Samuel Holstein, Benjamin Eastburn and Richard Miles to be the executors of this my last will and testament.

     PETER HOLSTEIN. [L. S.]

Signed, sealed, &c., in presence of us, his chosen witnesses.

  JESSE ROBERTS.
  M. BOWER.
  LYNE PRIEST.

WILL OF HUGH HUGHES.

I, Hugh Hughes, of the City of Philadelphia, gentleman, being in a good state of health and of a sound disposing and perfect mind and memory, calling to mind the certainty of death and the uncertainty of the time thereof, do make this my last will and testament in manner and form following:

FIRST. I do order that all my just debts and funeral expenses be paid and discharged by my executors hereinafter named.

Also, I give and devise unto my beloved wife Mary, the house and lot situate on Third street, in the said city, where I now live, with all the appurtenances, to hold to her during her natural life, in case she should not marry again. But if she should marry again then my mind and intention is that her estate in the premises shall immediately cease, expire and determine, and immediately after the determination of the estate of my said wife I give and devise the same house and lot, with the appurtenances, unto my son John Hughes, of the City of New

York, and the heirs of his body, forever, to hold to him and the heirs of his body forever. Also, I give and bequeath unto my said wife all the household furniture, goods, chattels and effects which she was possessed of at the time of our intermarriage and are now in my possession.

Also, I give and devise all that, my plantation and tract of two hundred and fifty-two acres of land, and, also, twenty-two acres adjoining thereto, situate in the County of Philadelphia, unto my son John Hughes, and his heirs, forever, to hold to him, my said son John Hughes, his heirs, forever.

Also, I give and bequeath unto my said wife the interest money of two hundred pounds, to be paid unto her yearly, and every year, during her widowhood, and if she doth not marry again during her natural life, which same two hundred pounds is now due me from my said son John, I do hereby order and enjoin my said son John to pay the said interest money to her as aforesaid, as the same shall become due, and immediately after the death or intermarriage of my said wife I do give and bequeath one hundred pounds, part of the principal of the said two hundred pounds, unto my said son John forever, and the remaining one hundred pounds I give and bequeath to my daughter Sarah DeHaven, forever.

Also, I give and bequeath the sum of two hundred pounds unto my said daughter Sarah DeHaven, forever.

Also, I give and bequeath the sum of two hundred pounds to my grandson Hugh DeHaven, son of my daughter Sarah, to be paid unto him when he shall arrive at the age of twenty-one years, together with the interest thereof. But if he shall happen to die before that age, then I give and bequeath the same two hundred pounds unto my said daughter, Sarah forever.

Also, I give and bequeath unto my son Hugh, the sum of six hundred pounds, to be paid to him out of the first moneys that shall come into my executors' hands from a certain debt or mortgage hereafter to become due from John Evans, of Lancaster county.

Also, I give and bequeath unto my son William, the yearly sum of twelve pounds, to be paid him every year during his natural life; for which purpose I do hereby order my executors to put out the sum of two hundred pounds on some good land security and with the interest thereof to pay the sum of twelve pounds, as aforesaid; and immediately after his death I give and bequeath the said sum of two hundred pounds unto such of his children as shall be then living, but if he should die without issue then I give and bequeath the said sum of two hundred pounds unto my two sons, John and Hugh, equally to be divided between them, forever.

Also, I give and bequeath the bed, bedstead and the furniture whereon I now lie and use in the front chamber and my silver watch, unto my said son Hugh, forever.

Also, I give and bequeath half dozen leather bottom chairs, Stackhouses' Bdy. of Divinity, The Whole Duty of Man, The Practice of Piety, and the looking glass in front chamber, to my daughter Sarah DeHaven, forever.

And my walnut desk I give to my son-in-law Peter DeHaven, forever.

Also, I give to my son William three rush bottom chairs.

Also, I give, devise and bequeath unto my said son John Hughes, my large bible and also all the rest, residue and remainder of my estate, both real and personal, forever.

And lastly, I do hereby nominate and appoint my said son John Hughes, my son-in-law Peter DeHaven, and Sarah, his wife, the executors of this my last will and testament, revoking, disannulling and holding for void all former and other wills and testaments heretofore made and ratifying and confirming this to be my last will and testament.

In witness whereof, I have hereunto set my hand and seal this first day of May, in the year of our Lord, 1756.

HUGH HUGHES. [SEAL.]

WILL OF JOHN HUGHES,

STAMP OFFICER OF THE PROVINCE OF PENNSYLVANIA.

January 31, 1772.

In the name of God. Amen.

I, John Hughes, late of the Province of Pennsylvania, but now collector of His Majesty's customs at Charles Town, in South Carolina, being extremely reduced by long illness, but of sound mind, memory and understanding, do make, declare and publish this my last Will and Testament, in manner and form following, that is to say:

First. My Will is, that if John Baynton and Samuel Wharton should obtain a grant which they are soliciting for, and clear off the bonds wherein I stand bound with them, then the following donations and bequests shall take place. Otherwise, so much of my estate, either real or personal, as shall be found necessary to clear off such bonds, must be sold, or otherwise collected, and the said bonds be discharged.

I give and bequeath my lands in Nova Scotia between my two sons, John Hughes and Isaac Hughes, to be equally divided between them, share and share alike, and held by them, their heirs and assigns forever. Provided always, that in case the above-named John Baynton and Samuel Wharton do obtain their grant wherein I am concerned, then my will is, that my share therein be equally divided between my five children, to-wit: Hugh Hughes, Ruth Coates, John Hughes, Isaac Hughes and Catharine Pritner, to them, their heirs and assigns forever.

I give and bequeath to my son John Hughes, my house in Fourth street, which I bought of William Gardner, to him, his heirs and assigns forever, from and immediately after the decease of his mother, Sarah Hughes, and not otherwise.

I give and bequeath to my son Isaac Hughes, the house and lot on Fourth street, which I bought of Jacob Croft, near the academy, to hold to him, his heirs and assigns forever, from and immediately after the decease of his mother, Sarah Hughes, and not otherwise.

I give and bequeath my lot of land in the Northern Liberties, which I bought of Samuel Burge, to my four children, John Hughes, Isaac Hughes, Ruth Coates and Catharine Pritner, to be equally divided between them, and held by them, their heirs and assigns forever.

I give and bequeath to my son Isaac Hughes, Walnut Grove, situate in Upper Merion, to hold to him, his heirs and assigns forever. He paying the sum of twenty pounds, Pennsylvania currency, a year, to his mother, Sarah Hughes, during her natural life, after whose decease it is my will that my said son, Isaac Hughes, shall have, hold, occupy, possess and enjoy the said Walnut Grove, which is composed of divers parcels of land purchased of divers persons and at different times, and every part and parcel thereof to himself, his heirs and assigns forever. If John Baynton and Samuel Wharton shall fail in discharging the incumbrance I am under on their account, then, and in that case, I shall hereafter impower my executors to sell so much of the rest and residue of my estate as with bonds and mortgages and sundry pieces of land, houses, and so forth, not yet bequeathed, will be sufficient to fully discharge the same, as it is not my intent that any part of my estate heretofore or now bequeathed shall be sold to pay my debts, there being, in my opinion, sufficient to do it without.

I give and bequeath the tract of land I bought of John Bannin, the Jerseys, and heretofore divided into lots, to four of my children, in manner following, to-wit: Numbers one and two, to my son John Hughes, his heirs and assigns forever. Lot number three, to my son, Isaac Hughes, his heirs and assigns forever. Lot number four, to my daughter Ruth Coates, her heirs and assigns forever.

I give, devise and bequeath to my eldest son, Hugh Hughes, his heirs and assigns forever, the residuary part or undivided moiety of all and singular the lands, mills, forges, negroes, stock of cattle, hereditaments and appurtenances whatsoever hereinbefore held in partnership between me and Jacob Stern, and by the said Stern conveyed to my said son and me as joint tenants. So that I hereby make my said son Hugh Hughes, complete master of the whole interest therein, real and personal.

I give and bequeath to Sarah Hughes, my loving wife, all and singular my household goods and plate, to be at her disposal either at or before her decease among such of her children as she shall think fit.

I do give and bequeath to my said wife, Sarah Hughes, all my wearing apparel and ready moneys and the rents, issues and profits of my two houses on Fourth street, and the sum of twenty pounds, Pennsylvania currency, a year, to be paid to her yearly by my son Isaac Hughes, during her natural life.

I give and bequeath to my son Isaac Hughes, the eight-day clock and my four-wheel chaise, which I left at the Grove, to him, his heirs and assigns forever.

I give and bequeath to my son John Hughes, my desk and large glass case, which I left at the Grove, to him and his heirs forever.

And, whereas, I have heretofore given several negroes to my children named in the Will, without any instrument or deed in writing, therefore, it is my Will, that the said several gifts be confirmed to them respectively, and I do hereby confirm them accordingly. As to the rest and residue of my estate both real and personal whereinsoever situated—

I give, devise and bequeath the same to be divided, share and share alike, between my two sons, John Hughes and Isaac Hughes, to them, their heirs and assigns forever.

Lastly, I do hereby nominate and appoint my two sons, John Hughes and Isaac Hughes, executors of this my last Will and Testament, hereby giving and granting to them for completely fulfilling the same, full power and authority to grant, alien, bargain, sell, convey and assure such part or parts of my estate as may be necessary for that purpose; hereby, also, revoking and annulling all and every form of Will or Wills by me made.

In witness whereof, I have hereunto set my hand and seal at Charles Town, in South Carolina, this thirty-first day of January, in the year of our Lord, one thousand seven hundred and seventy-two.

JOHN HUGHES. [L. S.]

Witnesses:

    SAMUEL WRIGHT.
    WILLIAM WORKMAN.
    JOHN SEWRIGHT.
    PETER TIMOTHY.

Probated, Philadelphia, April 24, 1772.
Recorded in Will Book P, page 248.

SYNOPSIS OF WILL OF LT. COL. ISAAC HUGHES.

It was written 3d of April, 1782. He gives to his son John Hughes, his plantation, situated in Upper Merion township, and called Walnut Grove, except the part his father purchased of Jacob Wigherline, containing about ninety-six acres, he gives to his four daughters, Rachel, Ruth, Sarah and Hannah, to be equally divided between them, their heirs and assigns forever. He also gives to these four daughters his plantation situated in Sussex county, West New Jersey, which was devised to him by his father, John Hughes.

He gives to his son John Hughes, his desk and book-case, together with all his books, and his eight-day clock.

He gives to his beloved wife Hannah, all the rents, issues and emoluments which may arise from the said devised plantation until his son John shall arrive at the age of twenty-one, after which time John is to pay a certain sum yearly to his mother during her life. All the rents and emoluments of his New Jersey estate to be paid to his wife until his youngest child arrives at the age of eighteen years, for the support and education of all his children, after which time his wife is to have a certain sum paid her from the New Jersey plantation during her life. He also provides a horse and carriages for her use, cow, etc. She is also to have six silver tablespoons, six teaspoons, silver cream-pot and tea-tongs. The remainder of his plate and furniture is to be divided equally between his four daughters, share and share alike. His wife to have the use of plate and furniture until the daughters are of age, or married.

His Nova Scotia lands he divides equally between his five children; his negroes he gives to his wife and children, which she may either employ for the common benefit of herself and children, or dispose of by sale. If sold, the proceeds to be equally divided between his four daughters.

The executors of his estate were his beloved wife, Hannah Hughes, his brother-in-law, Lindsay Coates, and his uncle, Peter DeHaven.

The estate was appraised by Jonathan Roberts, Samuel Holstein and Peter Holstein. In the inventory of property are three entries of Continental money, one of one hundred pounds, another of five hundred pounds, and another of two hundred and fifty pounds, with many articles on the farm and in the house.

SYNOPSIS OF THE WILL OF PETER DE HAVEN.

WHO DIED IN PHILADELPHIA, 1816; THE WILL WAS WRITTEN 1806.

He gives to his great granddaughter, Sarah Rawle DeHaven, one hundred pounds; to his great-great-grandson, Atlee DeHaven, two hundred pounds, in gold or siver current money of Philadelphia, when they are twenty-one.

All the rest and residue of his estate his son Hugh is to have the income of during all the time of his natural life and no longer.

After his death, his granddaughter, Harriet DeHaven, is to have a brick house on the east side of Sixth street, between Mulberry and Cherry, and after the death of his son Hugh, his granddaughter, Amelia DeHaven, is to have the brick house adjoining the one left to his granddaughter Harriet.

Emma Maria DeHaven, another granddaughter, is to have a brick house on the same street, adjoining the others.

The remainder of his estate, real, personal and mixed, of what kind or nature and wheresoever situate, he gives every part and parcel thereof unto his said son, Hugh DeHaven, who is his only child, his heirs, executors, administrators and assigns forever.

He appoints his son, Hugh DeHaven, and his grandson, Peter DeHaven, executors of this his last will and testament. December 27, 1806.

LIST OF PORTRAITS.

Von Alten, Adelaide Augusta Nina Edwina
Von Alten, Augusta Louisa, Baroness
Von Alten, Fomgard Stella
Amies, Mary Holstein
Clay, Hannah Holstein Hughes
Dewees, Francis Percival
Dewees, Rachel Bartholomew
Ellis, Alice Holstein
DeHaven, Edwin Augustus
DeHaven, Holstein
DeHaven, Holstein Joseph
DeHaven, Joseph Edwin, Captain
Henderson, Eliza Branton
Holstein, Anna Morris
Holstein, Branton
Holstein, Constance Pritner
Holstein, George W., Colonel
Holstein, George W., M. D.
Holstein, Matthias, Major
Holstein, Peter Blake
Hughes, Benjamin Bartholomew
Hughes, Dixon G.
Hughes, Francis Wade
Hughes, Henry C., Lieutenant
Hughes, Isaac Wayne, M. D.
Hughes, James Miles, General
Hughes, John
Potts, Robert Barnhill
Potts, Thomas Isaac
Potts, William John
Potts, William Lukens
Rittenhouse, James H.
Roberts, Rachel
Stacker, Hannah Hughes
Thomas, Emily Wayne
Williams, Martha L. Rittenhouse

Letter Fac-Simile Nicholas Collin, D. D.
Letter Fac-Simile Benjamin Franklin.
DeHaven Coat of Arms.

APPENDIX.

Mr. William John Potts, of Camden, New Jersey, has contributed several valuable articles relating to the persons named in this family record, which were received too late to appear in their proper place, and are therefore found in this Appendix.

DECLARATION OF THE CONGRESS HELD AT NEW YORK, OCTOBER 1, 1765.

The members of this Congress, sincerely devoted with the warmest sentiments of affection and duty to His Majesty's person and government, inviolably attached to the present happy establishment of the Protestant succession, and with minds deeply impressed by a sense of the impending misfortunes of the British Colonies on the Continent having considered maturely the circumstances of the said Colonies, esteem it our indispensable duty to make the following declaration of our Humble Opinion respecting the most Essential rights and Liberties of the Colonies, and of the Grievances under which they labor by reason of several late Acts of Parliament.

1st. That his Majesty's Subjects in these Colonies owe the same allegiance to the Crown of Great Britain that is owing from his Subjects born within the Realm, and all due subordination to that august body, the Parliament of Great Britain.

2d. That His Majesty's Subjects in these Colonies are entitled to all the Inherent Rights and Liberties of his natural born Subjects within the Kingdom of Great Britain.

3d. That it is inseparably essential to the Freedom of a people, and the undoubted right of Englishmen, that no Taxes be imposed on them but with their own consent given Personally, or by their own Representatives.

4th. That the People of these Colonies are not, and from their local circumstances cannot be, represented in the House of Commons in Great Britain.

5th. That the only Representatives of the people of these Colonies are persons chosen therein by themselves, and that to Taxes ever have been, or can be, constitutionally imposed on them but by their Respective Legislatures.

6th. That all Supplies to the Crown being free Gifts of the people, it is unreasonable and inconsistent with the principles of the British Constitution for the people of Great Britain to grant to His Majesty the property of the Colonies.

7th. That trial by jury is the Inherent and Invaluable Right of every British subject in these Colonies.

8th. That the late Act of Parliament, entitled an Act for granting and applying certain Stamp Duties and other duties in the British Colonies and Plantations in America, &c., by Imposing Taxes on the Inhabitants of these Colonies, and the said act, and several other acts, by Extending the Jurisdiction of the Courts of Admiralty beyond its Ancient Limits, have a manifest tendency to subvert the Rights and Liberties of the Colonists.

9th. That the Duties imposed by several late acts of Parliament, from the peculiar Circumstances of these Colonies, will be extremely Burthensome and Grievous, and from the Scarcity of Specie the payment of them absolutely impracticable.

10th. That as the profits of the Trade of these Colonies ultimately center in Great Britain, to pay for the Manufactures which they are obliged to take from thence, they contribute very largely to all supplies granted there to the Crown.

11th. That the restrictions imposed by several late acts of Parliament on the Trade of these Colonies will render them unable to purchase the manufactures of Great Britain.

12th. That the Increase, Prosperity and Happiness of these Colonies depend on the full and free Enjoyment of their Rights and Liberties, and an Intercourse with Great Britain mutually affectionate and advantageous.

13th. That it is the right of the British subjects in these Colonies to petition the King, or either House of Parliament.

Lastly. That it is the Indispensable Duty of these Colonies to the best of Sovereigns to the Mother Country and to themselves to Endeavor, by a Loyal and Dutiful address to His Majesty and Humble Application to both Houses of Parliament, to procure the repeal of the Act for granting and applying certain Stamp Duties, and of all clauses of any other Acts of Parliament whereby the Jurisdiction of the Admiralty is extended as aforesaid, and of the other late acts for the restriction of American commerce.

NEW YORK
LIBRARY.

ASTOR, LENOX AND
TILDEN FOUNDATIONS.

In an another part of this book the history of the Stamp Act is briefly given, with date of its repeal, etc. The following is a correct copy of a Bill of Stamps sent from London to John Hughes, Esq., Philadelphia:

Shipp'd, by the Grace of God, in good order and well conditioned, by Francis Mollison, in and upon the good ship called the Royal Charlotte, whereof is Master, under God, for this present voyage, Benjamin Holland, and now riding at anchor in the River Thames, and, by God's grace, bound for Philadelphia, to say:

3 cases, 7 Packs of Stamps, for Pennsylvania.
2 cases, 1 Pack of Stamps, for Maryland.
1 case, 2 Packs of Stamps, for New Jersey.

Being mark'd and numbered as in the margent, and are to be delivered in the like good order and well conditioned at the aforesaid port of Philadelphia (the danger of the seas only excepted), unto John Hughes, Esq., at Philadelphia, or to their assigns, he, or they, paying Freight for the said Goods, with Primage and Average accustomed.

In witness whereof, the Master or Purser of the said Ship hath affirmed to these Bills of Lading, all of this Tenor and Date, the one of which three Bills being accomplish'd, the other two to stand void. And so God send the good Ship to her desired Port in safety. Amen.

Dated in London, July 16, 1765.

BENJAMIN HOLLAND.

BEN'N FRANKLIN'S LETTER.

John Hughes held the office of Collector of Customs for the United States from this date, September 4, 1769, until his death in Charles Town, South Carolina, in 1772.

An account book of fees received in the Custom House in Piscataqua, by the collector, from September 4, 1769, to September 4, 1770, has many entries. Here are also recorded the names of the officers in the customs at Charles Town, July 13, 1770:

John Hughes, Collector.
John Morris, Comptroller.
William Coates, Searcher.
George Roupell, Searcher. Etc., etc.

Copy of part of a power of attorney left with Jonathan Roberts in 1770, when John Hughes went as Collector of Customs to Charles Town, South Carolina:

Know all men by these presents, That I, John Hughes, of the Township of Upper Merion, in the County of Philadelphia, have made, ordained and constituted, and by these Presents do make, ordain and constitute, and in my Place and Stead, put and depute my trusty and loving Friend, Jonathan Roberts, and Isaac Hughes and my wife, Sarah Hughes, all of the Township and County aforesaid, my true and lawful Attorneys, for me and in my name, and for my use, to ask, demand, sue for, recover and receive all such Sum and Sums of money, etc., which are, or shall be, due and belonging to me, by any manner of Ways or Means whatsoever, by any person or persons. And do also Empower my Attorneys, or any Two of them (the s'd Jonathan Roberts always being one of the Two) to Do and perform any other matter or thing that to them shall appear necessary for the preservation of all or any part of my Interest or Estate, giving and granting unto my said Attorney by these Presents my full and whole Power, Strength and Authority in and about the Premises, to have, use and take all lawful Ways and Means in my name for the Recovery thereof, etc. And in my name to do, execute and perform as fully, largely and amply to all Intents and Purposes as I myself could do if I was personally present, etc. Ratifying, allowing all and whatsoever my said Attorney shall lawfully do in and about the Premises by Virtue hereof.

In Witness whereof, I have hereunto set My hand and Seal, this 29th day of June, in the —— year of His Majesty's Reign, Annoque Domini, one Thousand Seven Hundred and Seventy.

JOHN HUGHES.

Sealed and delivered in the presence of
    LINDSAY COATES.
    RUTH COATES.

Other notes from papers belonging to John Hughes, the "stamp officer," were in the possession of his great grandson Benjamin B. Hughes, of Bridgeport. After his decease his executors permitted me to copy from them such matters as might interest the descendants.

The manuscript was at that time ready for the press, which will account for the position in which they are placed.

In a package of deeds, all over one hundred years of age, was a draft of Isaac Hughes' land, made in pursuance of an order from the Surveyor-General, John Lukens, Esq., by William Anderson, on the 8th day of December, 1774, in the township of Upper Merion, county of Philadelphia, and is surveyed as part of nine hundred acres which by warrant under the hand of John Penn, bearing date of September 8, 1764, is directed to be surveyed for the use of Priscilla Wragg, of London, who, by her attorney, Jacob Cooper, sold the nine hundred acres to John Hughes, Esq., &c.

Another is, The Exemplification of the Record of a Patent to Edward West, &c., dated 9th day of 5th month, being the third year of the reign of James the Second of England, Kinge, Anno Domino, 1687. This is beautifully written, clear and legible; was recorded 9th of 5th, 1687.

In 1751 is a lease for life, between Hugh Hughes, of the township of Upper Merion, and county of Philadelphia, and John Hughes, of the City of Philadelphia, &c. John Hughes to pay twenty pounds per annum rent.

A deed from James Logan and Samuel Carpenter, attorneys for parties in England, conveys to John Hughes two hundred and fifty-seven acres of land, the 12th day of September, in the sixth year of the Reign of our Sovereign Lady, ANNE, Queen of Great Britain; Anno Domino 1707, &c.

There are many others from this date to 1754.

One for two lots of land in Providence township, this county, to Isaac Hughes, from Samuel Seely and his wife, recalls Evert In Hoff, the first known American ancestor of the DeHaven line, in these words, which refer to the second son of Evert:

"Herman DeHaven, by his last will and testament, dated November 10, 1749, deviseth as follows: That Anica DeHaven, my wife, shall have the plantation whereon I now live during her natural life, and after my wife's decease, shall be my youngest son Isaac DeHaven's, his heirs and assigns forever," &c.

In a letter written by Samuel Wharton to Benjamin Franklin, from Philadelphia, October 13, 1765, he says: "In the evening a large mob was collected at the coffee-house, and the party declared that your house (i. e., Benjamin Franklin's), Mr. Hughes', Mr. Galloway's and mine should be level'd with the Street, for that you had obtained the Stamp Act, and we were warm advocates of the carry[ing] of it into execution."

John Hughes (stamp officer) and Joseph Galloway were owners of steel works, which was one of the earliest Pennsylvania industries of that kind.

Benjamin Franklin writing to his wife from London, June 10, 1758, says: "I think nobody ever had more faithful correspondents than I have in Mr. Hughes and you. It is impossible for me to keep out of your debt."—Spark's Life and Works of Franklin, 1838, Volume VII, page 168.

In an account book belonging to John Hughes, the stamp officer, are found many names that appear in this book, which are still familiar to old residents of Montgomery county.

Scattered among the accounts are numerous entries, of which the following is a fair sample, giving a glimpse of the home life and surroundings of a gentleman who stood high in the community in which he resided:

October 17, 1761, he states, that "Old Peggy began to spin."

In July, 1773, Andrew Supplee was paid £9-13-8, for weaving sixty-one yards of cloth, thirty-five yards of check, thirty-three yards of linen, thirty yards of tow linen and six yards of flannel.

Many memoranda are found of spinning and weaving done by different persons for the family, and sales of all kinds of farm products from "Walnut Grove Farm."

December 13, 1761, a few lines note that he "Lent Matthias Holstein four books; three of Peregrine Pickle, returned Sunday."

"Lent Charles Holstein two volumes Guardian."

"Polly Coates, Roderick Brandon."

"Mrs. Jones, Gil Bla, returned."

"Lent Mrs. Jones four volumes G. Bla, and two volumes Modern Travels."

"Lent Jinny Elliott one volume Shakspear."

"Lent Mr. Coates fifth volume Shakspear."

Entries of moneys paid to different parties is given sometimes in pounds and shillings, again "Continental Money" is written; frequently the words "hard money" are used.

During the seventeenth century, and also in the eighteenth, until the erection of dams for the use of the Navigation Company, the shad fisheries on the Schuylkill River were considered a matter of great value to the inhabitants residing on its banks, as well as to the families accessible to it by wagon roads. The following paper, in the writing of John Hughes—though the signature is lost—shows how it was appreciated:

WHEREAS, Peter Rambo, in his lifetime, applied to me to lay an old right on the island by the Ford, in order to secure the right of fishing for shad on the upper end of it, and at the same time said, that he desired a share for himself, and a share for his brother Jonas, and as I have got the said island surveyed and returned it into the Surveyor-General's Office, I hereby do bind and oblige myself to convey and assign forever one share or part in the fishery, and also another share or part in the said fishery, to Jonas Rambo and his heirs forever, as fully and effectually as the whole is vested in me, they paying me their proportion of the first cost and other charges at the delivery of a deed for each share aforesaid. In witness whereof, I have hereunto set my hand this 15th day of March, 1768.

As the "Gulf Hills" are familiar to all persons who have been resident in this locality, or who have visited them, I copy a paper addressed to Mr. John Hughes, in Philandadelphia, endorsed upon the back, "An account of the Gulph Hills, from James Logan's Book."

Extract from James Logan's Book of Accounts, relating to his sales of lands in the Manor of Mount Joy:

"Have sold the Gulph Hills twice or thrice, containing by estimation above two hundred acres, and as the purchasers declined it I sold it at last to Joseph Williams, a friend and preacher, for twenty pounds, but he declined it, as John Hughes, Benjamin Davis," etc.

In a letter written by John Hughes to his son Isaac, from Piscataqua, dated September 5, 1769, he mentions that on his return home he expects to find him a married man, and adds, "You may then expect to receive a deed for Weigherline's place."

Among the old deeds is an agreement between John Hughes, of Philadelphia, merchant, and Jacob Weigherline, of Upper Merion, County of Philadelphia, yeoman, for the sale of a farm of ninety acres, the price of which is named as being three hundred and ninety-four pounds. Signed by John Hughes and Jacob Weigherline, and witnessed by Griffith Thomas and Robert Findley.

BIBLE RECORD OF THE HUGHES FAMILY.

Quarto Bible in possession of Miss Elizabeth Potts, 1007 Vine street, Philadelphia:

"London. Printed by Charles Bill, and the executor of Thomas Newcomb, deceased; Printers to the Queen's Most Excellent Majesty, 1708."

At the head of the Book of Job is written in a different and older style hand from the other entries:

"John Hughes his Book given him by his father Hugh Hug[hes] in the [year] 1711."

Evidently Hugh Hughes followed a custom sometimes in vogue in England of giving a Bible to his son on his birth. John Hughes, the stamp officer, was born in 1711.

On the back of one of the title pages is in a large, bold hand, well written:

Ages of the children of John and Sarah Hughes:
Prudence Hughes, born the 7th of July, A. D. 1740.
Jane Hughes, born the 15th of June, A. D. 1741.
Hugh Hughes, born the 7th of September, A. D. 1742.
Ruth Hughes, born the 16th of November, A. D. 1743.
John Hughes, born the 14th of December, A. D. 1745.
Isaac Hughes, born the 1st of December, A. D. 1747.
Catharine Hughes, born the 29th of June, A. D. 1750.
James Hughes, born the 29th of November, A. D. 1752.

On another leaf in the handwriting of the clergyman, a different hand from the above:

Prudence, daughter of John and Sarah Hughes: Baptized 27th day of July, 1740. Pr. me, William Currie.

Jane, the daughter of John and Sarah Hughes was Baptized ye 5th of July, 1741. Pr. William Currie.

Hugh, son of John and Sarah Hughes was baptized on ye 12th day of September, 1742. Pr. me Willm Currie.

ADVERTISEMENT.

To be sold wholesale or retail by John Hughes and son, at their store on Fourth street, above Market street, Raven Duck prime linen, Ticklenburg, Oznabrigs, Buckram, checks and Irish Linen, muslins, Rosnall's Tandems, Tandem Garlix, Long Lawns, spotted and cotton, chintses, calicoes and stamped linens, cross-bar and striped [word obliterated], Tinksets flannen, half thicks bed bunts, Leghorn hats, Shaloon, fam— [word obliterated], diaper, worsted and thread, men's and wo— [obliterated], hair and worsted plush, hunting and everlastings, Silk handkerchiefs, Linen [words lost], cuffs and table knives, Razors, scissors, Sleeve buttons, mohair and silken hair, metal and hair buttons, Satin and padusoi flower'd and plain ribbons, ferret gartering, Women's leather and Silk mitts, silk caps, sewing silk, thread, Breeches patterns, knee garters, men's gloves, pipe and Spike Tomahocks, Iron Candle-sticks, pewter, pins, Needles, thimbles, Snuff-boxes, awl hafts, blades and Shoe tacks, Snuffers, Shoe and knee Buckles, watch keys and Seals, Holman's ink powder, Mariners' Compasses, Spectacles, Cotton and Silk Laces, women's fans, horse-whips, Cart-boxes, Curtain-rings, writing paper, Shirt Buttons, Wigg springs, small and large Brass Kettles, Gun flints, al— [obliterated], and New England rum, molasses, Loaf and Muscovada sugar, Rice, Tea, Coffee, Chocolate, Ginger, pepper, Allspice, French indigo, Rozin, Brimstone, bar iron, whale-bone, fine salt, Train oyl, Starch, nutmegs, cloves, mace, Cinnamon, coperas, Braseel cotton and wool cards, and sundry other things at most reasonable rates.

Copy of inventory of the personal estate of John Hughes, late of Philadelphia:

	£	s	d
1 Negro man,	30	0	0
1 Negro woman,	50	0	0
1 desk and book case, black walnut,	9	0	0
1 large book case,	1	15	0
1 chaise and harness,	30	0	0
1 large looking-glass,	6	0	0
1 eight-day clock,	25	0	0
1 large brass pan,	3	0	0
6 small iron back plates,	2	5	0
1 iron baking plate,	0	4	6
pair of mill stones, Rhine and spindle,	4	0	0
10 cwt. cart boxes,	4	0	0
5 Moravian stoves,	20	0	0
13 five plate stoves,	26	0	0
4 cwt. old iron,	2	0	0
Grey's Debates in the House of Commons, 10 vols.,	2	10	0
Historical Registers, 2 vols.,	0	15	0
Virginia Laws, 1 vol.,	0	5	0
21 Welsh, Latin and English old books,	0	5	0
13 pamphlets,	0	2	6
Pennsylvania Laws, 1 vol.,	0	6	0
Welsh Bible and Concordance,	1	10	0
Votes of the Assembly, 1 vol.,	0	7	6
Bonds,	1788	17	8
Notes,	275	3	6½

	£	s	d
Mortgages,	878	12	6
Book accounts,	2054	13	8
	£5581	6	7½

Appraised this 22d of May, 1772.

By JONATHAN ROBERTS.

JNO. PRICE, Affirmed.

	£	s	d
Hugh Hughes' bond to W. L. Smith and interest,	300	0	0
The Honorable Commissioners of His Majesty's Customs for the salary from the 11th of July, 1770, to 1st of February, 1772, 1 Yr., 6 Mo. and 20 Days at £60 Sterling,	150	0	0
Executors of Edwd. Scull,	70	0	0
Michael Gratz,	12	10	0
Jacob Ehrenzeller,	8	15	0
Martin Summers,	7	0	0
Michael Hall,	5	0	0
Christian Deirk,	12	0	0
Sarah Hughes for money she rec'd from the Custom House for incidental expenses due from the Comm'rs Ster. 126, 8, 5¼,	202	5	6
Grant & Graham's Protested Bills,	419	0	0
Joshua Brakett,	4	2	10
Wm. Ware's Note,	3	3	12
Saml. Potts for old Right sold Ashbridge,	50	0	0
Linnen Manufactory,	20	0	0
Benjn. Franklin on N. Scotia Business,	28	10	7½
Anthony Wayne, Note,	30	0	0
Joseph Pugh, P. Bill and Int'st,	32	0	0
John Wilday, do. and Int'st,	7	5	0
Benjn. Davis, do. and Int'st,	23	7	0
Wm. Busson, do. and Int'st,	31	0	0
Baynton Wharton, Old Bond and Int'st,	876	8	0
Saml. Martin, Bond and Int'st,	14	0	0
Arthur O'Neal, P. Bill and Int'st,	9	15	0
Wm. Stanley, Note,	40	0	0
Jas. Cosgrove, Note,	4	4	4
James Thompson, do.,	9	9	9
Joseph Williams, do.,	18	18	0
Jonas Seeley, do.,	50	0	0
Hugh Hughes, do. and Int'st,	107	16	0
Saml. Humphrey's Bond and Int'st,	12	10	0

Received, April 16, 1773, of John Hughes, one of the executors of John Hughes, deceased, one hundred and eight pounds, being the Legacy with Interest, bequeathed to my late wife, Sarah DeHaven, by her Father, Hugh Hughes, on the death or marriage of his wife, Mary Hughes, who is deceased.

Rec'd the above by me as administrator to the S'd Sarah DeHaven.

PETER DEHAVEN.

Baptism from Christ Church, Philadelphia's Parish Register:

"John, ye son of Hugh and Sarah Hughes, baptized August ye 1, aged 3 weeks and 3 days, 1711.

Marriages from Christ Church, Philadelphia, records as quoted in Pennsylvania Archives, second series, Volume VIII:

1748, October 31, Elizabeth Holstein and Ezekiel Rambo.
1775, April 27, Sarah Holstein and Hugh DeHaven.
1742, March 13, Andrew Holston and Mary Jones.
1799, July 4, George Holston and Mary McGill.
1766, August 13, Lawrence Holston and Ann Taylor.
1767, May 5, Martha Holston and Joseph Woodfield.
1740, February 23, Elizabeth Houlston and Enoch Story.

From First Baptist Church, Philadelphia, from Archives, second series, Volume XIII:

1793, February 16, William Holston and Rebecca Lownsborough.

From Swedes' Church, Philadelphia. Ibid:

1777, February 6, Lindsay Coates and Rachel Hollsten.
1789, November 24, Matthias Hollstein and Jane Johnson.
1775, March 13, Magdalena Hollsten and John Black.

From Christ Church, Philadelphia. Ibid:

1765, May 1, Ruth Hughes and Lindsay Coates.
1767, June 11, John Hughes, Jr., and Margaret Paschal.
1754, May 18, Hugh Hughes and Mary Morris.

Query if this latter is a second marriage of one Hugh Hughes, deceased, 1756?

Swedes' Church, Philadelphia. Ibid:

1773, January 18, Prudence Hughes and John Ruth. Query if of our family?

The following paper was received from Mr. William John Potts, of Camden, New Jersey. He says: " It is a copy of a paper in my possession, which descended to me from my grandmother Potts' (Rachel Hughes) family. She was the daughter of Lieutenant-Colonel Isaac Hughes, of the Pennsylvania Militia, and the paper, apparently in the handwriting of John Hughes, of "Walnut Grove," Upper Merion, refers to his son Isaac, her father. It is endorsed on the back:

"Inventory of things given to Isaac, also an account of things left on the place but not given."

[The front reads as follows, the spelling is exactly copied.]

Account of things given to my son Isaac, November 29, 1770:

 Three Feather Beds, bedstids and cloathes.
 Four Cows and a Heifer, and two oxen.
 Two Horses, Two Mares, Two Coults.
 Nine Sheep and three Goates.
 Three Hogs and four Shoates.
 One Couch and nine Walnut Chairs.
 Two Looking Glasses.
 One Cart and Ox Yoke and Chain.
 One Bar Shear plow and Irons and an old pair shear coulter and plow.
 Swingle trees, clevises, &c.
 Some pewter, some Iron Pots, Tea furniture and house utensils.
 Some kitchen furniture.
 [Erased as in the original.]
 A Moravian Stove.
 Sundry plantation Utensils, syder mill, crib and press and syder-casks.

$$8 - 565 - 128 - 1 \quad 14$$

There is the Shears and Gears, one clock, one Looking Glass, and One Large Brass pan Left and not given away, but are for Isaac's use whilst Left at the place.

There is also my Desk and Book case, which are to stand in My Room until I order otherwise, they being for my Wife. Only N. B. The crop that Peter Matson and my Negroes put in the Ground the fall that Isaac married is also left for him, he giving his Sister Caty seed corn and also bread corn until harvest of 1771. I also ordered seed corn for my son John, which has been Delivered.

There is also two Negro men, one negro woman and Two Negro children Left on the place. Negro man Jack and his wife Dinah, I give to my son Isaac, and the labour of Julius unless otherwise ordered by me.

One large Walnut Chest.
One cross-cut Saw.
One Whip Saw.
One Bottle Case and Some Bottles.
One Large pair Handirons.
Two Small pr. Do.
One Dining Table and Stand.
One large Kitching Tongs.
One Small Shovel and Tongs

5 Pictures Glazed.
Two Market Hampers.
One Large Kitchen Table.
Two Flat Irons.
Pensilvania Laws.

Copy of an old paper endorsed on the back in John Hughes' handwriting:

"Catherine's
Effects."

3 horsses, 3 cows, 8 sheep, three Hogs.
1 plow and swingle tree and plow line, Gears,
1 Cart, 1 Grubing hoe, 1 ax, and 1 Hatchet.
3 pitchforks and 3 Rakes, 1 Mans Saddle and Bridle,
1 Womans Siddle and Bridle, 6 Hhds,
And 3 Barrels, 1 Hammer, 1 old handsaw,
2 Gimlets, 20 harrowtine, 3 Beds,
Seven Black walnut Chairs, 1 Do. Table,
1 case of Drawers, 2 Looking Glasses, some
Pots, pans, pewter, Tea ware, 1 Coffee Mill,
1 frying pan, 1 sled, 2 pair of hand Yrons,
Tongs, and fire Shovel, some Books, a Spinnet,
And such other things as is in the house to be Divided.
My Negro Man Peter, his wife, and a child 1½ (?) years old, called Harriot.

[I presume the above to have been taken about 1770.]

The portrait of Mrs. Hannah Holstein Hughes Clay was painted when she was about eighty-two, by Miss Jane Sully.

The portrait of Mrs. Rachel Hughes Potts was painted by Mr. Sully at the same time; the latter was said to be a good picture, but not a good likeness, though Mr. Sully was a remarkably able artist.

While examining the two portraits, Mr. Sully is said to have turned to his daughter with the remark: "Jane, you have surpassed your father."

RACHEL HUGHES' ACROSTIC.

Written in elegant hand, the author unknown. As she was married to William Lukens Potts, it was written, of course, before that date.

Resistless charms the beauteous maid displays,
And to the mind the loveliest form conveys,
Cold, formal looks which converse oft destroys,
Her soul disdains, and soars to friendship's joys,
Engaging sweetness, charms no tongue can tell,
Like kindred virtues in her bosom dwell.

Her heart which ne'er by flattery's art would move,
Unaw'd by censure glows with virtuous love,
Gentle and mild with unaffected ease,
Humane and tender every wish to please,
Endow'd with all that various charms diffuse,
Such the description of the lovely Hughes.

An Inventory of the Goods and Chattels, Rights and Credits of Isaac Hughes, of Upper Merion township, in the County of Philadelphia, deceased, appraised by us the Subscribers, thus:

FRONT ROOM.

	£	s	d
Cash,	2	6	0
Wearing Apparel,	5	0	0
Books,	6	0	0
Desk and Book Case,	6	0	0
Looking Glass,	5	0	0
Walnut Table,	1	10	0
Clock,	20	0	0
Tea Table,	1	0	0
Stone Table,	1	10	0
Stove,	4	0	0

	£	s	d
Hand Irons, Tongs and Fire Shovel,	1	0	0
5 Windsor Chairs,	1	10	0
Stand,	0	10	0
12 Pictures,	1	10	0
Plate,	28	13	0
China and Glass,	3	10	0
Tea Kettles,	1	0	0
Thermometer,		15	0
Case and Bottles,	0	12	0

BACK ROOM.

	£	s	d
Bedstead, Bed, Bedding and Curtains,	20	0	0
Walnut Chairs,	2	10	0
Case of Drawers,	6	0	0
5 Pictures,	0	15	0
1 Walnut Card Table,	1	10	0
And Irons,	0	10	0
Looking Glass,	2	10	0
Scales,	0	7	6

UP STAIRS.

	£	s	d
Dressing Table,	2	0	0
2 Looking Glasses,	5	0	0
6 Walnut Chairs, Leather Bottomed,	2	0	0
Bedstead, Bed and Bedding and Curtains,	12	0	0
Bed and Bedding,	7	10	0
Truckle Bedstead, Bed and Bedding,	2	0	0
Brought forward,	£155	17	6
Walnut Chest,	0	10	0
7 Yard of Cloth,	2	12	6
Carpet,	2	0	0
2 Pairs of Andirons,	0	15	0

GARRET.

	£	s	d
Brass Pan,	5	0	0
Geers for a four wheeled carriage,	0	15	0
3 Spinning Wheels,	1	10	0
Bed,	0	5	0
Big Spinning Wheel,	0	7	6
Old Cart Tire,	2	0	0
Old Whip Saw,	0	5	0

KITCHEN.

	£	s	d
Iron Pots and Skillet,	2	0	0
Brass Kettle,	1	10	0
Andirons, Shovel and Tongs,	0	15	0
Dutch Oven,	7	6	0
2 Coffee Pots	0	15	0
Iron Plank,	0	3	9
2 Frying Pans and Grid Iron,	0	7	6
2 Pair Flat Irons,	0	7	6
Watering Pot,	0	3	9
Lantern,	0	1	0
Candlesticks,	0	7	6
Warming Pan,	0	10	0
Coffee Mill,	0	7	6
Tables and Dough-Trough,	0	7	6
Steel Yards,	0	10	0
Tubs, Buckets and Churn,	0	10	0
Pewter,	1	10	0
Crockery	0	5	0
Knives and Forks,	0	5	0
Saddle,	2	10	0

ON THE FARM.

	£	s	d
Waggon,	3	0	0
Riding Chair and Geers,	7	10	0
4 Milch Cows,	20	0	0
Grey Mare,	40	0	0
Sorrel Colt,	5	0	0
Roan Mare,	18	0	0
Plough and Geers belonging to it,	3	0	0
Harrow,	1	0	0
Wind Mill,	2	5	0
9 Shoats,	6	15	0

AT THE OLD FARM.

	£	s	d
An old Table and Pine Desk,	0	15	0
Paper Case,	0	5	0
Couch,	0	3	9
A Number of Bottles,	1	0	0
14 Bushels of Wheat,	18	10	0
7 Bushels of Rye,	1	8	0

	£	s	d
Wheat in the Ground, 15 acres, at £1 per acre,	15	0	0
Rye do 5 acres at 15s. per acre,	3	15	0
Barley do 2 acres at 20s. per acre,	2	0	0
An old cart,	1	10	0
3 Bulls,	4	10	0
The Iron of an old Waggon Bed,	0	10	0
11 Acres of Grain in the Ground at the new place,	10	0	0
Two Old Negroes, Jack and Dinah,	5	0	0
Negro Boy Pompey,	40	0	0

BONDS, ETC.

	£	s	d
Bond, Hugh Hughes,	200	0	0
Note, Moses Coates,	10	19	6
Bill Single, John Coates, dated March 19, 1778, Continental Money,	100	0	0
Bond, Thomas Coates, dated July 15, 1778, one-half thereof belonging to Jesse Roberts,	500	0	0
Book Debt, Isaac Thomas,	23	0	0
Account, John Coates, March 12, 1778, Continental Money,	200	0	0
	£1446	7	3

[COPY.]

May ye 4th, 1782————

Then received of Hannah Hughes in full for her Husbands Coffing [sic] two pound Ten Shillinges.

£2 10s 0. pr Me NATHAN STURGIS.

Pennsylvania Archives, Second Series, Volume I, pp. 501, 502 and 503.

" In December, 1747, the Assembly having made no provision for the defence of the City and Province, many of the inhabitants became alarmed and voluntarily entered into an association for defence. Companies were formed, which proceeded to choose officers, who, in turn, assembled and chose their superior officers, all being commissioned by the direction of the Provincial Council.—*Colonial Records, Volume V, pages 172 and 174.*"

The result of this movement is detailed in the message of Anthony Palmer, President, to the Assembly, dated May 17, 1748:

"The Province which very lately was in a defenceless state is now, through the zeal and activity of some, who have the love of their country sincerely at heart, rendered capable, with the blessing of God, of defending itself against the designs of our enemies, many thousands of the inhabitants having voluntarily entered into the most solemn engagements for that purpose, in consequence whereof arms have been provided and every one appears assiduous in qualifying himself for the defence of his country. They have likewise, at considerable expense, erected batteries on the River, so situated and of such strength and weight of metal, as to render it very dangerous for an enemy to attempt the bringing any ships before the city. We have granted commissions to such general and other officers, as have from time to time been presented to us for that purpose by the Association. Since these measures tend so manifestly, under God, for the security of this Province, and the preservation of its metropolis, we think they justly deserve the assistance and encouragement of your House.—*Votes of Assembly, Volume IV, page 72.*"

"Officers of the Associated Regiment of Foot of Philadelphia."—December 29, 1747.

Judging from the names of these officers, I presume the regiment had a carefully selected membership, as they are some of the best known men of the day. It was probably a fashionable organization:

Colonel, Abraham Taylor; Lieutenant-Colonel, Thomas Lawrence; Major, Samuel McCall; Captain, John Inglis; Lieutenant, Lynford Lardner; Ensign, Thomas Lawrence, Jr.

Among officers of the other companies in this regiment are William Bradford, William Bingham, Charles Willing, Atwood Shute, James Claypole, Thomas Bond, Richard Farmer, William Rush, Richard Nixon, James Coultas, George Gray, Junior.

We find in the company, "Captain, John Hughes; Lieutenant, Matthias Holstein; Ensign, Frederick Holstein."

Copy of a paper endorsed on the back in John Hughes' hand-writing, and, with the exception of course of the signatures, written by him, " Anthony Wayne's Agreement."

OBSERVATIONS TO BE MADE IN A NEW SETTLEMENT.

1. Good Land, and navigable water.
2. The heads of Navigation in Rivers, that is the Tide.
3. Convenient place for ferries.
4. Passes through Mountains in fertil valleys or country.
5. Iron Oar and cole mines.
6. Mill seats and other water works.
7. Places where many Roads are Like to meet.
8. Any Beeches or Islands with Black Sand washed up by ye Tide.
9. Mast or pine Swamps on Navigation.
10. Lime Stone or other Stones on Navigation. If stones are scarce.
11. Meadow Lands and Marsh.
12. Large Springs or any Mineral Springs.

Upon these principles we the subscribers Do Agree to be Concerned Equally in taking up and Improving as Tenants in Common Such Tracts or pieces of Land in Nova Scotia as we Shall from time to time get Laid out and Secured in the said Colony And we Do Agree for our Selves our Heirs, Executors or Administrators as Tenants in Common to bear and pay Equally all Expenses attending Each and Every Tract of Land taken up and Secured by us as aforesaid, and that all Such Tracts Shall be and is hereby Declared to be too and for our Joint use and behoof as Tenants in Common and not as Joint Tenants and too and for no other use or Intent whatsoever And that we will Constantly write to Each other and Mention or Describe Each Tract we are to be concerned in from Time to time as the same shall be located. And that Each of us his Heirs, Executors and Administrators shall and may at all Times hereafter paying his or their proportion as aforesaid Take, Occupy, possess and Enjoy one moiety or Equal half part of Each Tract of Land so Secured or Taken up as Aforesaid. In Witness whereof we have hereunto Set our hands and Seals the fourteenth day of March One Thousand Seven Hundred and Sixty-five.

[Signed] Anthy. Wayne. [Seal.]
Jno. Hughes. [Seal.]

Sign'd, Seal'd and Deliver'd in the presence of us.
Isaac Hughes.
Jno. Hughes, Junr

Entirely in the hand of John Hughes, though unsigned and endorsed on the back by him, is a " Letter to Coll. McNutt, May 29, 1764."

Philada, May 29th, 1764.

Dear Sir:

In Consequence of the Directions and orders I have Received from you, together with the Advertisements you sent me Some Time Ago, I have proceeded to inform my friends and Acquaintance, not only in this but the Neighboring Governments, with the Contents of your Orders, and the purport of your Advertisements, whereupon Several persons of Merit and fortune Undertook at my Instance to Engage Settlers for the Colony of Nova Scotia, and have on the Strength of my Engagements and Letters procured Great Numbers to put themselves in a posture for Removing this Spring, and many are now and have been some time past on Expences to their Great Disappointment and Damages, So that Some of them are Determined to go Elsewhere, Others continue to wait, But all threaten to Arrest me, and Some I believe will, and I make no Doubt will Recover Considerable Damages, as many put themselves out of Business in the way of their Trades, and many others Sold or Gave up their Little farms, being fully perswaded of the truth of our Informations, however I shall Do all I can to keep them Easy, but must be at Large Expences to Do it to any purpose. I therefore Earnestly beseech you on the Receipt of this (as I hope you will be Arrived) to take the most Speedy and Effectual Methods to have the Land Reserved for the Several Companies I have Engaged, and as soon as it is Done Send me an Account that I may Inform the people who are Ready to tear me to pieces, and I must Say not without a Cause, for it is Really very Extraordinary that you Shou'd Enter into Such Engagements as you have Done with me, and as I have Done with others on your Credits and by your Orders, and afterwards to Leave the place and go home to Brittain and Leave me a Sacrifice to the people, and my character as an honest man Call'd in Question. It is true that in your Last Letters you Complain of being delay'd by the Government, And say you have been Disapointed (and all that), but that is nothing to the people. They have been Disapointed, and Sorely too, by us, but they say by me, and therefore are Loud in their Complaints, And I Do without further Ceremony Insist that you Comply with your promises and have the Land Reserved, or I must be Obliged in my own Defense to use you as the people use me. Therefore, Dr. Sir, Let me beg and Intreat you to be Expeditious after your Arrival, which I believe by your Last Letter will be before this can Reach Hallifax, for I should be very sorry to be obliged to Sew you for breach of contract, for you know you are to Indemnifie me by your Agreement, but I hope you will on your arrival fully come up to your Agreements and the purport of your Advertisements. Please to Observe Strictly the Requests of the Several Companies in Respect to their Lands, for the Leaders or heads of Each company that I have Engaged are men of Reputation and Interest, and will be of Singular use to the Settlement. I will be concern'd with none Else, and there is one thing I had like to have forgot, and that is that we are told many Gentlemen in England are applying for Land, and are Like to have Large Tracts Granted them. We therefore, one and all, particularly Request that our Lands may not be near those Tracts, as we cannot believe they will be soon settled by great men at such a Distance, and therefore have no Desire to be in their Neighborhood, for we are all come to a Determination to make very Considerable Improvements with as much Speed as the Nature of the thing will admit, or that the Dint of Industry and a considerable share of property will naturally produce, and we are no strangers to new Settlements, and therefore know what methods to pursue for our common advantage, and Doubt not but a few Years will Give our part of the country a new face, much to the satisfaction of all concern'd. I have not sent you any List of Subscribers to the Several Companies, as this unexpected Delay has broke some part of our Scheam, and the first subscribers cannot all be Depended on, and Some others are Dayly Subscribing in one Company or Others. But when Ever they are wanted I will procure coppy's of Each and send them to you by Post. For God's sake, Sir, Do not procrastinate any Longer, or our plan may miscarry and we be put to a monstrous Expence, besides the Loss of

Reputation, which as I am not only a merchant but a farmer and Iron Master, will injure me Extremely in my Business in Each Branch.

Endorsed on the back by Mr. Hughes, "Coll: McNutt's Rect."

PHIL'ADA., Jan'y 1st, 1765.

Whereas, I the subscriber have promised Messrs. Benjamin Franklin, John Foxcraft, John Hughes, John Cox, John Reed, Samuel Miles and Benjamin Davis, that I will use my Best Endeavors, to have four Townships alotted in the province of Nova Scotia, for them and their associates, I do hereby also acknowledge to have Rec'ived from th s'd John Hughes a paper bearing Even Date herewith, Sign'd by him and them, which paper contains Some further Agreements on their parts. And as I have no Doubts of their fully Complying with Every part of their Engagements, I therefore Do promise them and each of them that no Endeavors of mine shall be wanting to fulfill Every Expectation I have Given them. As witness my hand the Day and Year Above Written.

ALEX'R McNUTT.

Addressed "To John Hughes, Esq., in Philadelphia."
"Pr. Favor of Capt. McNeal, via Boston."

HALIFAX, April the 10, 1765.

DEAR SIR:

We arrived here on the 20th of March after a passage of thirteen days we met a geal of wind off the East end of Long Island which Continued three days without Intermition. We were introduc'd by Con'l. McNutt, To the Governor and Councell and was very kindly rec'd, I had the Honour of Dining with his Excelleney in a day or two after we arr'd and with Several Gentlemen of the place Since, I can give you no acct. of the Quality of the land as yet only by heresay, the gentleman who have estates in the country says the land is very good and capable of Producing any Kind of grean, they raize excellent Spring wheat, which Yields 60 or 70 Bushels to the acre and Likewise hemp in all their dike Lands. I likewise am told there is great bodies of Iron oar on the river Petitcoodiack and the bay of Vert, but nobody to carry on Iron works for want of Money. Capt. Caton and Mr Jacobs sails the day after to-

riors for the river Saint Johns, in order to Survey all the good land they find there, and in a few days, Coml. McNutt, Parson Lyon and myself Sails Westward all along the Coast to mines bason, and so up the bay of Founday and river Petitcoodiack and meet Capt. Caton and Mr. Jacobs at the head of Said river. When you write pray Direct your letters to the care of Michael Franklin, Esqr., Merchant in Halifax, he is a gentleman of character, and one of the Councell, tho I believe Nothing related to our worthy friend Benjn. Franklin, Esquire.

We expect to return by the first of June to this place, at which time I hope I shall be able to give you a satisfactory Acct. My Compyliments to your Spouse and family and likewise to Mistress Frackling [Franklin] tho unacquainted.

I am, Dear Sir, your friend and Humble Servant,

ANTHY. WAYNE.

To JOHN HUGHES, ESQR.

N. B. This comes by the way of Boston.

Endorsed on the back in John Hughes' hand, "Copy of a letter sent to Anto. Wayne, June 3, 1765."

D'R SIR:

I Received your Favour by Way of Boston and also another by some Captain. The first brought the agreeable News of your safe Arrival after a passage of 13 Days and a smart Gale of Wind. We were in pain about you, as we had a most Dreadful Snow Storm after you sail'd, the like hardly ever known at that Season.

In the other, after some small Hints of the country as far as you could Learn by the Information you got from Gentlemen there, you seem to Insinuate the Country is full as good as we Expected.

I am also pleased with the Reception you meet with, and hope you will improve all advantages.

As to persons' names which you mention, I can confide in the following Gentlemen, Viz: John Baynton, Samuel Wharton, John Jones, Christian Deirk, Lindsay Coates, John Coates, Joseph Galloway, John Roberts, George David, John Coryel, George Hitner. These are all men of Reputation and Character, and are my particular Friends. I shall speak to your Father in a few Days. I was at his House last Week, but he was not at home.

I am now to inform you I am appointed the Officer to put the Stamp Act in Execution, which gives the Proprietary

Party no small pain. My Compliments to Coll. McNutt, and Let him know I am surprized I have no Letter from him.
I am, D'r Wayne, Your
Real Friend,
JNO. HUGHES.

P. S.—Mrs. Franklin Returns the Compliment, and is Obliged to you for Remembering her.

Addressed, "John Hughes, Esq're, in Philadelphia (via Boston).

HALIFAX, July 9th, 1765.
DEAR SIR:

I rec'd your favor of the 1st of June this day week. I returned here about nine days agoe after waiting three weeks at Port Roseway for Col'n McNutt. (I wrote you the 30th of May from Cape Negro, which I presume you have got by Mr. Lisket, who has obtained a reserve for five townships, three on Saint Johns river and two Between that and Peticoojack.) He has Embibed a notion in many of the Gentlemen of the Councell here that he will be the only man that is Capable of Complying with the firms of Settlement, and Has done his Endeavour to make the Other Company's Insignificant and not Equal to the Undertaking.

I have been very Deligent ever Since my return in trying to Obtain a reserve for a Number of townships. I waited on Severall Gentlemen of the Councell and got a promise from them for a reserve in any part of the province not already reserved or granted. They met the 5th Instant and Voted Sixteen townships for as many Companies, Each to Contain 100,000 Acres, and to be Situated in the following places, viz.: 10 on the river St. Johns, 1 on Peticoojack, 1 on St. Mary's bay, Situate between Cape Sables and Annopolis Royal; 1 on Milford bay, 1 on the river St. Mary's, 1 at pictoo, and 1 at Merimeche. These last four are to the East of Halifax.

I have joined some of the Gentlemens Names you sent me Along with your's, Mr. Franklin's and my own, for two townships, which I shall transmit you a Copy of the first Opportunity with the terms granted in it, which is not as agreeable as I could wish, but I am pretty well assured we shall Obtain better before I have this. Mr. Lisket, by his Dutch Policy, has got a large reserve, but poor terms. As Col'n McNutt and his Asso'ts are Mentioned in the reserve, Each of us may have what Quantity of Land we please in it.

I Congratulate you upon your Appointment of Stamp Officer (and do assure you if it gave the Proprietary party pain on the one part), it gives me Intimate pleasure on the Other. I am greatly Indebted to Mrs. Frankling for her Comp's, and would return it thrice.

Please to remember me to your Spouse and family, and believe me, Dear Sir, your Sincere friend,

ANTHY WAYNE.

P. S.—I forgot to tell you that the 16 townships is left to me to Chuse, which Can't be attended with any Disadvantage on our Side. Our Sloop Sailed yesterday for Mines bason, where I meet his, and so proceed up the river St. Johns.

Mr. Jacobs has just returned for Viewing St. Johns, and is well pleased with the land, but Out of Humer with Mr. Lisket. W.

ANTHONY WAYNE'S LETTER, OCT. 7, 1765.

"To John Hughes, Esq'r, in Philadelphia. Pr favour of Mr. Robinson."

HALIFAX, Oct'r 7th, 1765.

DEAR SIR:

I rec'd yours of the 28th of July, by way of Boston; Likewise of the 19th August, by Mr. Clarkson, and note the Contents.

As to the Disaprobation of the Terms Contained in the General reserves, was what I foresaw, and what every thinking person who was any way Interested would Disaprove of.

Mr. Jacobs and myself did whatever lay in our Power to get them Relaxed. We applied to Col'n McNutt and Dr. Lyon to joyn us in A memorial for that purpose, telling them at the same time we were well Satisfied. No Company Concerned would spend their Money and time upon such Unreasonable and Unjust terms without any prospect of remitances. But they Declined it.

We likewise Sounded the Councill man by man, representing the Necessity of altring them, in the Strongest light that we were Capable of, and had the greatest reason to believe from the private Sentiments of many of those Gentlemen, that we would meet with no Difficulty in Obtaining them that we required.

But to our great Surprise, when they met in Councill, notwithstanding the repeated assurances of the Majority of them that they would do all that lay in their power for us, and they look'd upon our request nothing but what was reasonable and just.

They very Lively [sic] tould us it was not in their power to Grant any other terms than those they had afore proposed.

But my surprise has since been reversed, for I have been Informed by several Gentlemen of the Council that Col'n McNutt had made Interest privately against us, and Said that we had Nothing to do with the terms or anything Else, and was only Employed as Surveyors under him; that he was the person Applyed to by all the Company's Concerned, and Produced his Applications.

This Despicable and Unjust proceedings of McNutt I did not find out till my return here the 18th of Sep'r, Which threw me Under the necesity of producing your Letters, and our Agreement, to shew them that I had a rite to ask for terms and act in the manner I did. To give you *a true* and full Detail would take up Many pages of paper.

Laving that and coming to our Proceeding since we arrived last from St. Johns. Upon our arrival, Mr. Clarkson Informed us he had put in a Memorial to the Governor and Council representing the Disaprobation of the Company's Concerned in taking up lands in this Province, of the terms proposed, &c., and at the Same time Proposing such others as he thought would answer.

I imadiately drew up an other, to strenthin his, and was joined by Capt. Caton and Mr. Jacobs in it. We waited on the Council next Day when they made the following proposals to us, Viz:

To Issue Grants to the principal Undertakers Imadiately. The terms for every 100,000 Acres 100 families, each family to consist of 5 persons, to be Introduced in four years, at the yearly Quota of families p. year, Quitrents at 2t p. every hundred acres, one half to Commence in five years, and the whole in 10, to Close or Improve ⅓ d in 10 Years, ⅓ in 20 years and the remainder in 30 years, and all not so complyed with to be forfited, and all so complyed with to be to us and our Heirs forever.

They have agreed to have a Clause in the Grants, " that if we can obtain better terms at any time from his Majesty it shall be Inserted in this Grant, and they shall be the terms on which we hold our lands." Which I took upon a good Proviso, as well as that of forfiting what lands we don't Enclose or Settle, for I do assure you there is a great deal of Land in Each township that will be better to forfit than pay the Quitrents on them.

We meet with great Dificulty in Obtaining our Grants, tho we have a reserve on the Lands that we apply for, which is one 4 Township on St. Johns river at the head of Navigation, 1 on St. Mary's Bay and 2 on Peticoodiack.

There is a Sort of a miss between the Council and us and things Dont go on as fast as I could wish. If we Carrie our Matters thro, you and I are to have one Quarter of each township. Mr. Clarkson, Mr. Caton and Mr. Jacobs each a Quarter. But one thing which I do not approve of is, that McNutt is mentioned in each of our Grants. We shall try to exclude him if possible, as he has been rather a Determent than of Service to us.

It has been a Costly Voiage to us all and if we Obtain our Grants, which is the thing that now Detain us, the Office fees will amount to near £70 Sterling for each township, the lands will pay sufficiently for it.

They want to Cull part of the best lands on Petticoodiack for some of the favorite Gentlemen of Halifax, which has caused the Difference between them and us, to prevent which we have made a faint as if we would lave the Province without taking up any Lands, and have set up our names for that purpose.

I believe Matters will Shortly be accomodated, as the[y] dont think it will be Consistant with their Interest to lose such a number of Settlers.

I have Drawn on you for £78 of Penn'sa Currency, payable to Mr. James Robertson on 10 day sight, which you will please to Honor. If it may Sute you to let him Have it Sooner, provided he should want it would greatly

Oblige Your Sincere friend,

And Most Huml. Sert.,

ANTHY. WAYNE.

N. B. My Compts to Mrs. Hughes' family ; as to lands on Mines Bason there is none, worth accepting, but what is gr[anted?] and as to St. Johns Island there is positive Orders [torn] not to grant any part of it to any person whatsoev[er].

In removing the oil painting of Mrs. Hannah Holstein Hughes Clay from the frame in November, 1892, for the purpose of having another photograph of it taken, the following inscription, written, as it is supposed, by Mr. Thomas Sully, the artist, was found upon the canvas:

<blockquote>
MRS. HANNAH CLAY,
BORN DECEMBER 4TH, 1748.
PAINTED JANUARY, 1826,
BY MISS JANE SULLY,
PHILADELPHIA.
</blockquote>

MARRIAGES WITH DATES.

YEAR.		PAGE.
1851.	Amies, Elizabeth Holstein and Charles E. Morris	145
1879.	Amies, Emily Thomas and Abram Walker	145
1866.	Atlee, Emma Maria and Hiram Hendrixon	132
1878.	Atlee, Hugh DeHaven and Mary M. Carmany	177
1882.	Atlee, John Stewart and Elizabeth Stewart	177
1836.	Atlee, Julianna DeHaven and Robert Louis Williams	132
1847.	Atlee, Samuel John and Jane Stewart	132
1885.	Blackiston, Josephine and Henry Augustus Newland	167
1876.	Blackiston, Lizzie and Henry Augustus Newland	167
1873.	Blackiston, Mary Eugenia and J. Woodbridge Patton	167
1868.	Blackiston, Samuel Hepburn and Mrs. Sarah T. Brooke	167
1862.	Brandt, George and Susan Orr	187
1859.	Brandt, Georgianna and Louis Lyman Albee	138
1868.	Brandt, Hannah and Daniel Preston	187
1865.	Brandt, Henry and Catharine Humphrey	187
1862.	Brandt, Mary and James Groves	187
1866.	Brandt, Sarah and William Howard	187
1869.	Brandt, William and Sarah Harman	187
1881.	Brooke, Ida Longinire and J. Howard Lewis, Jr.	194
1881.	Brooke, William Thomas and Rebecca H. Chapman	194
1869.	Brown, Annie Louisa and Albert S. Furst	169
1879.	Brown, Gertrude Mary and Thomas Hilton	169
1887.	Campbell, Elizabeth Anna and Boyd Henry	190
1788.	Clay, Ann and Samuel Hepburn	102
1845.	Clay, Ann and Joseph Potts	128
1821.	Clay, Charles Holstein and Maria Evans	103
1841.	Clay, Emily and William Pollock	128
1822.	Clay, George and Emma DeHaven	102
1855.	Clay, Dr. Geo. Bolton Lownes and Clara J. Tiers	128
1853.	Clay, George Henry and Amelia Donnel	129
1848.	Clay, Harriet P. and Rev. Edmund Leaf	128
1814.	Clay, Rev. Jehu Curtis and Margaret Annan	102
1828.	Clay, Rev. Jehu Curtis, 2d, and Simmons Edy	103
1847.	Clay, Julia Frances and Dr. John T. Evans	128
1863.	Clay, Richard Edy and Louisa Ann Pollock	129
1819.	Coates, Ann and William Halloway	106
1853.	Coates, Ann E. and Thomas Maitland	135
1857.	Coates, Annie Hayman and William Mason	174
1864.	Coates, Aaron Yerkes and Margaret Ann Sheard	172

YEAR.		PAGE
1857.	Coates, Davis P. and Anne Worral	134
1841.	Coates, Jane and William Knight	135
1865.	Coates, John and Sarepta Stringfield	134
1837.	Coates, Levi Pawling and Mary Yerkes	129
1857.	Coates, Louisa and Jacob Shainline	134
1852.	Coates, Margaret and Francis A. Drew	135
1850.	Coates, Mary Holstein and George Saunders	135
1846.	Coates, Mary Moore and John Smiley	130
1836.	Coates, Matthew Henderson and Beulah W. Allen	130
1875.	Coates, Matthew Henderson and Mary B. Drom	174
1866.	Coates, Matthias and Mary Augusta McMullen	172
1859.	Coates, Matilda P. and Alexander McCurdy	135
1851.	Coates, Nicholas Collin and Elizabeth Stewart	130
1815.	Coates, Samuel Holstein and Margaret Owens	107
1850.	Coates, Susan and Jacob Hurst	135
1865.	Coates, Susan Yerkes and Charles Wilkinson Castor	172
1860.	Colket, Emily Thomas and Harrison Koons Caner	105
1862.	Dewees, Francis Percival and Emma Loeser	149
1862.	Dewees, Isaac Holstein and Olivia Camilla Ledyard	149
1872.	Dewees, James Collin and Charity Eye Packer	151
1861.	Dewees, John Hughes and Sarah Hammer	148
1887.	Dewees, John Hughes and Emily J. Milliken, 2d	148
1869.	Dewees, Theodore Lyng and Amelia Louisa Fiske	151
1860.	Hampton, Emma and B. P. Sloan	178
1867.	Hampton, Sophia M. and S. D. Adams	178
1853.	DeHart, Jane Gaul and Wm. Wilson Harvey	130
1860.	DeHaven, Alex'r Henry and Clara Robinson	133
1864.	DeHaven, Alex'r Henry and Mary A. Townsend	133
1869.	DeHaven, Amelia and Jos. Augustus Atlee	105
1882.	DeHaven, Augusta Louisa and Baron Eberhard Curd von Alten	175
1846.	DeHaven, Charles Elliott and Mary Anne Carman	132
1875.	DeHaven, Charles Elliott and Anne Traquair Henderson	178
1844.	DeHaven, Emma C. and William H. Hampton	132
1875.	DeHaven, Emma and Francis Bright	178
1822.	DeHaven, Emma M. and George Clay	100
1809.	DeHaven, Harriett and Nathaniel Barber	105
1818.	DeHaven, Holstein and Sophia Elliott	105
1801.	DeHaven, Holstein and Annah Colket Gallup	178
1775.	DeHaven, Hugh and Sarah Holstein	85
1825.	DeHaven, Hugh and Christiana Lyng Bunting	105
1852.	DeHaven, Hugh and Zipporah Dill White, 2d	105
1842.	DeHaven, Hugh and Mary L. Cleaver	132
1862.	DeHaven, Hugh and Clara Boyd Brinton	133
1874.	DeHaven, Josephine Amelia and Towson Caldwell	202
1856.	DeHaven, Joseph Edwin and Amelia Louisa Bigelow	134

YEAR		PAGE
1875.	DeHaven, Joseph Edwin and Augusta W. Borek, 2d	131
1880.	DeHaven, Mary Anna and Malcolm W. Bryan	178
1801.	DeHaven, Peter and Sarah Atlee	105
1884.	DeHaven, Sarah Elizabeth and Dr. Hans Frederick Carl-Moritz von Campe	175
1878.	DeHaven, Sarah Carman and Richard Meade Bache	178
1870.	DeHaven, Sallie Letitia and David T. Boyd	134
1850.	DeHaven, Samuel White and Emma Thompson	133
1847.	DeHaven, Susannah Sholer and Samuel White	133
1870.	DeHaven, William Neill and Lizzie Regina Hildreth	131
1885.	Henderson, Elizabeth Branton and Edwin Burrough Campion	189
1877.	Henderson, Jane and Charles W. Kellogg	189
1887.	Henderson, John and Marian Agnes Hagan	189
1886.	Henderson, Matthias Holstein and Lucy Bower	189
1845.	Henderson, Samuel Holstein and Jane Cunningham	140
1849.	Henderson, Samuel Holstein, Second, and Emmaline Satterfield	140
1849.	Hepburn, Emma and Lieutenant J. Hogan Brown	127
1855.	Hepburn, Hannah Maria and William Henry Blackiston	123
1840.	Hepburn, James Curtis and Clara M. Leet	123
1885.	Hepburn, Louisa Harriet and Edwin C. McClure	127
1847.	Hepburn, Mary and L. A. Mackey	127
1882.	Hepburn, Samuel Boyd and Sarah R. Booth	168
1873.	Hepburn, Samuel Dyer and Clara Shaw	167
1837.	Hepburn, Sarah Ann and James Pollock (Governor)	125
1849.	Hepburn, Slator Clay and Anna M. Boyd	127
1872.	Holstein, Alexander and Elinor E. Rosensteel	184
1856.	Holstein, Annabel and Alexander Armstrong	136
1870.	Holstein, Anna Elizabeth and F. M. McKiernan	141
1845.	Holstein, Andrew Johnston and Margaret H. Fulton	136
1820.	Holstein, Ann Sophia and Andrew Shainline	110
1830.	Holstein, Branton and Constance Pritner	110
1815.	Holstein, Christiana and Henry Makemson	108
1888.	Holstein, Constance and D. M. Hadley	142
1870.	Holstein, Ella and William W. Potts	147
1863.	Holstein, Eliza Branton and Smith K. Campbell	141
1822.	Holstein, Elizabeth and Samuel Love	108
1819.	Holstein, Elizabeth Branton and John Henderson	109
1882.	Holstein, Elizabeth Brookfield and David M. Ellis	147
1849.	Holstein, Elizabeth Wayne and Dr. Joseph Brookfield	111
1822.	Holstein, Elizabeth and Samuel Love	108
1836.	Holstein, Emily Wilson and William Brooke Thomas	112
1871.	Holstein, Frances Jones and John James Forster	141
1753.	Holstein, Frederick and Magdalena Jones	18
1890.	Holstein, George Meade and Sarah Corson Highley	147
1847.	Holstein, George Washington and Abby T. Brower	115

YEAR.		PAGE.
1801.	Holstein, George Washington and Elizabeth Wayne Hayman	43
1871.	Holstein, George Wolf and Emma Hand Eagle	140
1769.	Holstein, Hannah and Isaac Hughes	26
1861.	Holstein, Hannah and Louis S. Kochersperger	185
1854.	Holstein, Isaac Wayne and Alice Hallowell	116
1841.	Holstein, Jane and James Keir	136
1883.	Holstein, Jane Henderson and Gilbert C. Kennedy	141
1803.	Holstein, John and Jane Parkinson	108
1811.	Holstein, John Jonse and Elizabeth Williamson	107
1859.	Holstein, John and Christiana Riter	185
1885.	Holstein, John Jones and Annie M. Pearl	182
1846.	Holstein, Louisa Brooke and George W. Dewees	113
1843.	Holstein, Louis Ducardree and Sarah Klingman	136
1843.	Holstein, Margaret and John Ellwood	136
1841.	Holstein, Margaret and William Hunter	138
1845.	Holstein, Mary and John McLoo	136
1880.	Holstein, Mary Alice and William A. Armstrong, Jr.	148
1828.	Holstein, Mary Atlee and William Antes	112
1688.	Holstein, Mats and Katharine	13
1705.	Holstein, Matthias and Brita Rambo	13
1876.	Holstein, Matthias and Alice Emery	141
1795.	Holstein, Matthias and Elizabeth Branton	39
1872.	Holstein, Malinda and Thomas A. Craft	183
1842.	Holstein, Peter Blake and Eliza Ann Cassell	138
1759.	Holstein, Peter Jonse and Catharine Blake	32
1777.	Holstein, Rachel and Jordan Coates	27
1830.	Holstein, Rachel M. and Thomas J. Molony	111
1781.	Holstein, Rebecca and Jesse Roberts	28
1874.	Holstein, Robert and Mattie Coulter	183
1771.	Holstein, Samuel and Rachel Moore	24
1840.	Holstein, Samuel and Anna Pritchett	110
1775.	Holstein, Sarah and Hugh DeHaven	29
1829.	Holstein, Sarah and Robert Love	108
1868.	Holstein, Sarah Eastburn and James McDowell	141
1841.	Holstein, Susan and Wm. B. Roberts	115
1848.	Holstein, William Hayman and Anna Morris Ellis	113
1871.	Holloway, Anna Mary and George M. White	180
1882.	Holloway, Bertha and Oliver Burnett	181
1888.	Holloway, Ella May and Roger Evarts	218
1880.	Holloway, Henry M. and Libby DuMont	181
1877.	Holloway, Ida and David M. Jarrett	180
1873.	Holloway, Sam'l Eastburn and Sarah Hardcastle	180
1844.	Holloway, Thomas and Mary Ann Eastburn	134
1869.	Holloway, William H. and Ida Virginia Buzby	180
1850.	Hubley, Louisa Harriet and Edward Burd Peale	161

YEAR.		PAGE.
1882.	Hughes, Ann Bryan and Basil Manley	200
1885.	Hughes, Annette and Geo. Ringgold Kaercher	159
1880.	Hughes, Annie Smallwood and Harry Allen Lowe	201
1829.	Hughes, Benj'n Bartholomew and Mary Rambo	117
1858.	Hughes, Benj'n B., married 2d, Mary J. Brooke	117
1882.	Hughes, Bertram and Caroline Cordelia Love	202
1877.	Hughes, Catharine Dewees and Edmund M. Evans	158
1860.	Hughes, Charles Collin and Emily Pechin	157
1892.	Hughes, Charles Collin and Elizabeth Marple Wills	202
1881.	Hughes, Clara Stevenson and Walter Parker Williamson .	201
1884.	Hughes, Donnel, M. D., and Sarah Summers Burton	202
1875.	Hughes, Eliza McLin and Thomas Forbes	200
1884.	Hughes, Emily Irene and Wm. Harrison Yerkes	203
1890.	Hughes, Fanny Farquhar and Joseph Cloude Smith	202
1864.	Hughes, Frances and Guy E. Farquhar	159
1839.	Hughes, Francis Wade and Elizabeth Silliman	118
1786.	Hughes, Hannah Holstein and Rev. Slater Clay	100
1878.	Hughes, Hannah and Chas. Cottingham Calvert	160
1871.	Hughes, Henry Clay and Kate Longacre	158
1748.	Hughes, Hugh and Charity Smith	84
1829.	Hughes, Isaac Wayne, M. D., and Eliza A. McLin	117
1853.	Hughes, Isaac Wayne, 2d, and Annie M. Smallwood	133
1855.	Hughes, Isaac Wayne, M. D., and Alice E. Donnel	156
1878.	Hughes, Isaac Wayne, 2d, Emilie Baker	156
1862.	Hughes, Jane Augusta and Robert Carmer Hill	159
1859.	Hughes, Dr. James Bettner and Laura A. W. Bryan	153
1851.	Hughes, John Curtis Clay and Mrs. Emma R. Heebner	120
1738.	Hughes, John (Stamp Officer) and Sarah Jones	84
1767.	Hughes, John, Jr., and Margaret Paschall	84
1854.	Hughes, John and Jane Daves	153
1851.	Hughes, John J. and Hannah Brooke	156
1858.	Hughes, John Jarrett and Mary E. Clark	159
1889.	Hughes, John Robert and Sallie Nelson Harding	161
1884.	Hughes, Kathleen Cawthorne and Wm. Lightfoot Ross	201
1882.	Hughes, Louis Curtis and Charlotte Tritle	160
1872.	Hughes, Mary Ann and Hubert O. Blackfan	157
1874.	Hughes, Mary Elizabeth and Rev. Nathaniel Harding	160
1881.	Hughes, Mary Rambo and Winfield Scott Stacker	201
1864.	Hughes, Nathan Rambo and Amanda E. Stacker	159
1848.	Hughes, Nicholas Collin (Rev.) and Adaline Williams . .	120
1880.	Hughes, Nicholas Collin, Jr., and Martha Elizabeth Harding .	161
1783.	Hughes, Peter and Sarah Ann Ward	93
1801.	Hughes, Rachel and William Lukens Potts	86
1820.	Hughes, Rachel and Dr. Jacob Dewees	110
1765.	Hughes, Ruth and Lindsay Coates	84

HOLSTEIN FAMILY HISTORY. 285

YEAR.		PAGE.
1801.	Hughes, Sarah and David Rittenhouse	86
1836.	Hughes, Slator Clay and Susan Jarrett	117
1844.	Hughes, Theodore Jones and Caroline Fonville	120
1855.	Hughes, Theodore J. and Clara Filman Stevenson	154
1879.	Hurst, Margaret A. and John B. Sommers	182
1865.	Hurst, Jane and Robert W. Ballenger	212
1870.	Jolly, Elizabeth Ashton and Reuben D. Neff	190
1851.	Jolly, Mary Anna and Henry P. Rutter	140
1870.	Jolly, Mary Anna and Samuel W. Loomis	190
1850.	Jolly, Matthias Holstein and Anna Ashton Squire	140
1876.	Keir, Sarah Love and George A. McCracken	183
1880.	Knight, Blanche Eva and T. R. Vernon	184
1869.	Knight, Emily Jane and John R. Pugh	184
1879.	Knight, Grace Irene and Dr. L. L. Adams	184
1879.	Knight, Kate Gertrude and Harry T. Walter	184
1872.	Knight, Margaret Ann and George Frantz	184
1860.	Knight, Paul Gardiner and E. J. Gotwaltz	184
1873.	Knight, Samuel Coates and F. J. McBride	184
1877.	Knight, William Thomas and E. P. McDowell	208
1876.	Lichtenthaler, Annie Mary and Thomas P. Mann	169
1886.	Lichtenthaler, Henry Curtis (M. D.) and Annie Keeser	169
1886.	Lightner, Julia Jane and Willis A. Jolly	214
1854.	Lodge, Abel and Mary Magdalene DeHart	131
1885.	Love, Annette and J. Calvin Elder	185
1859.	Love, J. Holstein and Jane Love	137
1864.	Love, John Serson and Jane R. Harvey	137
1885.	Love, Lelia Ada and Joseph Chesnut	184
1851.	Love, Martha Jane and James McCafferty	137
1871.	Love, Rebecca and David F. Norris	137
1859.	Love, Sarah Ann and Robert Love	137
1869.	Mackey, Annie Hepburn and Dr. Joseph Hayes	168
1883.	Mackey, Mary Louise and Fr. Frank P. Ball	169
1872.	Maitland, Margaret M. and Wm. Caldwell	182
1881.	Morris, John Roberts and Nellie Woolston	194
1884.	Pollock, Ann Clay and Samuel M. Riley	168
1889.	Pollock, Emma and Charles Corss	168
1879.	Pollock, James Crawford and Mary Agnes Kelsey	168
1882.	Pollock, James and Mary Douglass Leisenring	170
1885.	Pollock, Juliet Campbell and Louis L. Hubley	170
1863.	Pollock, Louisa Ann and Richard Ely Clay	168
1861.	Pollock, Margaret Annan and Wm. Gould Meigs	170
1875.	Pollock, Mary Wilson and Edward Burd Hubley	170
1872.	Pollock, Sarah Margaret and Henry T. Harvey	168
1868.	Pollock, William Curtis and Ella M. Burr	168
1882.	Potts, Emily Frances and Edward Kneass Landis	171

YEAR.		PAGE.
1866.	Potts, Harriett and Wm. Potts Rockhill	162
1881.	Potts, Henry W. and Eleanor S. Powell	170
1862.	Potts, Julia H. and Samuel H Grey	163
1829.	Potts, Rachel Hughes and Francis S. Hubley	121
1820.	Potts, Robert Barnhill and Sarah Page	121
1837.	Potts, Thomas Isaac and Mary Frances Johnson	121
1837.	Potts, William Frances and Caroline Tryon	121
1840.	Rittenhouse, Charles Edwin and Sarah M Whittall	122
1885.	Rittenhouse, Charles Edwin and Grace Hubbell	166
1868.	Rittenhouse, Clementina Crawford and R. S. T. Cissel	165
1887.	Rittenhouse, David and Mary Tilghman	165
1854.	Rittenhouse, Elizabeth Scott and Wm. Henry Fitzhugh Gurley	164
1864.	Rittenhouse, Fannie and Thomas Hyde	166
1858.	Rittenhouse, Hannah Hughes and (Judge) Alexander Jordan	122
1858.	Rittenhouse, Henrietta W. and Capt. Thomas Wilson	164
1853.	Rittenhouse, Isobel L. and Jos. Harvey Nourse	164
1878.	Rittenhouse, James Hall and Ida R. Cole	165
1847.	Rittenhouse, John (Rev.) and Jane L. Simonton	122
1837.	Rittenhouse, Mary Elizabeth and A. B. Shuman	122
1868.	Rittenhouse, Mary W. and Leonard Gunnel	166
1874.	Rittenhouse, Samuel White and Caroline Lockwood	166
1866.	Roberts, Eliza Ann and David Connard	146
1884.	Roberts, George Holstein and Clara Fries	147
1888.	Roberts, George Holstein, 2d, and Mrs. Jennie Bowman	147
1882.	Roberts, Jonathan John and Sarah Louisa Beidler	147
1869.	Roberts, Matthew and Clara Connard	146
1866.	Roberts, Sarah Louisa and William Wills	146
1876.	Roberts, William Holstein and Laura Massey	147
1886.	Shainline, Ann Sophia and Daniel S. Middleton	192
1850.	Shainline, DeWitt Clinton and Catharine Davis	144
1840.	Shainline, Elizabeth Holstein and George W. Bishing	142
1892.	Shainline, Florence Ella and Harvey H. Smith	193
1864.	Shainline, George Holstein and Sarah Forsythe	144
1866.	Shainline, Henry Harrison and Abbie S DeHaven	144
1882.	Shainline, William Henry and Caddie Ganer	192
1866.	Shainline, William Holstein and Mary Emily Potter	144
1837.	Smith, Charles Moore and Mrs. Rebecca Moore Grant	129
1849.	Smith, Charles Moore, 2d, and Adaline O'Connor	129
1873.	Smith, Henderson Coates and Flora C. Allison	172
1876.	Smylie, Ellen and Alfred Morris Herkness	173
1883.	Smylie, Mary Elizabeth and Frank Dallett	173
1870.	Smylie, Matthias Coates and Virginia Maria Peters	173
1882.	Smylie, Robert Sayres and Virginia Wright Kiehl	173
1844.	Smylie, William Duff and Sarah Alice Keiser	173
1858.	Thomas, Anna Elizabeth and Nathan Brooke	145

YEAR.		PAGE.
1867.	Thomas, Rebecca Brooke and Geo. Hamilton Colket	146
1874.	Thomas, Mary Ames and Hunter Brooke	146
1883.	Travis, Robert Williams and Mary Singleton	215
1882.	White, Christiana Bunting and Charles L. Bams	179
1889.	White, Emily Louisa and Dr. E. H. Neall	179
1850.	Williams, Amelia A. and David Sterrett Lightner	176
1873.	Williams, Amelia A., 2d, and Casper Frederick Goodyear	176
1875.	Williams, Joseph Atlee and Mrs. Mary Reed, nee Goodyear	177
1800.	Williams, Priscilla Martin and Geo. Thompson Travis	176
1889.	Williams, Robert Lewis and Mary Emma Wileman	177
1804.	Williams, Susan Miles and Wm. Martin Travis	176
1862.	Wills, Elizabeth Marple and Charles Collin Hughes	196
1890.	Wills, Susan Roberts and Harry Stoner Welch	195
1887.	Wilson, Henrietta Rittenhouse and Lt. David Hall Boughton	207
1882.	Wilson, Mary D. and Warren Switzler	207

MARRIAGES WITHOUT DATES.

Atlee, Hugh DeHaven and second wife, Lizzie Cary
Atlee, John Stewart and second wife, Clara Funk
Atlee, Joseph Augustus and Mamie Harper
Blackiston, Slator Clay (Rev) and Margaret Monroe
Brandt, Catharine and David Walton
Brandt, John and Ann Eliza Helms
Brandt, Maria and John Lincoln
McCafferty, James and Eva Thompson
McCafferty, John Andrew and Emma Pames
McCafferty, Robert and Ellie Elliott
Cissel, Mary C. and Samuel Berry
Coates, Caroline P. and Abner Brown
Coates, Hannah and John Young
Coates, John and Martha Pugh
Coates, Matthias and Sophia Hayman
Coates, Rachel and Nathaniel Smith
Coates, Rebecca and Nathaniel Henderson
Coates, Ruth and William Elliott
Coates, Sarah and Ebeneezer Rambo
Coates, Sarah and Charles Moore
Coates, Sarah and Henry Bush
McCurdy, Adelaide and Charles Hank
McCurdy, Herbert and Minerva Davis
Dickerson, Edward Nicoll and Mary C. Nystrom
Dickerson, John Henry and Maria Kirby
Dickerson, Louise Adele and Charles W. Gould
Dickerson, Maria E. and Nathaniel Coles
Dickerson, Mary and John M. Gould
Drew, George and Ada Bittings
Drew, Laura J. and Charles Caldwell
Gurley, Ralph R. and Ella A. Gibbon
Gurley, William Fitzhugh and Elizabeth S. Buckey
DeHart, Mary Margaret and Abel Lodge
DeHaven, Alexander and Rebecca Virginia Townsend
DeHaven, Atlee Augustus and Anna Courtney
DeHaven, Augustus Juliana and Richard Henry Ranson
DeHaven, William Niell and Miss Wamsley
DeHaven, William Niell, 2d, and Miss Dodge
Holstein, Andrew and Mary Jones

HOLSTEIN FAMILY HISTORY. 289

	PAGE
Holstein, Andrew and Miss Patterson	108
Holstein, Catharine B. and John DeHart	109
Holstein, Elizabeth and Samuel Love	108
Holstein, John and Elizabeth	17
Holstein, John Jonse and Elizabeth Williamson	107
Holstein, Mary and Septimus Coates	31
Holstein, Mary Magdalena and Abel Lodge	109
Holstein, Matthias and Magdalena Hulings	18
Holstein, Matthias (son of John) and Mary Jonse	31
Holstein, Matthias (son of Frederick) and Jane Johnston	32
Holstein, Peter and Abigal Jones	23
Holstein, Peter Jones and Hannah Leech	109
Holstein, Rachel Moore and Thomas Mayberry Jolly	109
Holstein, Rebecca and Evan Davis	107
Holstein, Samuel and Mary Henderson	108
Holstein, Sarah and George Brandt	109
Holstein, Susanna Jonse and Charles Vaugn	107
Holstein, William Sims and Phœbe Urian	185
Hoopes, Lydia and William Davidson	187
Hoopes, Pratt and Rebecca	187
Hoopes, Thomas L. M. and Mary Bongardner	187
Hoopes, Walker J. and Miss Huber	187
Hurley, Edward Bard and Mary Louisa Pollock	164
Hughes, Catharine and Mr. Pritner	85
Hughes, Charles and Ann Dixon	93
Hughes, Charles Hugh and Ann Lawton	94
Hughes, Dixon G. and Mary L. Storer	95
Hughes, Hannah and Francis Wade	48
Hughes, Hugh and Laura Bostwick	94
Hughes, James Miles and Maria Bailey	93
Hughes, Jasper Ward and Catharine Conely	94
Hughes, John and Hannah Bartholomew	44
Hughes, Peter and Naomi Gould	93
Hughes, Ruth and David Jones	45
Hughes, Sarah and Peter DeHaven	84
Hughes, Sarah and Capt. John Stotesbury	93
Hughes, Sarah Ann and Dr. Nathan Farnsworth	93
Hughes, Susan and William Gamble	93
Hughes, William M. and Annie Gould	95
Hull, Joseph and Elizabeth Mahaffey	166
Hull, William R. and Jerusha Willard	165
Hunter, Benjamin Parkinson and Mary Dearborn	186
Hunter, Catharine Ann and Jesse Murray	185
Hunter, James Blake and Annie Johnson	186
Hunter, John Carson and Maggie Littlefield	185

	PAGE.
Hunter, John Carson, 2d, and Emma Johnson	185
Hunter, Rachel Pocohontas and James Benjamin Flinn	185
Hyde, Emily Rowland and Barry Buckley	207
Hyde, Thomas and Nellie Augur	207
Jones, Harriet and Benjamin Evans	122
Jones, Theodore and Laura Rutter	122
Lodge, Abel and Mary Margaret DeHart	139
Lodge, Abel and Anna Hall	188
Lodge, Catharine and Azariah Bane	139
Lodge, Ella and Andrew Ford	188
Lodge, Elizabeth and John Hoopes	139
Lodge, Elizabeth and Frank Baldwin	188
Lodge, Emmor and Hannah Mary Eachus	187
Lodge, Frank and Lizzie Ewe	188
Lodge, Henry and Elizabeth McClellan	139
Lodge, Ida and Homer E. Hoopes	188
Lodge, John and Caroline Green	139
Lodge, Matilda E. and William Eachus	187
Lodge, Mary M. and Alexander Crozier	139
Lodge, Sallie and George Griswold	188
Lodge, Thomas and Hettie Hetson	188
Lodge, Walter and Annie Morgan	188
Makemson, Catharine and Benjamin Yerkes	138
Makemson, George and Margaret Fullerton	138
Makemson, Henry and Susan Myers	138
Makemson, Mary and Jonathan Urid	138
Makemson, Peter and Hannah Fadden	138
Makemson, William and Margaret Simpson	138
Maitland, Martha and D. Kunkle	182
Potts, Charles Clay and Mary Joy Ridgway	121
Potts, Charles W. Tryon and Adelaide Kelly	163
Potts, Ellen and Jacob M. Armbruster	163
Potts, Horace Turley and Annie O'Harra	163
Potts, Kate B. and Capt. Charles Hobbs	163
Pritner, Caroline and Dr. John T. Huddleson	87
Pritner, Elizabeth and Benjamin Bartholomew	86
Pritner, Isaac Hughes and Rebecca Conard	87
Pritner, Rebecca and John A. Colwell	87
Rambo, William and Mary Ann Supplee	134
Ransom, Joseph Morgan and Miss Smith	174
Rittenhouse, Benj. Franklin and Isobel Laurie	122
Rittenhouse, Benj. Franklin, 2d, and Henrietta Waring Davidson	122
Rittenhouse, Benj. Franklin and Elizabeth Shapter	165
Rittenhouse, Charles Edwin and Helen S. Goode	165
Rittenhouse, Emily Josepha and Rev. David Hull	122

	PAGE
Rittenhouse, James Delesier and Dolores Casillas	105
Rittenhouse, Martha L. and Joshua Williams	109
Rittenhouse, Mary D. and Rev. A. Miller Woods	104
Rittenhouse, Mary E. and D. D. Lambie	100
Roberts, Magdalena and Edward Lane	104
Smith, Collin Coates and Emma Kennedy	172
Stotesbury, Sydney Maria and Philemon Dickerson	93
Urol, Elizabeth and Robert Egner	180
Urol, Susanna and William Bell	180
Wach, George and Sophia De Pathion	123
Williams, Ellen Harriet and Claudius B. Hess	170

GENERAL INDEX.

	PAGE
Adams, Clara Jessup	217
Adams, Douglass	217
Adams, Emma H	217
Adams, S. Francis	217
Adams, Thomas Birdsall	219
Adams, William Knight	219
Allee, George B.	187
Von Alten, Adelaide Augusta Nina Edwina	213
Von Alten, Fomgard Stella	214
Amies, Charles Thompson	145
Amies, Elizabeth Holstein	145
Amies, Emily Thomas	145
Amies, Joseph Washington	145
Armbruster, Carrie Tryou	209
Armstrong, Lillie Etta	198
Armstrong, William A., 3d	198
Armstrong, Wayne Holstein	198
Atlee, Emma Maria	132
Atlee, Eva	216
Atlee, Hugh DeHaven	177
Atlee, Jane Amelia	177
Atlee, John Stewart	177
Atlee, Joseph Augustus	177
Atlee, Julianna DeHaven	131
Atlee, Lizzie	216
Atlee, Mary Emma	177
Atlee, Margaret Gray	216
Atlee, Mary Black	216
Atlee, Samuel John	132
Atlee, Stewart Lee	216
Atlee, Thomas James	177
Bache, Edith	216
Bains, Charles	217
Bains, Helen White	217
Bains, Otis Tiffany	217
Ball, Mary Hepburn	210
Ballenger, Clinton Summerfield	221
Ballenger, Franklin Lee	221
Ballenger, Jane Parkinson	221
Ballenger, Nannie Hunter	221

	PAGE
Ballenger, Peyton Rowe	221
Bane, Abel	187
Bane, Elton	187
Bane, Hannah	187
Bane, Louis	187
Bane, Mary	187
Bartleson, Hilary	109
Bishing, Anna Holstein	192
Bishing, Maria Streeper	192
Bishing, William Holstein	192
Bishing, Winfield Scott	192
Blackiston, Alice Medford	209
Blackiston, Anne	167
Blackiston, Anne J.	209
Blackiston, Clara	167
Blackiston, Emma	167
Blackiston, Helen	209
Blackiston, Helen Hepburn	204
Blackiston, Henry Curtis	167
Blackiston, Henry Curtis	209
Blackiston, Josephine	167
Blackiston, Josephine	209
Blackiston, Lizzie	167
Blackiston, Martha M.	209
Blackiston, McCall	204
Blackiston, Slater Clay	209
Blackiston, Martha M.	209
Blackiston, Mary Eugenia	167
Blackiston, McCall	209
Blackiston, Samuel Hepburn	167
Blackiston, Slator Clay	167
Blackiston, Slator Clay	209
Boughton, George Wilson	227
Boyd, David Thompson	179
Boyd, Etheldreda Holstein	179
Boyd, Harold DeHaven	179
Boyd Helen	179
Brandt, Anne	222
Brandt, Catharine	138
Brandt, Charles	187
Brandt, Daniel	222

	PAGE.		PAGE.
Brandt, Ella	187	McCafferty, William	184
Brandt, Frances	222	Calvert, Adaline	204
Brandt, Frank	187	Calvert, Charles Cottingham	204
Brandt, George	187	Calvert, Lalla	204
Brandt, George	222	Calvert, Nicholas Collin Hughes	204
Brandt, Georgianna	138	Calvert, Zoe Ella	204
Brandt, Hannah	187	Calvert, Zoe Frost	204
Brandt, Henry	187	Caldwell, Anna Lillian	220
Brandt, Henry	222	Caldwell, Barton	220
Brandt, Ida	222	Caldwell, H. W.	220
Brandt, Ida	222	Caldwell, Mackey	213
Brandt, John	138	Caldwell, Mary Coates	219
Brandt, John	221	Caldwell, Thomas	220
Brandt, Kate	222	Campbell, Alice Colwell	190
Brandt, Maria	138	Campbell, Elizabeth Anna	190
Brandt, Mary	138	Campbell, Holstein Primer	190
Brandt, Mary	187	Von Campe, Alice Hedwig-Clara Maria	214
Brandt, Mary	222		
Brandt, Sarah	187	Von Campe, Edwin Gothard-Edmund Hans	214
Brandt, Sarah	221		
Brandt, Sarah	222	Von Campe, Hans Uster Bigelow	214
Brandt, William	187	Von Campe, Otto Joseph Carl Herman	214
Bright, Holstein DeHaven	217		
Bright, Mary DeHaven	217	Caner, Harrison Koons, Jr	225
Brooke, Emily Thomas	195	Castor, Levi Coates	212
Brooke, Gertrude Chapman	224	Castor, Lewis David	212
Brooke, Helen	195	Castor, Mary Coates	212
Brooke, Hugh Jones	195	Chesnut, Sarah Edith	220
Brooke, Hunter	195	Cissel, Atkinson	207
Brooke, Ida Lewis	224	Cissel, Clementina S.	207
Brooke, Ida Longmire	134	Cissel, Helen M.	207
Brooke, Josephine Atmore	224	Cissel, Henrietta D.	207
Brooke, Mary Thomas	195	Cissel, Katharine B.	207
Brooke, William Thomas	194	Cissel, Margaret S.	207
Brown, Anna	182	Cissel, Mary C.	207
Brown, Annie Louisa	109	Clay, Ann	101
Brown, Gertrude Mary	199	Clay, Ann	128
Brown, Mary Emily	182	Clay, Annie A.	171
Brown, Samuel Curtis	109	Clay, Charles Holstein	103
Bryan, Guy	217	Clay, Charles H.	171
Bryan, Malcolm Guy	217	Clay, Clara Isabel	171
Burnett, Den Silas	218	Clay, Ellen Lane	129
Bush, Adelia A.	181	Clay, Emily	128
Bush, Helen M.	181	Clay, George	102
Bush, Samuel Holstein	181	Clay, Geo. Bolton Lownes	128
McCafferty, Ethel	220	Clay, George Henry	129
McCafferty, Grace Bell	220	Clay, Hannah Maria	129
McCafferty, James	184	Clay, Harriet P.	128
McCafferty, John Andrew	184	Clay, Henry	171
McCafferty, Mabel Grey	220	Clay, Jehu Curtis	102
McCafferty, Martha Ellen	184	Clay, Julia Frances	128
McCafferty, May Jane	184	Clay, Lillie	171
McCafferty, Mary Love	220	Clay, Mary Evans	129
McCafferty, Nannie Bell	184	Clay, Richard Edy	128
McCafferty, Robert	184	Clay, Richard Edy, Jr	210
McCafferty, Sarah Ann	184	Coates, Ann	106

HOLSTEIN FAMILY HISTORY. 295

	PAGE.		PAGE.
Coates, Ann E.	135	Colket, Emily Thomas	195
Coates, Ann Hayman	130	Colket, George Hamilton	195
Coates, Annie Hayman	174	Colket, Mary Walker	195
Coates, Aaron York	172	Colket, Tristram Colfin	195
Coates, Betsy	104	Connard, Catharine Styer	195
Coates, Caroline P.	135	Connard, Clara Virginia	195
Coates, Charles	130	Connard, Elizabeth Styer	195
Coates, Charles	173	Connard, Laura Roberts	195
Coates, Collin	213	Connard, Mary Schlater	195
Coates, Davis Pugh	134	Connard, Reese	195
Coates, Emma	104	Connard, Sarah Louisa	195
Coates, Frank Raymond	212	Connard, Susan Holstein	195
Coates, Hannah	104	Craft, Andrew	220
Coates, Hannah	109	Crozier, Helen	188
Coates, Henry	134	Crozier, Susanna	188
Coates, Jane	135	McCurdy, Adelaide	182
Coates, Joanna Potts	180	McCurdy, Havilah J.	182
Coates, John	109	McCurdy, Herbert	182
Coates, John	134	Davidson, Elizabeth Hoopes	223
Coates, John Hughes	130	Davidson, Sidney Hoopes	223
Coates, Katie Louisa	180	Dewees, Alfred Rollin	199
Coates, Levi Pawling	129	Dewees, Catharine Alliene	199
Coates, Levi Pawling	212	Dewees, Emma Loeser	198
Coates, Lindsay, Jr.	85	Dewees, Ethel Hughes	198
Coates, Lindsay	129	Dewees, Eva Amelia	146
Coates, Louisa	134	Dewees, Frances Farquhar	199
Coates, Magdalena	106	Dewees, Francis Percival	149
Coates, Mary	85	Dewees, George Holstein	146
Coates, Mary Moore	130	Dewees, Isaac Holstein	146
Coates, Mary Mumford	174	Dewees, James Collin	199
Coates, Mary Holstein	135	Dewees, James Collin	151
Coates, Margaret	135	Dewees, John Hughes	148
Coates, Martha Louisa	180	Dewees, Lennis	100
Coates, Matilda P.	135	Dewees, Louis Loeser	198
Coates, Matthew Henderson	130	Dewees, Louisa Fisks	199
Coates, Matthew Henderson	173	Dewees, Mary Catharine	148
Coates, Matthias	103	Dewees, Mary Hughes	146
Coates, Matthias	172	Dewees, Percival	198
Coates, N. Collin	130	Dewees, Phœbe James	199
Rachel	103	Dewees, Rachel Hughes	199
Rebecca	103	Dewees, Theodore John	199
Roland	212	Dewees, Theodore Lyng	151
Ruth	85	Dewees, William Henry	151
Coates, Sarah	85	Dewees, William Holstein	130
Coates, Sarah	109	Dickerson, Edward Nicoll	95
Coates, Sarah	135	Dickerson, John Henry	94
Coates, Samuel	135	Dickerson, Louisa Adele	95
Coates, Samuel Holstein	107	Dickerson, Maria P.	94
Coates, Septimus	135	Dickerson, Mary	94
Coates, Sherman	180	Dickerson, Mary Caroline	95
Coates, Slator Clay	107	Dickerson, Philemon	94
Coates, Sophia Louisa	174	Dickerson, Philemon	94
Coates, Susan	135	Dickerson, Susan S.	94
Coates, Susan Yerkes	172	Dickerson, Theodore	94
Coates, William Hayman	129	McDowell, Branton Holstein	191
Coates, William Holstein	135	McDowell, Charles Hamilton	191

	PAGE.		PAGE.
McDowell, Constance	191	Gurley, George Hull	206
Drew, Adelaide	182	Gurley, Ralph R.	206
Drew, George	182	Gurley, Wm. Fitzhugh	206
Drew, Laura J.	182	Hampton, Emma	178
Drew, Samuel	182	Hampton, Sophia M.	178
Drew, Wm. Bridenbaugh	182	Hampton, William Henry	178
Drew, William Corson	182	Hank, Ida	219
Eachus, George	223	Hank, Pearl Adelaide	219
Eachus, Walter	223	Harding, Adelaide Williams	204
Elder, Robert Brown	220	Harding, Collin Hughes	204
Ellis, Alice Holstein	197	Harding, Frederick Harriman	204
Ellis, William Holstein	198	Harding, Martha	204
Ellwood, Alexander Donalson	183	Harding, Mary Elizabeth	204
Ellwood, Thomas	183	Harding, Nathaniel	204
Evans, Benjamin Hughes	203	Harding, Robert	204
Evans, Ellen	164	Harding, William Blount	204
Evans, Eva Frances	171	DeHart, Christiana G.	139
Evans, Harriet	164	DeHart, Jane Gaul	139
Evans, Mary Hughes	203	DeHart, Mary Margaret	139
Evans, Ray Wright	203	DeHart, Rachel	139
Evarts, Ida May	227	DeHart, William Henry	139
Farquhar, Annette	203	Harvey, Henry Thomas	210
Farquhar, Elizabeth Hughes	203	Harvey, James Pollock	210
Farquhar, Francis Hughes	203	Harvey, John B. N.	188
Farquhar, George Wildman	203	Harvey, Mary Margaret	188
Farquhar, Marion Amelia	203	Harvey, Newman	188
Farquhar, Otto Edward	203	Harvey, Sallie Hepburn	210
Farnsworth, Monroe	94	DeHaven, Alexander Henry	133
Farnsworth, Nathan Hughes	94	DeHaven, Amelia	105
Forbes, Bessie	225	DeHaven, Anna	174
Forbes, Edward Ripley	225	DeHaven, Atlee Augustus	130
Forbes, Frank Andrew	225	DeHaven, Augusta	174
Forbes, Gifford Thomas	225	DeHaven, Augusta Julianna	131
Forbes, Randolph Hughes	225	DeHaven, Augusta Louisa	175
Forbes, Thomas Gifford	225	DeHaven, Caleb	134
Frantz, Jennie Coates	219	DeHaven, Charles Elliott	132
Furst, J. Hogan	210	DeHaven, Charles Elliott	217
Furst, Richard Clay	210	DeHaven, Charles Elliott	178
Gamble, Ruth Hughes	94	DeHaven, Charles Bunting	133
Goodyear, Helen Louisa	215	DeHaven, Clara Brinton	179
Goodyear, Joseph Atlee	214	DeHaven, Edwin Augustus	175
Goodyear, Margaret Priscilla	215	DeHaven, Emma C.	132
Goodyear, Robert Conrad	214	DeHaven, Emma	178
Gould, Ann Eliza	94	DeHaven, Emma M.	105
Gould, Catharine Holsman	94	DeHaven, George Clay	134
Gould, Sydney Maria	94	DeHaven, George Lewis	174
Grey, Alice Croasdale	206	DeHaven, Harriet	105
Grey, Charles Phillip	206	DeHaven, Henry	174
Grey, Ethel	206	DeHaven, Holstein	105
Grey, Julia Ridgway	206	DeHaven, Holstein	178
Grey, Mary Joy	206	DeHaven, Holstein Joseph Atlee	175
Groves, Edward Brandt	222	DeHaven, Hugh	85
Groves, Ida Brandt	222	DeHaven, Hugh	105
Groves, William Brandt	222	DeHaven, Hugh	132
Gunnel, Leonard	208	DeHaven, Hugh	133
Gurley, Franklin R.	206	DeHaven, Hugh Hill	179

	PAGE.		PAGE.
DeHaven, Jane Cleaver	178	Herkness, Sidney	213
DeHaven, John	132	Herkness, Walter Lindsay	213
DeHaven, John White	134	Herkness, Wayne	213
DeHaven, Joseph	134	Hess, Agnes Amelia	215
DeHaven, Joseph	174	Hess, Joseph Atlee	215
DeHaven, Josephine Amelia	175	Hess, Julia Elizabeth	215
DeHaven, Joseph Edwin	131	Hess, Lewis Claudius	216
DeHaven, Julianna	105	Hess, Martha Lewis	215
DeHaven, Lindsay Coates	105	Hess, Sarah Bell	215
DeHaven, Maria	105	Hess, Susan Rebecca	215
DeHaven, Maria S.	178	Hilton, Edwin Norris	211
DeHaven, Mary	105	Hilton, Norris Hepburn	211
DeHaven, Mary	174	Holds, Horace Potts	205
DeHaven, Mary Anna	178	Holstein, Abraham	108
DeHaven, Mary Florence	179	Holstein, Alexander	184
DeHaven, Neill Montgomery	174	Holstein, Alice	192
DeHaven, Peter	105	Holstein, Amy	23
DeHaven, Sallie Letitia	134	Holstein, Ann	107
DeHaven, Samuel John	131	Holstein, Ann	109
DeHaven, Samuel White	133	Holstein, Ann Sophia	110
DeHaven, Sarah	105	Holstein, Anna	192
DeHaven, Sarah Carman	178	Holstein, Annabell	136
DeHaven, Sarah Cole	179	Holstein, Anna Elizabeth	141
DeHaven, Sarah Elizabeth	175	Holstein, Anna Fenner	221
DeHaven, Sarah Rawle	130	Holstein, Anna Margaret	183
DeHaven, Sophia M.	178	Holstein, Andrew	17
DeHaven, Susannah Shoder	133	Holstein, Andrew	108
DeHaven, Wallace Henderson	217	Holstein, Andrew	13
DeHaven, Walter Townsend	179	Holstein, Andrew	17
DeHaven, William Niell	131	Holstein, Andrew Johnston	139
Hayes, E. N. Mackey	210	Holstein, Branton	110
Hayes, William Bruce	210	Holstein, Branton	192
Henderson, Branton Holstein	139	Holstein, Brichard	18
Henderson, Elizabeth Branton	189	Holstein, Brita	17
Henderson, Florence	223	Holstein, Catharine	13
Henderson, Jane	189	Holstein, Catharine	15
Henderson, John	189	Holstein, Catharine B.	109
Henderson, Matthias Holstein	189	Holstein, Charles	42
Henderson, Samuel Holstein	139	Holstein, Charles	110
Hendrixon, William	177	Holstein, Charles Elliott	147
Hepburn, Amy Louisa	210	Holstein, Christiana	107
Hepburn, Anna Bayard	210	Holstein, Christiana	108
Hepburn, Emma	127	Holstein, Christiany	33
Hepburn, Hannah Maria	123	Holstein, Constance	142
Hepburn, James Curtis	123	Holstein, Delora	17
Hepburn, Jane	127	Holstein, Earl R.	220
Hepburn, Louisa Harriet	127	Holstein, Edith Lawrence	190
Hepburn, Mary	127	Holstein, Eliza	109
Hepburn, Samuel Boyd	168	Holstein, Eliza Ann	221
Hepburn, Samuel Dyer	167	Holstein, Eliza J.	138
Hepburn, Sarah Ann	125	Holstein, Elizabeth	18
Hepburn, Slator Clay	127	Holstein, Elizabeth	108
Herkness, Alfred Morris	213	Holstein, Elizabeth	138
Herkness, Gilbert	213	Holstein, Elizabeth Branton	109
Herkness, John Smylie	213	Holstein, Elizabeth Branton	141
Herkness, Malcolm	213		

Holstein, Elizabeth Branton	100
Holstein, Elizabeth Brookfield	147
Holstein, Elizabeth Matson	107
Holstein, Elizabeth Mary	183
Holstein, Elizabeth Wayne	111
Holstein, Ella	147
Holstein, Ellen Douglass	135
Holstein, Ellwood Harvey	147
Holstein, Emma Gertrude	221
Holstein, Emily Wilson	112
Holstein, Frances Jones	141
Holstein, Frederick	10
Holstein, Frederick	17
Holstein, Frederick	18
Holstein, Frederick	108
Holstein, Frederick	13
Holstein, Frederick Riter	221
Holstein, George Meade	147
Holstein, George Washington	42
Holstein, George Washington	115
Holstein, George Washington	221
Holstein, George Wolf	140
Holstein, Gustavus Adolphus	113
Holstein, Hannah	27
Holstein, Hannah	107
Holstein, Hannah	185
Holstein, Henry	13
Holstein, Henry Kochersperger	221
Holstein, Isaac	32
Holstein, Isaac Wayne	110
Holstein, James	136
Holstein, James Bartman	109
Holstein, Jane	130
Holstein, Jane	184
Holstein, Jane Henderson	141
Holstein, Jemima	184
Holstein, Jeremiah	31
Holstein, Jesse	192
Holstein, John	17
Holstein, John	108
Holstein, John	185
Holstein, John	221
Holstein, John Jones	182
Holstein, John Jonse	107
Holstein, John Parkinson	138
Holstein, Joseph	137
Holstein, Josephine Cora	140
Holstein, Josephine Prichett	190
Holstein, Lawrence	14
Holstein, Lawrence	17
Holstein, Lawrence Montgomery	141
Holstein, Lavinia	184
Holstein, Linnaeus	136
Holstein, Louisa Brooke	113
Holstein, Louis Ducardree	136
Holstein, Louis Kochersperger	221
Holstein, Magdalena	23
Holstein, Magdalena Jones	18
Holstein, Margaret	138
Holstein, Margaret	136
Holstein, Martha	23
Holstein, Mary	17
Holstein, Mary	17
Holstein, Mary	37
Holstein, Mary	107
Holstein, Mary	108
Holstein, Mary	108
Holstein, Mary	136
Holstein, Mary Ann Jones	136
Holstein, Mary Alice	148
Holstein, Mary Atlee	112
Holstein, Mary Magdalena	109
Holstein, Matts	9
Holstein, Matthias	13
Holstein, Matthias	17
Holstein, Matthias	17
Holstein, Matthias	18
Holstein, Matthias	31
Holstein, Matthias	32
Holstein, Matthias	39
Holstein, Matthias	110
Holstein, Matthias	141
Holstein, Matthias	141
Holstein, Melinda	183
Holstein, Mina A.	220
Holstein, Nathan B.	109
Holstein, Nicholas Collin	107
Holstein, Peter	13
Holstein, Peter	23
Holstein, Peter Blake	138
Holstein, Peter Jones	32
Holstein, Peter Jones	109
Holstein, Peter Jonse	32
Holstein, Peter Jonse	107
Holstein, Rachel	27
Holstein, Rachel	107
Holstein, Rachel Moore	109
Holstein, Rachel Moore	111
Holstein, Ralph	192
Holstein, Rebecca	28
Holstein, Rebecca	107
Holstein, Rebecca	107
Holstein, Rebecca Ellen	183
Holstein, Robert	136
Holstein, Robert	183
Holstein, Ruth C.	183
Holstein, Sarah	17
Holstein, Sarah	29
Holstein, Sarah	108
Holstein, Sarah	109
Holstein, Sarah	184
Holstein, Sarah Eastburn	141

HOLSTEIN FAMILY HISTORY.   299

	PAGE		PAGE
Holstein, Sadie B.	220	Hubley, Jennette Schuyler	205
Holstein, Samuel	24	Hubley, Jennette Schuyler	211
Holstein, Samuel	105	Hubley, Julia Harriet	164
Holstein, Samuel	119	Hubley, Louisa Harriet	164
Holstein, Samuel	184	Hubley, Mary Louisa	205
Holstein, Silas	184	Hubley, Mary Louisa	211
Holstein, Stephanus	23	Hubley, William Potts	164
Holstein, Susan	115	Hughes, Adaline Wiliams	205
Holstein, Susanna	17	Hughes, Alice Donnel	220
Holstein, Susanna Jouse	107	Hughes, Ann C.	199
Holstein, William	44	Hughes, Ann Bryan	200
Holstein, William Blake	221	Hughes, Anna Brooke	202
Holstein, Will C.	230	Hughes, Annette	159
Holstein, William Hallowell	148	Hughes, Annie M.	159
Holstein, William Hayman	112	Hughes, Annie Smallwood	201
Holstein, William Simes	185	Hughes, A. W. Sidney	93
Holstein, William Simes	221	Hughes, Benjamin Bartholomew	117
Holloway, Anna Elizabeth	180	Hughes, Benjamin Bartholomew	202
Holloway, Anna Mary	180	Hughes, Benjamin B., 2d	202
Holloway, Anna Mary	218	Hughes, Benjamin Francis	100
Holloway, Bertha	181	Hughes, Benjamin Raymond	202
Holloway, Egbert Benson Buzby	218	Hughes, Bertram	202
Holloway, Ella May	218	Hughes, Bertram	220
Holloway, Elizabeth H.	218	Hughes, Burton Donnel	226
Holloway, Frank Eastburn	218	Hughes, Caroline Virginia	204
Holloway, George W.	181	Hughes, Catharine	85
Holloway, Hannah Ella	150	Hughes, Catharine Dewees	158
Holloway, Harry Pawling	218	Hughes, Catharine Louise	65
Holloway, Henry M.	181	Hughes, Catharine L.	95
Holloway, Ida	180	Hughes, Charles	93
Holloway, James Garfield	218	Hughes, Charles Collin	157
Holloway, Mabel	218	Hughes, Charles Collin	202
Holloway, Malvina Richards	218	Hughes, Charles Hugh	94
Holloway, Samuel Eastburn	180	Hughes, Charles M.	95
Holloway, Septimus	134	Hughes, Charles Wood	95
Holloway, Thomas	218	Hughes, Charity	93
Holloway, Thomas H.	218	Hughes, Clara Stevenson	201
Holloway, Walter Buzby	218	Hughes, Collins	201
Hoopes, Edith Bomgardener	222	Hughes, Cordelia Nass	201
Hoopes, Ellis S.	187	Hughes, David Porter	202
Hoopes, John	222	Hughes, Dixon G.	95
Hoopes, Lydia	187	Hughes, Donnel	202
Hoopes, Mary	222	Hughes, Edward S.	159
Hoopes, Pratt	187	Hughes, Edward Hall	160
Hoopes, Thomas J. M.	187	Hughes, Eliza A.	199
Hoopes, Walker Y.	187	Hughes, Eliza Knox	200
Howard, Charles	222	Hughes, Elizabeth G.	199
Howard, Gertrude	222	Hughes, Eliza McLin	203
Howard, Harrison	222	Hughes, Emma Augusta	95
Howard, John	222	Hughes, Emma Augusta	95
Howard, Joseph	222	Hughes, Emily Irene	203
Howard, Serena	222	Hughes, Ethel	200
Hubley, Anna Elizabeth	161	Hughes, Fanny Farquhar	202
Hubley, Edward Burd	161	Hughes, Frances	159
Hubley, Francis Curtis	205	Hughes, Francis Wade	117
Hubley, Francis Curtis	211	Hughes, Francis Wade	159

300   HOLSTEIN FAMILY HISTORY.

	PAGE
Hughes, Francis Wade	159
Hughes, Francis Wade	226
Hughes, Frank Stacker	203
Hughes, George Stevenson	201
Hughes, Hannah	45
Hughes, Hannah	85
Hughes, Hannah	153
Hughes, Hannah	160
Hughes, Hannah	158
Hughes, Harriette M	95
Hughes, Harriette M	94
Hughes, Harriet M	95
Hughes, Helen May	160
Hughes, Harriet M	94
Hughes, Henry Clay	157
Hughes, Henry Warden	95
Hughes, Hugh	70
Hughes, Hugh	84
Hughes, Hugh	84
Hughes, Hugh	93
Hughes, Hugh	200
Hughes, Hugh	47
Hughes, Isaac	84
Hughes, Isaac Wayne	117
Hughes, Isaac Wayne	156
Hughes, Isaac Wayne	156
Hughes, Isaac Wayne	159
Hughes, Isaac Wayne	161
Hughes, Isaac Wayne	199
Hughes, Isaac Wayne	200
Hughes, Israel Harding	205
Hughes, James	85
Hughes, James Betmor	153
Hughes, James Bryan	200
Hughes, James Miles	93
Hughes, Jane	84
Hughes, Jane Augusta	159
Hughes, Jane Daves	199
Hughes, Jasper W	95
Hughes, Jasper Ward	94
Hughes, John Curtis Clay	120
Hughes, John	44
Hughes, John	84
Hughes, John, Jr	84
Hughes, John	86
Hughes, John	152
Hughes, John Daves	199
Hughes, John Hunter	201
Hughes, John Jarrett	159
Hughes, John Jones	156
Hughes, John Lamb	93
Hughes, John Roberts	160
Hughes, Julia Diefendorf	202
Hughes, Julia Washington	200
Hughes, Kathleen Cawthorne	201
Hughes, Laura	200
Hughes, Louis Curtis	160
Hughes, Lucretia Nash	204
Hughes, Lucy	159
Hughes, Mabel	200
Hughes, Mary Ada	95
Hughes, Mary Ann	157
Hughes, Mary Alice	199
Hughes, Mary Elizabeth	160
Hughes, Mary Rambo	201
Hughes, Nathan Brooke	202
Hughes, Nathan Rambo	156
Hughes, Nicholas Collin	120
Hughes, Nicholas Collin	154
Hughes, Nicholas Collin	161
Hughes, Nicholas Collin, Jr	161
Hughes, Nicholas Collin	200
Hughes, Nicholas Collin, 3d	204
Hughes, Paul	205
Hughes, Peter	93
Hughes, Peter Gould	93
Hughes, Prudence	84
Hughes, Rachel	45
Hughes, Rachel	86
Hughes, Rachel Bartholomew	116
Hughes, Ruth	45
Hughes, Ruth	84
Hughes, Ruth	86
Hughes, Ruth	93
Hughes, Sarah	44
Hughes, Sarah	45
Hughes, Sarah	84
Hughes, Sarah	86
Hughes, Sarah	93
Hughes, Sarah Ann	93
Hughes, Sarah Summers	226
Hughes, Slator Clay	117
Hughes, Stephen Decatur	94
Hughes, Stephen D	95
Hughes, Stephen Ward	93
Hughes, Susan	93
Hughes, Susan Mary	205
Hughes, Susan Taylor	200
Hughes, Susannah	93
Hughes, Theodore Jones	120
Hughes, Theodore Jones	154
Hughes, Theodore Jones	201
Hughes, Thomas Silliman	159
Hughes, Wayne	203
Hughes, Wayne Baker	202
Hughes, William	84
Hughes, William Corson	158
Hughes, William M	95
Hughes, Zophar Mills	201
Hull, Joseph	166
Hull, J. Frampton	207
Hull, William R	165

HOLSTEIN FAMILY HISTORY. 301

	PAGE		PAGE
Hunter, Benjamin Parkinson	186	Knight, Paul Gardiner	181
Hunter, Catharine Ann	185	Knight, Samuel Coates	181
Hunter, Jane	185	Knight, Thomas	181
Hunter, James Blake	186	Knight, William Thomas	181
Hunter, John Carson	185	Kochersperger, Henry	221
Hunter, Rachel Pocahontas	185	Lambie, D. Dale	208
Hurst, Harry H.	182	Lambie, Ethel	208
Hurst, Jacob M.	182	Lambie, Helen Rittenhouse	208
Hurst, Margaret A.	182	Landis, Isabel Potts	212
Hyde, Emily Rowland	207	Lane, Phœbe	130
Hyde, Thomas	207	Lane, Rebecca	130
Jarrett, Irene B.	218	Lane, Samuel	130
Jarrett, Jessie Mabel	218	Leaf, Charles Clay	171
Jarrett, Mary Ann	218	Leaf, Edmund Leonard	171
Jolly, Charles Frederick	227	Leaf, Ellen Lane	171
Jolly, Charlotte Reed	190	Leaf, George Herbert	171
Jolly, Charles Squire	190	Leaf, Samuel Bowman	171
Jolly, Elizabeth	140	Lewis, Anna Brooke	224
Jolly, Elizabeth Ashton	190	Lewis, Helen Brooke	224
Jolly, John	140	Lewis, Sarah Fallon	224
Jolly, Mary Anna	189	Lichtenthaler, Annie Mary	169
Jolly, Mary Anna	140	Lichtenthaler, Henry Curtis, M.D.,	169
Jolly, Matthias Holstein	140	Lichtenthaler, Mary Elizabeth	211
Jolly, Rebecca	140	Lightner, Julia Jane	214
Jolly, Rebecca Mayberry	190	Lodge, Abel	139
Jolly, Thomas Craig	140	Lodge, Abel	188
Jolly, Thomas Herbert	227	Lodge, Catharine	139
Jolly, Werner	190	Lodge, Caroline	223
Jones, Charles	122	Lodge, Corena	223
Jones, Harriet	122	Lodge, Ella	188
Jones, Laura	164	Lodge, Elizabeth	139
Jones, Marion	164	Lodge, Elizabeth	188
Jones, Theodore	122	Lodge, Emmor	187
Jones, Theodore	164	Lodge, Frances	139
Kercher, Francis	203	Lodge, Frank	188
Kercher, George Hughes	203	Lodge, Henry	139
Keir, Isabel	183	Lodge, Henry	188
Keir, Margaret	183	Lodge, Ida	188
Keir, Mary Ann	183	Lodge, Ida	223
Keir, Rebecca	183	Lodge, Jane Holstein	139
Keir, Samuel	183	Lodge, John	139
Keir, Sarah Love	183	Lodge, John	188
Keir, William	183	Lodge, Mary M	139
Kellogg, Alfred Galpin	223	Lodge, Matilda E.	187
Kellogg, Branton Holstein	223	Lodge, Phœbe	139
Kellogg, Charles Wetmore	223	Lodge, Sallie	188
Kellogg, Edith	223	Lodge, Susan	139
Kellogg, Henderson	223	Lodge, Thomas	188
Knight, Blanche Eva	181	Lodge, Walter	188
Knight, Emily Jane	181	Loomis, Charlotte Jolly	223
Knight, George McDowell	219	Loomis, Jennie Mallet	223
Knight, Gertrude Beatrice	219	Loomis, John Branan	223
Knight, Grace Irene	181	Love, Anna Bell	184
Knight, Kate Gertrude	181	Love, Annette	185
Knight, Margaret Ann	181	Love, Elizabeth	137
Knight, Mary Bertha	181	Love, J. Holstein	137

HOLSTEIN FAMILY HISTORY.

	PAGE.
Love, John Serron	137
Love, Lelia Ada	184
Love, Martha Jane	137
Love, Rachel } twins	137
Love, Rebecca }	
Love, Sarah Ann	137
Love, Sharp Serron	137
Mackey, Annie Hepburn	168
Mackey, Mary Louisa	169
Mackey, Samuel Hepburn	169
Mann, Jennie Hepburn	211
Maitland, Margaret M	182
Maitland, Martha	182
Makemson, Catharine	138
Makemson, Charles	186
Makemson, Christiana	186
Makemson, Ella	186
Makemson, George	186
Makemson, George	138
Makemson, Henry	138
Makemson, James	138
Makemson, Martha	186
Makemson, Mary	138
Makemson, Mary	186
Makemson, Peter	138
Makemson, Rachel	186
Makemson, Susan	186
Makemson, William	138
Makemson, William	186
Manley, Basil	225
Manley, Matthias S	225
Meigs, Curtis Clay	211
Meigs, William Pollock	211
Middleton, Varina Shainline	222
Middleton, William Shainline	224
Molony, George Holstein	145
Morris, Anna Ellis	194
Morris, Charles Ellis	224
Morris, Charles Wells	194
Morris, Courtland Southworth	224
Morris, Elizabeth Rooke	194
Morris, Emily Amies	194
Morris, Emily Walker	224
Morris, George Holstein	194
Morris, Herbert Holstein	194
Morris, John Roberts	194
Morris, Mary Amies	194
Morris, Russel DuPont	224
Morris, Virginia	194
Morris, William Ellis	194
Murray, Margaret Lee	185
Neff, Charles Jolly	225
Neff, Edith Virginia	224
Neff, Joyce Holstein	224
Neff, Robert Bruce	224
Newland, Augustus James	209

	PAGE.
Newland, Maria Hepburn	209
Newland, Mary Blakiston	209
Norris, Nannie Lelia	185
Norris, Pearl	185
Norris, Rachel Lucella	185
Norris, Robert Blain	185
Norris, Sadie Blanche	185
Norris, William Holstein	185
Nourse, Bessie	206
Nourse, Edward	206
Nourse, Emily	206
Nourse, Harvey	206
Nourse, Isabel	206
Nourse, Laurie	206
Nourse, Louisa	206
Patton, Agnes	209
Patton, Helen	209
Patton, Henry Blackiston	209
Patton, J. Woodbridge	209
Peale, Francis	205
Peale, Rubens	205
Pollock, Ann Clay	170
Pollock, Curtis Clay	169
Pollock, Emma	168
Pollock, Emily Clara	168
Pollock, Emily Clay	211
Pollock, Enoch Walton	211
Pollock, Ethel Hepburn	210
Pollock, Francis Hughes	170
Pollock, Henry Clay	211
Pollock, James	170
Pollock, James Crawford	168
Pollock, James Hepburn	209
Pollock, Juliet Campbell	170
Pollock, Laura Leisenring	211
Pollock, Louisa Ann	168
Pollock, Mabel Kelsey	210
Pollock, Margaret Annan	170
Pollock, Mary Louisa	210
Pollock, Mary Wilson	170
Pollock, Samuel Hepburn	167
Pollock, Sarah Margaret	168
Pollock, Walter	210
Pollock, William	211
Pollock, William Curtis	168
Pollock, William Curtis	209
Potts, Abby Holstein	197
Potts, Anna Frances	162
Potts, Brita Holstein	197
Potts, Carrie	197
Potts, Charles Clay	121
Potts, Charles W. Tryon	163
Potts, Ella Holstein	197
Potts, Eleanor Lee	212
Potts, Ellen	163
Potts, Emily Frances	171

HOLSTEIN FAMILY HISTORY.   303

	PAGE		PAGE
Potts, (Hannah) Elizabeth	121	Rittenhouse, Charles Edwin	105
Potts, Harriet	162	Rittenhouse, Charles Edwin	166
Potts, Harriet Provost	120	Rittenhouse, Charles Edwin	208
Potts, Harrison Isaac	205	Rittenhouse, Charles Edwin	166
Potts, Helen	107	Rittenhouse, Clementina Crawford	105
Potts, Helen	205	Rittenhouse, David	105
Potts, Henry W.	170	Rittenhouse, Elizabeth	207
Potts, Horace	205	Rittenhouse, Elizabeth Scott	164
Potts, Horace Turley	163	Rittenhouse, Emily	166
Potts, Joseph Henry	212	Rittenhouse, Emily Josepha	122
Potts, John H.	163	Rittenhouse, Fannie	166
Potts, Kate B.	163	Rittenhouse, Hannah Hughes	122
Potts, Margaret Annan	212	Rittenhouse, Helen Murray	165
Potts, Mary	163	Rittenhouse, Henrietta W.	164
Potts, Mary	163	Rittenhouse, Henry	208
Potts, Rachel Hughes	121	Rittenhouse, Howard	208
Potts, Robert Earnhill	121	Rittenhouse, Isabel L.	164
Potts, Robert E.	163	Rittenhouse, James Delosier	165
Potts, Sarah	163	Rittenhouse, James Hall	165
Potts, Sallie Hughes	163	Rittenhouse, John D.	165
Potts, Thomas Charles	205	Rittenhouse, John Hugh	209
Potts, Thomas Isaac	121	Rittenhouse, Rev. John Hughes	122
Potts, William Francis	121	Rittenhouse, Karl David	208
Potts, William John	163	Rittenhouse, Leonard Cole	208
Pritner, Caroline	87	Rittenhouse, Lucia Morse	208
Pritner, Catharine	87	Rittenhouse, Martha L.	166
Pritner, Constance	87	Rittenhouse, Mary D.	164
Pritner, Elizabeth	86	Rittenhouse, Mary Elizabeth	122
Pritner, Henry	87	Rittenhouse, Mary E.	166
Pritner, Henry, 2d	87	Rittenhouse, Mary W.	166
Pritner, Hughes	86	Rittenhouse, Mary W.	208
Pritner, Isaac Hughes	87	Rittenhouse, Norris	207
Pritner, John Thomas	86	Rittenhouse, Paul	208
Pritner, Lindsay Coates	86	Rittenhouse, Ralph Davidson	208
Pritner, Martha	87	Rittenhouse, Sadie	208
Pritner, Rebecca	87	Rittenhouse, S. Emily	164
Pritner, William	87	Rittenhouse, Sarah Louisa	166
Pugh, DeWitt	210	Rittenhouse, Samuel White	166
Pugh, Grace Frantz	210	Rittenhouse, Zen Delozier	208
Pugh, Jennie W.	210	Roberts, Anna Ellis	196
Pugh, Mina Knight	210	Roberts, Catharine Connard	196
Pugh, Willie Knight	210	Roberts, Clara Virginia	196
Rambo, Hiram	180	Roberts, David C.	190
Rambo, William	134	Roberts, Edith May	197
Ransom, Joseph Morgan	174	Roberts, Edward	147
Riley, Emily Clay	212	Roberts, Eliza Ann	146
Riley, Robert Annan	212	Roberts, Emma K. Dunwoody	196
Riley, Louis Adams	212	Roberts, George Holstein	147
Rittenhouse, Anna	166	Roberts, Greta Massey	196
Rittenhouse, Arthur	208	Roberts, Hannah	104
Rittenhouse, Benjamin Franklin	122	Roberts, John	147
Rittenhouse, Benjamin Franklin	105	Roberts, Jonathan John	147
Rittenhouse, Benjamin Franklin	207	Roberts, Magdalena	104
Rittenhouse, Carolyn	208	Roberts, Mary Davis	197
Rittenhouse, Catharine	209	Roberts, Matthew	146
Rittenhouse, Charles Edwin	122	Roberts, Rachel	104

	PAGE.		PAGE.
Roberts, Reese Connard	196	Shainline, William Davis	192
Roberts, Sarah	104	Shainline, William Ellis	193
Roberts, Sarah Louisa	146	Shainline, William Henry	192
Roberts, Susan H.	196	Shainline, William Holstein	144
Roberts, Susan Holstein	196	Shuman, Charles F.	165
Roberts, Walter Jonathan	197	Shuman, David R.	165
Roberts, William B.	196	Shuman, Emily A.	165
Roberts, William B.	197	Shuman, Helen M.	165
Roberts, William Holstein	147	Shuman, Mary R.	165
Rockhill, Anna Potts	205	Shuman, Sarah	165
Rockhill, Edward Potts	205	Sloan, Edward Holstein	217
Ross, Alfred Green	226	Sloan, Elizabeth Worral	25
Ross, Clara Hughes	226	Sloan, Helen DeHaven	217
Ross, William Lightfoot	226	Sloan, Kate	217
Rutter, Anne	190	Sloan, Louis H.	217
Rutter, James Leonard	190	Smith, Albert	172
Rutter, Sally Saylor	190	Smith, Charles Moore	129
Schofield, Elizabeth	136	Smith, Charles Moore	172
Shainline, Alda Bailey	224	Smith, Colin Coates	172
Shainline, Anna Elizabeth	193	Smith, Henderson Coates	172
Shainline, Ann Sophia	192	Smith, James O'Connor	172
Shainline, Anne Sophia	145	Smith, Levi Coates	172
Shainline, Andrew	192	Smith, Lindsay Coates	172
Shainline, Andrew Lawrence	193	Smith, Mary Emma	172
Shainline, Beulah May	194	Smith, Nathaniel	129
Shainline, Burton Tolen	194	Smith, Thomas Lowrey	172
Shainline, Charles R.	194	Smith, William Wayland	172
Shainline, DeWitt Clinton	144	Smylie, Dorothy	213
Shainline, DeWitt Clinton	224	Smylie, Ellen	173
Shainline, Elizabeth Bisbing	192	Smylie, Ellen	213
Shainline, Elizabeth DeHaven	193	Smylie, Ellen Morrison	173
Shainline, Elizabeth Holstein	142	Smylie, John	173
Shainline, Ella Baker	193	Smylie, John	213
Shainline, Ella May	193	Smylie, Mary Elizabeth	173
Shainline, Emily Rambo	192	Smylie, Matthias Coates	173
Shainline, Earnest Manning	193	Smylie Robert Sayres	173
Shainline, Florence Ella	193	Smylie, Virginia Wright	213
Shainline, Franklin Howard	194	Smylie, William Duff	173
Shainline, George Bisbing	193	Smylie, William M.	213
Shainline, George Henry	194	Stacker, Hannah Hughes	226
Shainline, George Holstein	144	Stotesbury, Susan	93
Shainline, Harriet Anna	193	Stotesbury, Sydney Maria	93
Shainline, Helen Anderson	193	Switzler, Alice R.	227
Shainline, Henry Harrison	144	Switzler, Robinson M.	227
Shainline, Isaac Holstein	193	Switzler, Thomas W.	227
Shainline, James Yocom	144	Thomas, Anna Elizabeth	145
Shainline, Joseph Brookfield	224	Thomas, Benjamin Thomas	146
Shainline, Joseph Potter	193	Thomas, Mary Amies	146
Shainline, Marianna	192	Thomas, Rebecca Brooke	146
Shainline, Martha Emily	180	Travis, Charles Gardiner	215
Shainline, Mary Louisa	144	Travis, Clara Ellen	215
Shainline, Rebecca Emily	144	Travis, Clarence Williams	227
Shainline, Sarah	192	Travis, Claude Laneton	215
Shainline, Sallie DeHaven	193	Travis, Ethel Ray	227
Shainline, Thomas William	224	Travis, James Herbert	215
Shainline, Varina Thomas	192	Travis, Julia Atlee	215

	PAGE		PAGE
Travis, Laura Bell	227	Wilson, William Lowe	207
Travis, Lewis Williams	215	Williams, Alice Jane	208
Travis, Oscar Hills	215	Williams, Alice Mabel	216
Travis, Robert Williams	215	Williams, Amelia Atlee	175
Urid, Elizabeth	186	Williams, Charles Rittenhouse	208
Urid, John Makemson	186	Williams, Ellen Harriet	176
Urid, Kate M.	186	Williams, Elizabeth Boal	177
Urid, Mary Ann M.	186	Williams, Emma Clay	176
Urid, Susanna	186	Williams, James Augustus	176
Vernon, Helen Roxanna	219	Williams, James Frederick	216
Vernon, Jennie Coates	219	Williams, John T.	216
Vernon, William Knight	219	Williams, Joseph Atlee	177
Wade, Emily	123	Williams, Julia DeHaven	177
Wade, Francis	123	Williams, Julia Elizabeth	216
Wade, Francis	166	Williams, Louis Hudson	208
Wade, George	123	Williams Louisa May	216
Wade, George	166	Williams, Priscilla Martin	176
Wade, Hannah Clay	123	Williams, Rachel Louisa	208
Wade, Sarah	123	Williams, Robert Conrad	216
Wade, Sophia	166	Williams, Robert Lewis	177
Wade, Susan	123	Williams, Sarah DeHaven	176
Walter, Frances Knight	219	Williams, Susan Miles	176
Walter, Meta	219	Williams, William Gibson	216
Welsh, James Harold	225	Williamson, Kathleen Hughes	226
White, Alice	218	Williamson, Theodore	226
White, Bertha Holloway	218	Wills, Anna Gorgas	196
White, Charles Gordon	179	Wills, Eleanora Wayne	196
White, Christianna Bunting	179	Wills, Elizabeth Marple	196
White, Emily Louisa	179	Wills, George Edward	196
White, George W.	218	Wills, Jonathan Roberts	196
White, Hugh DeHaven	179	Wills, Louis Andrew	196
White, Lillie	179	Wills, Mary Hannah	196
White, Mary Elizabeth	179	Wills, Sarah Tyson	196
White, Samuel	179	Wills, Susan Roberts	195
White, Sarah	179	Wills, William Wayne	196
White, Susan Shober	179	Woods, Franklin R.	206
White, Thomas Holloway	218	Woods, Henrietta R.	206
Wilson, Henrietta R.	207	Woods, James S.	206
Wilson, Margaret Stevens	207	Yerkes, Beatrice Hughes	227
Wilson, Mary D.	207	Yerkes, Eugene	186

www.ingramcontent.com/pod-product-compliance
Lightning Source LLC
Chambersburg PA
CBHW020105020526
44112CB00033B/934